Kenilworth. by the Author of 'waverley'.

Walter Scott

KENILWORTH.

PRINTED BY RIGNOUX,

Nº 8, RUE DES FRANCS-BOURGEOIS-S.-MICHEL.

KENILWORTH;

A ROMANCE.

BY THE AUTHOR OF «WAVERLEY,» «IVANHOE, etc.

No scandal about Queen Elizabeth, I hope?
The Critic.

IN TWO VOLUMES.

VOL. II.

———

PARIS.

BAUDRY, bookseller in foreign languages; n° 9, rue du Coq-S.-Honoré;
AMYOT, bookseller, n° 6, rue de la Paix;
PINARD, n° 5, quai Voltaire.
———
1821.

KENILWORTH.

CHAPTER XIX.

> *Pistol.* And tidings do I bring, and lucky joys,
> And happy news of price.
> *Falstaff.* I prythee now deliver them like to men of this world.
> *Pistol.* A foutra for the world, and worldlings base!
> I speak of Africa, and golden joys.
>
> *Henry IV. Part.* 2.

T HE public room of the Black Bear at Cumnor, to which the scene of our story now returns, boasted, on the evening which we treat of, no ordinary assemblage of guests. There had been a fair in the neighbourhood, and the cutting mercer of Abingdon, with some of the other personages whom the reader has already been made acquainted with, as friends and customers of Giles Gosling, had already formed their wonted circle around the evening fire, and were talking over the news of the day.

A lively, bustling, arch fellow, whose pack and oaken *ell-wand*, studded duly with brass points, denoted him to be of Autolycus's profession, occupied a good deal of the attention, and furnished much of the amusement, of the evening. The pedlars of these days, it must be remembered, were men of far greater impor-

II.   I

tance than the degenerate and degraded hawkers
of our modern times. It was by means of these
peripatetic venders that the country-trade, in
the finer manufactures used in female dress
particularly, was almost entirely carried on;
and if a merchant of this description arrived
at the dignity of travelling with a pack-horse,
he was a person of no small consequence,
and company for the most substantial yeoman
or Franklin whom he might meet in his wan-
derings.

The pedlar of whom we speak bore, accordingly, an active and unrebuked share in the
merriment to which the rafters of the bonny
Black Bear of Cumnor resounded. He had his
smile with pretty Mistress Cicely, his broad
laugh with mine host, and his jest upon dashing
Master Goldthred, who, though indeed without
any such benevolent intention on his own part,
was the general butt of the evening. The pedlar
and he were closely engaged in a dispute upon
the preference due to the Spanish nether stock
over the black Gascoigne hose, and mine host
had just winked to the guests around him, as
who should say, «You will have mirth presently,
my masters,» when the trampling of horses was
heard in the court-yard, and the hostler was
loudly summoned, with a few of the newest
oaths then in vogue to add force to the invocation. Out tumbled Will Hostler, John Tapster,
and all the militia of the inn, who had slunk
from their posts in order to collect some scat-

tered crumbs of the mirth which was flying
about among the customers. Out into the yard
sallied mine host himself also, to do fitting salu-
tation to his new guests; and presently returned,
ushering into the apartment, his own worthy
nephew, Michael Lambourne, pretty tolerably
drunk, and having under his escort the astrologer.
Alasco, though still a little old man, had, by
altering his gown to a riding-dress, trimming
his beard and eye-brows, and so forth, struck
at least a score of years from his apparent age,
and might now seem an active man of sixty, or
little upwards. He appeared at present exceedingly anxious, and had insisted much with
Lambourne that they should not enter the inn,
but go straight forward to the place of their
destination. But Lambourne would not be controuled. « By Cancer and Capricorn, » he vociferated, « and the whole heavenly host — besides
all the stars I saw in the southern heavens, to
which these northern blinkers are but farthing
candles, I will be unkindly for no one's humour
— I will stay and salute my worthy uncle here.
— Chesu! that good blood should ever be
forgotten betwixt friends! — A gallon of your
best, uncle, and let it go round to the health
of the noble Earl of Leicester! — What! Shall
we not collogue together, and warm the cockles
of our ancient kindness? — Shat we not collogue, I say? »

« With all my heart, » kinsman, » said mine
host, who obviously wished to be rid of him;

« but are you to stand shot to all this good
liquor? »

This is a question has quelled many a jovial
toper, but it moved not the purpose of Lambourne's soul. « Question my means, uncle? »
he said, producing a handful of mixed gold
and silver pieces; « question Mexico and Peru
— question the Queen's exchequer — God save
her Majesty! — She is my good Lord's good
mistress. »

« Well, kinsman, » said mine host, « it is my
business to sell wine to those who can buy it —
So, Jack Tapster, do me thine office. — But I
would I knew how to come by money as lightly
as thou doest, Mike. »

« Why, uncle, » said Lambourne, « I will
tell thee a secret — Dost see this little old fellow
here? as old and withered a chip as ever the devil put into his porridge — and yet, uncle, between you and me — he hath Potosi in that brain
of his — Sblood! he can coin ducats faster than
I can vent oaths. »

« I will have none of his coinage in my purse
though, Michael, » said mine host; « I know
what belongs to falsifying the Queen's coin. »

« Thou art an ass, uncle, for as old as thou
art — Pull me not by the skirts, doctor, thou
art an ass thyself to boot — so, being both asses,
I tell ye I spoke but metaphorically. »

« Are you mad? » said the old man; « is the
devil in you? — can you not let us begone without drawing all men's eyes on us? »

« Say'st thou? » said Lambourne; « Thou art deceived now — no man shall see you an I give. the word. — By heavens, masters, an any one dare to look on this old gentleman, I will slash the eyes out of his head with my poniard — So sit down, old friend, and be merry — these are mine ancient inmates, and will betray no man. »

« Had you not better withdraw to a private apartment, nephew, » said Giles Gosling; « you speak strange matter, » he added, « and there be intelligencers every where. »

« I care not for them, said the magnanimous Michael — « intelligencers, pshaw! — I serve the noble Earl of Leicester — Here comes the wine — Fill round, Master Skinker, a carouse to the health of the flower of England, the noble Earl of Leicester! I say, the noble Earl of Leicester! He that does me not reason is a swine of Sussex, and I'll make him kneel to the pledge, if I should cut his hams and smoke them for bacon. »

None disputed a pledge given under such formidable penalties; and Michael Lambourne, whose drunken humour was not of course diminished by this new potation, went on in the same wild way, renewing his acquaintance with such of the guests as he had formerly known, and experiencing a reception in which there was now something of deference, mingled with a good deal of fear; for the least servitor of the favourite Earl, especially such a man as Lambourne, was, for very sufficient reasons, an object both of the one and of the other.

In the meanwhile, the old man, seeing his guide in this uncontroulable humour, ceased to remonstrate with him, and sitting down in the most obscure corner of the room, called for a small measure of sack, over which he seemed, as it were, to slumber, withdrawing himself as much as possible from general observation, and doing nothing which could recal his existence to the recollection of his fellow-traveller, who by this time had got into close intimacy with his ancient comrade, Goldthred of Abingdon.

« Never believe me, bully Mike, said the mercer, « if I am not as glad to see thee as ever I was to see a customer's money! Why, thou canst give a friend a sly place at a mask or a revel now, Mike; ay, or, I warrant thee, thou canst say in my lord's ear, when my honourable lord is down in these parts, and wants a Spanish ruff or the like— thou canst say in his ear, there is mine old friend, young Lawrence Goldthred of Abingdon, has as good wares, lawn, tiffany, cambric, and so forth — ay, and is as pretty a piece of man's flesh too as is in Berkshire, and will ruffle it for your lordship with any man of his inches, and thou may'st say »——

« I can say a hundred damned lies besides, mercer, « answered Lambourne; what, one must not stand upon a good word for a friend! »

« Here is to thee, Mike, with all my heart, » said the mercer, » and thou canst tell one the reality of the new fashions too — Here was a rogue pedlar but now, was crying up the old-fashioned

Spanish nether stock over the Gascoigne hose, although thou seest how well the French hose set off the leg and knee, being adorned with parti-coloured garters and garniture in conformity. »

« Excellent, excellent, » replied Lambourne; « why, thy limber bit of a thigh, thrust through that bunch of slashed buckram and tiffany, shews like a housewife's distaff, when the flax is half spun off. »

« Said I not so ? » said the mercer, whose shallow brain was now overflowed in his turn; «where then, where be this rascal pedlar?—there was a pedlar here but now, methinks — Mine host, where the foul fiend is this pedlar ?»

« Where wise men should be, Master Goldthred, » replied Giles Gosling; « even shut up in his private chamber', telling over the sales of to-day, and preparing for the custom of to-morrow. »

« Hang him, a mechanical chuff, » said the mercer; « but for shame, it were a good deed to ease him of his wares, — a set of peddling knaves, who stroll through the land, and hurt the established trader. There are good fellows in Berkshire yet, mine host — your pedlar may be met withal on Maiden Castle. »

« Ay, » replied mine host, laughing, « and he who meets him may meet his match — the pedlar is a tall man. »

« Is he? » said Goldthred.

« Is he? » replied the host; « ay., by cock

and pye is he — the very pedlar he who raddled
Robin Hood so tightly, as the song says, —

> ' Now Robin Hood drew his sword so good,
>   The pedlar drew his brand;
> And he hath raddled him, Robin Hood,
>   Till he neither could see nor stand. »

« Hang him, foul scroyle, let him pass, »
said the mercer; « if he be such a one, there
were small worship to be won upon him. —
And now tell me, Mike — my honest Mike,
how wears the Hollands you won of me? »

« Why, well, as you may see, Master Goldthred, » answered Mike; « I will bestow a pot
on thee for the handsel. — Fill the flagon,
Master Tapster. »

« Thou wilt win no more Hollands, I think,
on such wager, friend Mike, said the mercer;
« for the sulky swain, Tony Foster, rails at thee
all to nought, and swears you shall ne'er darken
his doors again, for that your oaths are enough
to blow the roof of a Christian man's dwelling. »

« Doth he say so, the mincing hypocritical
miser? » vociferated Lambourne; — Why then
he shall come down and receive my commands
here, this blessed night, under my uncle's roof!
And I will ring him such a black sanctus, that
he shall think the devil hath him by the skirts
for a month to come, for barely hearing me. »

« Nay, now the pottle-pot is uppermost, with
a witness, » said the mercer. » Tony Foster

obey thy whistle!—Alas! good Mike, go sleep
— go sleep. »

« I tell thee what, thou thin-faced gull, »
said Michael Lambourne, in high chafe, « I
will wager thee fifty angels against the first five
shelves of thy shop, numbering upward from
the false light, with all that is on them, that
I make Tony Foster come down to this public
house, before we have finished three rounds. »

« I will lay no bet to that amount, » said the
mercer, something sobered by an offer which
intimated rather too private a knowledge, on
Lambourne's part, of the secret recesses of his
shop, « I will lay no such wager, » he said;
« but I will stake five angels against thy five,
if thou wilt, that Tony Foster will not leave his
own roof, or come to ale-house after prayer
time, for thee, or any man. »

« Content, » said Lambourne. — « Here,
uncle, hold stakes, and let one of your young
bleed-barrels there — one of your infant tap-
sters, trip presently up to The Place, and give
this letter to Master Foster, and say that I, his
ingle Michael Lambourne, pray to speak with
him at mine uncle's castle here, upon business
of grave import. — Away with thee, child, for
it is now sun down, and the wretch goeth to
bed with the birds, to save mutton-suet —
faugh! »

Shortly after this messenger was dispatched
— an interval which was spent in drinking and

buffoonery, — he returned with the answer, that Master Foster was coming presently.

« Won, won! » said Lambourne, darting on the stake.

« Not till he comes, if you please, » said the mercer, interfering.

« Why, 'sblood, he is at the threshold, replied Michael — « What said he, boy? »

« If it please your worship, » answered the messenger, « he looked out of window, with a musquetoon in his hand, and when I delivered your errand, which I did with fear and trembling, he said, with a vinegar aspect, that your worship might be gone to the infernal regions. »

« Or to hell, I suppose, » said Lambourne — « it is there he disposes of all that are not of the congregation. »

« Even so, » said the boy; « I used the other phrase, as being the more poetical. »

« An ingenious youth, » said Michael; « shalt have a drop to whet thy poetical whistle — And what said Foster next? »

« He called me back, answered the boy, « and bid me say, you might come to him, if you had aught to say to him. »

« And what next ? » said Lambourne.

« He read the letter, and seemed in a fluster, and asked if your worship was in drink — and I said you were speaking a little Spanish, as one who had been in the Canaries. »

« Out, you diminutive pint-pot, whelped of

an overgrown reckoning!» replied Lambourne — «Out! — But what said he then?»

« Why, he muttered, that if he came not, your worship would bolt out what were better kept in; and so he took his old fleet cap, and thread-bare blue cloak, and, as I said before, he will be here incontinent. »

« There is truth in what he said, » replied Lambourne, as if speaking to himself — « My brain has played me its old dog's trick — but couragio — let him approach! — I have not rolled about in the world, for many a day, to fear Tony Foster, be I drunk or sober. — Bring me a flagon of cold water, to christen my sack withal. »

While Lambourne, whom the approach of Foster seemed to have recalled to a sense of his own condition, was busied in preparing to receive him, Giles Gosling stole up to the apartment of the pedlar, whom he found traversing the room in much agitation.

« You withdrew yourself suddenly from the company, » said the landlord to the guest.

« It was time, when the devil became one among you, » replied the pedlar.

«It is not courteous in you to term my nephew by such a name, » said Gosling, « nor is it kindly in me to reply to it; and yet, in some sort, Mike may be considered as a limb of Satan.»

« Pooh — I talk not of the swaggering ruffian, » replied the pedlar, « it is of the other, who,

for aught I know—But when go they? or wherefore come they? »

, « Marry, these are questions I cannot answer, »
replied the host. « But, look you, sir, you have
brought me a token from worthy Master Tressilian — a pretty stone it is. » He took out the
ring, and looked at it, adding, as he put it into
his purse again, that it was too rich a guerdon
for any thing he could do for the worthy donor.
He was, he said, in the public line, and it ill
became him to be too inquisitive into other
folks' concerns; he had already said, that he
could hear nothing, but that the lady lived still
at Cumnor Place, in the closest seclusion, and,
to such as by chance had a view of her, seemed
pensive and discontented with her solitude. « But
here, » he said « if you are desirous to gratify
your master, is the rarest chance that hath occurred for this many a day. Tony Foster is coming
down hither, and it is but letting Mike Lambourne smell another wine-flask, and the Queen's
command would not move him from the ale-
bench. So they are fast for an hour or so —
Now, if you will don your pack, which will be
your best excuse, you may, perchance, win
the ear of the old servant, being assured of the
master's absence, to let you try to get some custom of the lady, and then you may learn more
of her condition than I or any other can tell
you. »

« True—very true, » answered Wayland, for
he it was; « an excellent device, but methinks

something dangerous — for say Foster should return ? »

« Very possible indeed, » replied the host.

« Or say, » continued Wayland, « the lady should render me cold thanks for my exertions?»

« As is not unlikely, » replied Giles Gosling. « I marvel, Master Tressilian will take such heed of her that cares not for him. »

« In either case I were foully sped, » said Wayland; «and therefore I do not, on the whole, much relish your device.»

« Nay, but take me with you, good master serving-man, » replied mine host, « this is your master's business and not mine; you best know the risk to be encountered, or how far you are willing to brave it. But that which you will not yourself hazard, you cannot expect others to risk. »

« Hold, hold, » said Wayland; « tell me but one thing — Goes yonder old man up to Cumnor ? »

« Surely, I think so, » said the landlord; « their servant said he was to take their baggage thither, but the ale-tap has been as potent for him as the sack-spiggot has been for Michael. »

« It is enough, » said Wayland, assuming an air of resolution— « I will thwart that old villain's projects—my affright at his baleful aspect begins to abate, and my hatred to arise.—Help me on with my pack, good mine host—And look to thyself, old Albumazar—there is a malignant influence in thy horoscope, and it gleams from the constellation Ursa Major. »

So saying, he assumed his burthen, and, guided by the landlord through the postern gate of the Black Bear, took the most private way from thence up to Cumnor Place.

CHAPTER XX.

Clown. You have of these pedlars, that have more in 'em than you'd think, sister.

Winter's Tale, Act IV. Scene 3.

In his anxiety to obey the Earl's repeated charges of secrecy, as well as from his own unsocial and miserly habits, Anthony Foster was more desirous, by his mode of housekeeping, to escape observation, than to resist intrusive cusiosity. Thus, instead of a numerous household, to secure his charge, and defend his house, he studied, as much as possible, to elude notice, by diminishing his attendants; so that, unless when there were attendants of the Earl, or of Varney, in the mansion, one old male domestic, and two old crones, who assisted in keeping the Countess's apartments in order, were the only servants of the family. It was one of these old women who opened the door when Wayland knocked, and answered his petition, to be admitted to exhibit his wares to the ladies of the family, with a volley of vituperation, couched in what is there called the *jowring* dialect. The pedlar found the means of checking this vociferation, by slipping a silver groat into her hand,

and intimating the present of some stuff for a coif, if the lady would buy of his wares.

« God ield thee, for mine is aw in littocks — Slocket with thy pack into gharn, mon—Her walks in gharn. » Into the garden she ushered the pedlar accordingly, and pointing to an old ruinous garden-house, said, « Yonder be's her, mon,—yonder be's her—Zhe will buy changes an zhe loikes stuffs. »

« She has left me to come off as I may, « thought Wayland, as he heard the hag shut the garden-door behind him. « But they shall not beat me, and they dare not murder me, for so little trespass, and by this fair twilight. Hang it, I will on —a brave general never thought of his retreat till he was defeated. I see two females in the old garden-house yonder—but how to address them ? —Stay—Will Shakespeare, be my friend in need. I will give them a taste of Autolycus. » He then sung, with a good voice, and becoming audacity; the popular play-house ditty,

« Lawn as white as driven snow,
Cyprus black as e'er was crow,
Gloves as sweet as damask roses,
· Masks for faces and for noses. »

« What hath fortune sent us here for an unwonted sight, Janet ? » said the lady.

« One of these merchants of vanity, called pedlars, » answered Janet, demurely, « who utters his light wares in lighter measures—I marvel old Dorcas let him pass. »

« It is a lucky chance, girl, » said the Countess; « we lead a heavy life here, and this may while off a weary hour. »

« Aye, my gracious lady, » said Janet; « but my father? »

« He is not *my* father, Janet, nor I hope my master, » answered the lady—I say, call the man hither—I want some things. »

« Nay, » replied Janet, » your ladyship has but to say so in the next packet, and if England can furnish them they will be sent.—There will come mischief on't—Pray, dearest lady, let me bid the man begone ! »

« I will have thee bid him come hither, » said the Countess,—« or stay, thou terrified fool, I will bid him myself, and spare thee a chiding. »

« Ah! well-a-day, dearest lady, if that were the worst, » said Janet, sadly, while the lady called to the pedlar, « Good fellow, step forward—undo thy pack—if thou hast good wares, chance has sent thee hither for my convenience, and thy profit. »

« What may your ladyship please to lack ? » said Wayland, unstrapping his pack, and displaying its contents with as much dexterity as if he had been bred to the trade. Indeed he had occasionally pursued it in the course of his roving life, and now commended his wares with all the volubility of a trader, and shewed some skill in the main art of placing prices upon them.

« What do I please to lack? » said the lady;

1*

« why, considering I have not for six long months bought one yard of lawn or cambric, or one trinket, the most inconsiderable, for my own use, and at my own choice, the better question is, what hast thou got to sell? Lay aside for me that cambric partlet and pair of sleeves — and those roundells of gold fringe, drawn out with cyprus—and that short cloak of cherry-coloured fine cloth, garnished with gold buttons and loops—is it not of an absolute fancy, Janet? »

« Nay, my lady, » replied Janet, « if you consult my poor judgment, it is, methinks, over gawdy for a graceful habit. »

« Now, out upon thy judgment, if it be no brighter, wench, » said the Countess; thou shalt wear it thyself for penance sake; and I promise, the gold buttons being somewhat massive, will comfort thy father, and reconcile him to the cherry coloured body. See that he snap them not away, Janet, and send them to bear company with the imprisoned angels which he keeps captive in his strong-box. »

« May I pray your ladyship to spare my poor father ! » said Janet.

« Nay, but why should any one spare him that is so sparing of his own nature? » replied the lady.—« Well, but to our gear—That head garniture for myself, and that silver bodkin, mounted with pearl;—and take off two gowns of that russet cloth for Dorcas and Alison, Janet, to keep the old wretches warm against winter comes—And stay, hast thou no perfumes and sweet bags, or any handsome casting bottles of the newest mode? »

« Were I pedlar in earnest, I were a made merchant, » thought Wayland, as he busied himself to answer the demands which she thronged one on another, with the eagerness of a young lady who has been long secluded from such a pleasing occupation. « But how to bring her to a moment's serious reflection. » Then as he exhibited his choicest collection of essences and perfumes, he at once arrested her attention by observing, that these articles had almost risen to double value, since the magnificent preparations made by the Earl of Leicester to entertain the Queen and court at his princely Castle of Kenilworth.

« Ha! » said the Countess, hastily; « that rumour then is true, Janet. »

« Surely, madam, » answered Wayland; « and I marvel it hath not reached your noble ladyship's ears. The Queen of England feasts with the noble Earl for a week during the Summer's Progress; and there are many who will tell you England will have a king, and England's Elizabeth, God save her, a husband, ere the Progress be over. »

« They lie like villains! » said the Countess, bursting forth impatiently.

« For God's sake, madam, consider, » said Janet, trembling with apprehension; who would cumber themselves about pedlar's tidings? »

« Yes, Janet! » exclaimed the Countess; « right,

thou hast corrected me justly. Such reports,
blighting the reputation of England's brightest
and noblest peer, can only find currency amongst
the mean, the abject, and the infamous. »

« May I perish, lady, » said Wayland Smith,
observing that her violence directed itself towards him, « if I have done any thing to merit this
strange passion!—I have said but what many
men say. »

By this time the Countess had recovered her
composure, and endeavoured, alarmed by the
anxious hints of Janet, to suppress all appearance
of displeasure. « I were loth, » she said, « good
fellow, that our Queen should change the virgin
style, so dear to us her people—think not of it. »
And then, as if desirous to change the subject,
she added, « And what is this paste, so carefully
put up in the silver box ? » as she examined the
contents of a casket in which drugs and perfumes
were contained in separate drawers.

» It is a remedy, madam, for a disorder, of
which I trust your ladyship will never have reason to complain. The amount of a small turkey-
bean, swallowed daily for a week, fortifies the
heart against those black vapours which arise
from solitude, melancholy, unrequited affection, disappointed hope »—

« Are you a fool, friend ? » said the Countess,
sharply; « or do you think, because I have good-
naturedly purchased your trumpery goods at
your roguish prices, that you may put any gul-
lery you will on me?—who ever heard that af-

fections of the heart were cured by medicines given to the body? »

« Under your honourable favour, » said Wayland, « I am an honest man, and I have sold my goods at an honest price—As to this most precious medicine, when I told its qualities, I asked you not to purchase it, so why should I lie to you? I say not it will cure a rooted affection of the mind, which only God and time can do; but I say, that this restorative relieves the black vapours which are engendered in the body of that melancholy which broodeth on the mind. I have relieved many with it, both in court and city, and of late one Master Edmund Tressilian, a worshipful gentleman in Cornwall, who, on some slight, received, it was told me, where he had set his affections, was brought into that state of melancholy which made his friends alarmed for his life. »

He paused, and the lady remained silent for some time, and then asked, with a voice which she strove in vain to render firm and indifferent in its tone, «Is the gentleman you have mentioned perfectly recovered? »

« Passably, madam, answered Wayland; « he hath at least no bodily complaint. »

« I will take some of the medicine, Janet, » said the Countess. « I too have sometimes that dark melancholy which overclouds the brain. »

« You shall not do so, madam, said Janet; « who shall answer that this fellow vends what is wholesome? »

« I will myself warrant my good faith, » said
Wayland; and, taking a part of the medicine,
he swallowed it before them. The Countess now
bought what remained, a step to which Janet, by
farther objections, only determined her the more
obstinately. She even took the first dose upon the
instant, and professed to feel her heart lighten-
ed and her spirits augmented, — a consequence
which, in all probability, existed only in her
own imagination. The lady then piled the purchases she had made together, flung her purse to
Janet, and desired her to compute the amount
and to pay the pedlar; while she herself, as if
tired of the amusement she at first found in conversing with him, wished him good evening, and
walked carelessly into the house, thus depri-
ving Wayland of every opportunity to speak with
her in private. He hastened, however, to attempt an explanation with Janet.

« Maiden, » he said, « thou hast the face of one
who should love her mistress. She hath much
need of faithful service. »

« And well deserves it at my hands, » replied
Janet; » but what of that? »

« Maiden, I am not altogether what I seem, «
said the pedlar, lowering his voice.

« The less like to be an honest man, » said Janet.

« The more so, » answered Wayland, « since I
am no pedlar. »

« Get thee gone then instantly, or I will call
for assistance, » said Janet; « my father must ere
this be returned. »

« Do not be so rash, » said Wayland ; you
will do what you may repent of. I am one of
your mistress's friends; and she had need of
more, not that thou should'st ruin those she
hath. »

« How shall I know that ? » said Janet.

« Look me in the face, » said Wayland Smith,
« and see if thou dost not read honesty in my
looks. »

And in truth, though by no means handsome, there was in his physiognomy the sharp,
keen expression of inventive genius and prompt
intellect, which, joined to quick and brilliant
eyes, a well-formed mouth, and an intelligent
smile, often gives grace and interest to features
which are both homely and irregular. Janet looked at him with the sly simplicity of her sect,
and replied, « Notwithstanding thy boasted honesty, friend, and although I am not accustomed to read and pass judgment on such volumes
as thou hast submitted to my perusal, I think I
see in thy countenance something of the pedlar
—something of the picaroon. »

« On a small scale, perhaps, » said Wayland
Smith, laughing. « But this evening, or to-morrow, will an old man come hither with thy father, who has the stealthy step of the cat, the
shrewd and vindictive eye of the rat, the fawning wile of the spaniel, the determined grasp
of the mastiff—of him beware, for your own
sake and that of your mistress. See you, fair
Janet, he brings the venom of the aspic under

the assumed innocence of the dove. What precise mischief he meditates towards you I cannot guess, but death and disease have ever dogged his footsteps. — Say nought of this to thy mistress — my art suggests to me that in her state, the fear of evil may be as dangerous as its operation — But see that she take my specific, for — (he lowered his voice and spoke low but impressively in her ear,) it is an antidote against poison — Hark, they enter the garden! »

In effect, a sound of noisy mirth and loud talking approached the garden door, alarmed by which, Wayland Smith sprung into the midst of a thicket of overgrown shrubs, while Janet withdrew to the garden-house that she might not incur observation, and that she might at the same time conceal, at least for the present, the purchases made from the supposed pedlar, which lay scattered on the floor of the summer-house.

Janet, however, had no occasion for anxiety. Her father, his old attendant, Lord Leicester's domestic, and the astrologer, entered the garden in tumult and in extreme perplexity, endeavouring to quiet Lambourne, whose brain had now become completely fired with liquor, and who was one of those unfortunate persons, who, being once stirred with the vinous stimulus, do not fall asleep like other drunkards, but remain long partially influenced by it, for many hours, until at length, by successive draughts, they are elevated into a state of uncontroulable frenzy. Like many men in this state also, Lambourne neither lost the power of motion, speech, or expression; but, on the contrary, spoke with unwonted emphasis and readiness, and told all that at another time he would have been most desirous to have kept secret.

« What! » ejaculated Michael, at the full extent of his voice, « am I to have no welcome — no carouse, when I have brought fortune to your old ruinous dog-house in the shape of a devil's ally, that can change slate-shivers into Spanish dollars? — Here, you Tony Fire-the-Faggot, papist, puritan, hypocrite, miser, profligate, devil, compounded of all men's sins, bow down and reverence him who has brought into thy house the very mammon thou worshippest. »

« For God's sake, » said Foster, « speak low — come into the house — thou shalt have wine, or whatever thou wilt. »

« No, old puckfist, I will have it here, » thundered the inebriated ruffian — « here *al fresco,* as the Italian hath it. — No, no, I will not drink with that poisoning devil within doors, to be choked with the fumes of arsenic and quicksilver; I learned from villain Varney to beware of that, »

« Fetch him wine, in the name of all the fiends, » said the alchemist.

« Aha! and thou wouldst spice it for me, old Truepenny, wouldst thou not? Ay, I should have coperas, and hellebore, and vitriol, and aquafortis, and twenty devilish materials, bub-

II.   2

bling in my brain-pan like a charm to raise the
devil in a witch's cauldron: Hand me the flask
thyself, old Tony Fire-the-Faggot — and let it
be cool — I will have no wine mulled at the pile
of the old burned bishops — Or stay, let Leicester be king if he will — good — and Varney,
villain Varney, grand vizier — why, excellent,
— and what shall I be then ? — why, emperor
— Emperor Lambourne. — I will see this choice
piece of beauty that they have walled up here
for their private pleasures — I will have her this
very night to serve my wine-cup, and put on my
night-cap. What should a fellow do with two
wives, were he twenty times an Earl ? — answer
me that, Tony boy, you old reprobate hypocritical dog, whom God struck out of the book
of life, but tormented with the constant wish
to be restored to it — You old bishop-burning,
blasphemous fanatic, answer me that. »

« I will stick my knife to the haft in him, »
said Foster, in a low tone, which trembled with
passion.

« For the love of heaven, no violence, » said
the astrologer. « It cannot but be looked closely
into. — Here, honest Lambourne, wilt thou
pledge me to the health of the noble Earl of
Leicester and Master Richard Varney ? »

« I will, mine old Albumazar — I will, my
trusty vender of rat's-bane — I would kiss thee,
mine honest infractor of the Lex Julia, (as they
said at Leyden,) didst thou not flavour so
damnably of sulphur, and such fiendish apothe-

caries stuff.—Here goes it, up seyes—to Varney
and Leicester! — two more noble mounting
spirits — and more dark-seeking, deep-diving,
high-flying, malicious, ambitious miscreants —
well, I say no more, but I will whet my dagger
on his heart-spone, that refuses to pledge me!
And so, my masters.»———

   Thus speaking, Lambourne exhausted the cup
which the astrologer had handed him, and which
contained not wine, but distilled spirits. He
swore half an oath, dropped the empty cup from
his grasp, laid his hand on his sword without
being able to draw it, reeled, and fell without
sense or motion into the arms of the domestic,
who dragged him off to his chamber and put him
to bed.

   In the general confusion, Janet regained her
lady's chamber unobserved, trembling like an
aspen leaf, but determined to keep secret from
the Countess the dreadful surmises which she
could not help entertaining from the drunken
ravings of Lambourne. Her fears, however,
though they assumed no certain shape, kept
pace with the advice of the pedlar; and she con-
firmed her mistress in her purpose of taking the
medicine which he had recommended, from
which it is probable she would otherwise have
dissuaded her. Neither had these intimations escaped the ears of Wayland, who knew much
better how to interpret them. He felt much compassion at beholding so lovely a creature as the
Countess, and whom he had first seen in the

bosom of domestic happiness, exposed to the machinations of such a gang of villains. His passions, too, had been highly excited, by hearing the voice of his old master, against whom he nourished, in equal degree, the passions of hatred and fear. He nourished also a pride in his own art and resources; and, dangerous as the task was, he that night formed a determination to attain the bottom of the mystery, and to aid the distressed lady, if it were yet possible. From some words which Lambourne had dropped amongst his ravings, Wayland now, for the first time, felt inclined to doubt that Varney had acted entirely on his own account, in wooing and winning the affections of this beautiful creature. Fame asserted of this zealous retainer, that he had accommodated his lord in former love intrigues; and it occurred to Wayland Smith, that Leicester himself might be the party chiefly interested. Her marriage with the Earl he could not suspect; but even the discovery of such a passing intrigue with a lady of Mistress Amy Robsart's rank, was a secret of the deepest importance to the stability of the favourite's power over Elizabeth. « If Leicester would hesitate to stifle such a rumour by very strange means, » said he to himself, « he has those about him who would do him that favour without waiting for his consent. If I would meddle in this business, it must be as my old master uses to compound his manna of Satan, with a close mask on my face. So I will quit Giles Gosling

to morrow, and change my course and place
of residence as often as a hunted fox. I should
like to see this little puritan, too, once more.
She looks both pretty and intelligent, to have
come of such a caitiff as Antony Fire-the-Faggot. »

Giles Gosling received the adieus of Wayland
rather joyfully than otherwise. The honest publican saw so much peril in crossing the course
of the Earl of Leicester's favourite, that his virtue was scarce able to support him in the task,
and he was well pleased when it was likely to
be removed from his shoulders; still, however,
professing his good will, and readiness, in case
of need, to do Mr Tressilian or his emissary any
service, in so far as consisted with his character
of a publican.

CHAPTER XXI.

Vaulting ambition, that o'erleaps itself,
And falls on t'other side.

Macbeth.

THE splendour of the approaching revels at
Kenilworth was now the conversation through
all England; and every thing was collected at
home, or from abroad, which could add to the
gaiety or glory of the prepared reception of Elizabeth, at the house of her most distinguished
favourite. Meantime, Leicester appeared daily
to advance in the Queen's favour. He was perpetually by her side in council, willingly listened
to in the moments of courtly recreation — favoured with approaches even to familiar intimacy — looked up to by all who had aught to
hope at court — courted by foreign ministers
with the most flattering testimonies of respect
from their sovereigns — the *Alter Ego*, as it
seemed, of the stately Elizabeth, who was now
very generally supposed to be studying the time
and opportunity for associating him, by marriage, into her sovereign power.

Amid such a tide of prosperity, this minion of
fortune, and of the Queen's favour, was probably
the most unhappy man in the realm which seemed

at his devotion. He had the Fairy King's superiority over his friends and dependants , and saw
much which they could not. The character of
his mistress was intimately known to him; it was
his minute and studied acquaintance with her
humours, as well as her noble qualities, which,
joined to his powerful mental qualities, and his
eminent external accomplishments, had raised
him so high in her favour; and it was that very
knowledge of her disposition which led him to
apprehend at every turn some sudden and overwhelming disgrace. Leicester was like a pilot
possessed of a chart, which points out to him
all the peculiarities of his navigation, but which
exhibits so many shoals, breakers, and reefs of
rocks, that his anxious eye reaps little more from
observing them, than to be convinced that his
final escape can be little else than miraculous.

In fact, Queen Elizabeth had a character
strangely compounded of the strongest masculine sense, with those foibles which are chiefly
supposed proper to the female sex. Her subjects
had the full benefit of her virtues, which far pre-
dominated over her weaknesses; but her courtiers, and those about her person, had often to
sustain sudden and embarrassing turns of caprice,
and the sallies of a temper which was both jealous and despotic. She was the nursing-mother
of her people, but she was also the true daughter of Henry VIII; and though early sufferings
and an excellent education had repressed and
modified, they had not altogether destroyed, the

hereditary temper of that « hard-ruled King. »
—« Her mind , « says her witty god-son, Sir John
Harrington, who had experienced both the smiles
and the frowns which he describes, « was oftime
like the gentle air, that cometh from the western
point in a summer's morn — 'twas sweet and
refreshing to all around her. Her speech did win
all affections. And again, she could put forth
such alterations, when obedience was lacking,
as left no doubting *whose* daughter she was.
When she smiled, it was a pure sunshine, that
every one did chuse to bask in, if they could;
but anon came a storm, from a sudden gathering
of clouds, and the thunder fell, in a wondrous
manner, on all alike. » *

This variability of disposition, as Leicester
well knew, was chiefly formidable to those who
had a share in the Queen's affections, and who
depended rather on her personal regard, than
on the indispensable services which they could
render to her councils and her crown. The favour of Burleigh, or of Walsingham, of a description far less striking than that by which he
was himself upheld, was founded, as Leicester
well knew, on Elizabeth's solid judgment, not
on her partiality; and was, therfore, free from
all those principles of change and decay, necessarily incident to that which chiefly arose from
personal accomplishments and female predilec-
tion. These great and sage statesmen were jud-

* Nugæ Antiquæ, vol. I, pp. 355, 356—362.

ged of by the Queen, only with reference to
the measures they suggested, and the reasons by
which they supported their opinions in council;
whereas the success of Leicester's course depended on all those light and changeable gales
of caprice and humour, which thwart or favour
the progress of a lover in the favour of his mistress, and she, too, a mistress who was ever and
anon becoming fearful lest she should forget the
dignity, or compromise the authority of the
Queen, while she indulged the affections of the
woman. Of the difficulties which surrounded his
power, « too great to keep or to resign, » Leicester was fully sensible; and, as he looked
anxiously round for the means of maintaining
himsef in his precarious situation, and sometimes contemplated those of descending from it
in safety, he saw but little hope of either. At such
moments, his thoughts turned to dwell upon
his secret marriage, and its consequences; and
it was in bitterness against himself, if not against
his unfortunate Countess, that he ascribed to
that hasty measure, adopted in the ardour of
what he now called inconsiderate passion, at
once the impossibility of placing his power on
a solid basis, and the imminent prospect of its
precipitate downfall.

« Men say, » thus ran his thoughts, in these
anxious and repentant moments, « that I might
marry Elizabeth, and become King of England.
All things suggest this. The match is carolled
in ballads, while the rabble throw their caps

up — It has been touched upon in the schools — whispered in the presence-chamber — recommended from the pulpit — prayed for in the Calvinistic churches abroad — touched on by statists in the very council at home — These bold insinuations have been rebutted by no rebuke, no resentment, no chiding, scarce even by the usual female protestation that she would live and die a virgin princess. — Her words have been more courteous than ever, though she knows such rumours are abroad — her actions more gracious — her looks more kind — nought seems wanting to make me King of England, and place me beyond the storms of court-favour, excepting the putting forth of mine own hand to take that crown imperial, which is the glory of the universe! And when I might stretch that hand out most boldly, it is fettered down by a secret and inextricable bond. — And here I have letters from Amy, » he would say, catching them up with a movement of peevishness, « persecuting me to acknowledge her openly — to do justice to her and to myself — and I wot not what. Methinks I have done less than justice to myself already. And she speaks as if Elizabeth were to receive the knowledge of this matter, with the glee of a mother hearing of the happy marriage of a hopeful son! She, the daughter of Henry, who spared neither man in his anger, nor woman in his desire, — she to find herself tricked, drawn on with toys of passion to the verge of acknowledging her love to a subject, and he a married man! — Elizabeth to learn that she had been dallied with in such fashion, as a gay courtier might trifle with a country wench — We should then learn *furens quid fœmina!* »

He would then pause, and call for Varney, whose advice was now more frequently resorted to than ever, because the Earl remembered the remonstrances which he had made against his secret contract. And their consultation usually terminated in anxious deliberation, how, or in what manner, the Countess was to be produced at Kenilworth. These communings had for some time ended always in a resolution to delay the Progress from day to day. But at length a peremptory decision became necessary.

« Elizabeth will not be satisfied without her presence, » said the Earl ; « whether any suspicion hath entered her mind, as my own apprehensions suggest, or whether the petition of Tressilian is kept in her memory by Sussex, or some other secret enemy, I know not ; but amongst all the favourable expressions which she uses to me, she often recurs to the story of Amy Robsart. I think that Amy is the slave in the chariot, who is placed there by my evil fortune to dash and to confound my triumph, even when at the highest. Shew me thy device, Varney, for solving the inextricable difficulty. I have thrown every such impediment in the way of these accursed revels, as I could propound even with a shade of decency ; but to-

day's interview has put all to a hazard. She said
to me kindly, but peremptorily, We will give
you no farther time for preparations, my lord,
lest you should altogether ruin yourself. On
Saturday, the 9th of July, we will be with you
at Kenilworth — We pray you to forget none
of our appointed guests and suitors, and in
especial this light-o'-love, Amy Robsart. We
would wish to see the woman who could postpone yonder poetical gentleman, Master Tressilian, to your man, Richard Varney. — Now,
Varney, ply thine invention, whose forge hath
availed us so often; for sure as my name is
Dudley, the danger menaced by my horoscope
is now darkening around me. »

« Can my lady be by no means persuaded to
bear for a brief space the obscure character
which circumstances impose on her? » said
Varney, after some hesitation.

« How, sirrah! my Countess term herself *thy*
wife! — that may neither stand with my honour
nor with her's. »

« Alas! my lord, » answered Varney, « and
yet such is the quality in which Elizabeth now
holds her; and to contradict this opinion is to
discover all. »

« Think of something else, Varney, » said the
Earl, in great agitation; « this invention is
naught — If I could give way to it, she would
not; for I tell thee, Varney, if thou know'st it
not, that not Elizabeth on the throne has more
pride than the daughter of this obscure gentle-

man of Devon. She is flexible in many things, but where she holds her honour brought in question, she hath a spirit and temper as apprehensive as lightning, and as swift in execution. »

« We have experienced that, my lord, else had we not been thus circumstanced, » said Varney. « But what else to suggest I know not — Methinks she who gives rise to the danger, should do somewhat towards parrying it. »

« It is impossible, » said the Earl, waving his hand; « I know neither authority nor entreaties would make her endure thy name for an hour. »

« It is somewhat hard though, » said Varney, in a dry tone; and, without pausing on that topic, he added, « Suppose some one were found to represent her? Such feats have been performed in the courts of as sharp-eyed monarchs as Queen Elizabeth. »

« Utter madness, Varney, » answered the Earl; « the counterfeit would be confronted with Tressilian, and discovery become inevitable. »

« Tressilian might be removed from court, » said the unhesitating Varney.

« And by what means? ».

« There are many, » said Varney, « by which a statesman in your situation, my lord, may remove from the scene one who pries into your affairs, and places himself in perilous opposition to you. »

« Speak not to me of such policy, Varney, » said the Earl, hastily; « which, besides, would

avail nothing in the present case. Many others
may be at court, to whom Amy may be known;
and besides, on the absence of Tressilian, her
father or some of her friends would be instantly
summoned hither. Urge thine invention once
more. »

« My lord, I know not what to say, » answered
Varney; « but were I myself in such perplexity,
I would ride post down to Cumnor Place, and
compel my wife to give her consent to such
measures as her safety and mine required. »

« Varney, » said Leicester, « I cannot urge her
to aught so repugnant to her noble nature, as a
share in this stratagem — it would be a base
requital to the love she bears me. »

« Well, my lord, » said Varney, « your lordship is a wise and an honourable man, and
skilled in those high points of romantic scruple,
which are current in Arcadia, perhaps, as your
nephew, Philip Sidney, writes. I am your humble
servitor — a man of this world, and only happy
that my knowledge of it, and its ways, is such
as your lordship has not scorned to avail
yourself of. Now I would fain know, whether
the obligation lies on my lady or on you, in
this fortunate union; and which has most reason
to shew complaisance to the other, and to consider that other's wishes, conveniencies, and
safety? »

« I tell thee, Varney, » said the Earl, « that
all it was in my power to bestow upon her,
was not merely deserved, but a thousand times

overpaid , by her own virtue and beauty ; for never did greatness descend upon a creature so formed by nature to grace and adorn it. »

« It is well, my lord , you are so satisfied , » answered Varney , with his usual Sardonic smile, which even respect to his patron could not at all times subdue — « you will have time enough to enjoy undisturbed the society of one so gracious and beautiful — that is, so soon as such confinement in the Tower be over , as may correspond to the crime of deceiving the affections of Elizabeth Tudor — A cheaper penalty, I presume, you do not expect. »

« Malicious fiend ! » answered Leicester , « do you mock me in my misfortune ? — Manage it as thou wilt. »

« If you are serious, my lord , » said Varney, « you must set forth instantly , and post for Cumnor Place. »

« Do thou go thyself, Varney ; the devil has given thee that sort of eloquence , which is most powerful in the worst cause. I should stand self-convicted of villainy, were I to urge such a deceit. — Begone, I tell thee — Must I entreat thee to mine own dishonour ? »

« No , my lord , » said Varney — « but if you are serious in entrusting me with the task of urging this most necessary measure , you must give me a letter to my lady, as my credentials, and trust to me for backing the advice it contains with all the force in my power. And such is my opinion of my lady's love for your lordship,

and of her willingness to do that which is at
once to contribute to your pleasure and your
safety, that I am sure she will condescend to
bear, for a few brief days, the name of so
humble a man as myself, especially since it is
not inferior in antiquity to that of her own pa-
ternal house. »

Leicester seized on writing materials, and
twice or thrice commenced a letter to the Countess, which he afterwards tore into fragments.
At length he finished a few distracted·lines,
in which he conjured her, for reasons nearly
concerning his life and honour, to consent to
bear the name of Varney for a few days, during
the revels at Kenilworth. He added, that Varney
would communicate all the reasons which rendered this deception indispensable; and having
signed and sealed these credentials, he flung
them over the table to Varney, with a motion
that he should depart, which his adviser was
not slow to comprehend and to obey.

Leicester remained like one stupified, till he
heard the trampling of the horses, as Varney,
who took no time even to change his dress,
threw himself into the saddle, and, followed
by a single servant, set off for Berkshire. At
the sound, the Earl started from his seat, and
ran to the window, with the momentary purpose of recalling the unworthy commission with
which he had entrusted one, of whom he used
to say, he knew no virtuous property save
affection to his patron. But Varney was already

beyond call — and the bright starry firmament, which the age considered as the Book of Fate, lying spread before Leicester when he opened the casement, diverted him from his better and more manly purpose.

« There they roll, on their silent but potential course, » said the Earl, looking around him, « without a voice which speaks to our ear, but with influences which affect, at every change, the indwellers of this vile earthly planet. This, if astrologers fable not, is the very crisis of my fate! The hour approaches, of which I was taught to beware — the hour, too, which I was encouraged to hope for. — A King was the word — but how? — the crown matrimonial — all hopes of that are gone — let them go. The rich Netherlands have demanded me for their leader, and, would Elizabeth consent, would yield to me *their* crown. — And have I not such a claim, even in this kingdom? That of York, descending from George of Clarence to the House of Huntingdon, which, this lady failing, may have a fair chance — Huntingdon is of my house. — But I will plunge no deeper in these high mysteries. Let me hold my course in silence for a while, and in obscurity, like a subterranean river — the time shall come that I will burst forth in my strength, and bear all opposition before me. »

While Leicester was thus stupifying the remonstrances of his own conscience, by appealing to political necessity for his apology, or losing

2*

himself amidst the wild dreams of ambition,
his agent left town and tower behind him, on
his hasty journey to Berkshire. *He* also nourished high hope. He had brought Lord Leicester
to the point which he had desired, of commit-
ting to him the most intimate recesses of his
breast, and of using him as the channel of his
most confidential intercourse with his lady.
Henceforward it would, he foresaw, be difficult
for his patron either to dispense with his services, or refuse his requests, however unreason-
able. And if this disdainful dame, as he termed
the Countess, should comply with the request
of her husband, Varney, her pretended husband,
must needs become so situated with respect to
her, that there was no knowing where his audacity might be bounded, perhaps not till circumstances enabled him to obtain a triumph,
which he thought of with a mixture of fiendish
feelings, in which revenge for her previous
scorn was foremost and predominant. Again he
contemplated the possibility of her being totally
intractable, and refusing obstinately to play the
part assigned to her in the drama at Kenilworth.

« Alasco must then do his part, » he said—
« Sickness must serve her Majesty as an excuse
for not receiving the homage of Mrs Varney—
ay, and a sore and a wasting sickness it may
prove, should Elizabeth continue to cast so favourable an eye on my Lord of Leicester. I will
not forego the chance of being favourite of a
monarch for want of determined measures,

should these be necessary. — Forward, good horse, forward—ambition, and haughty hope of power, pleasure, and revenge, strike their stings as deep through my bosom as I plunge the rowels in thy flanks—On, good horse, on —the devil urges us both forward. »

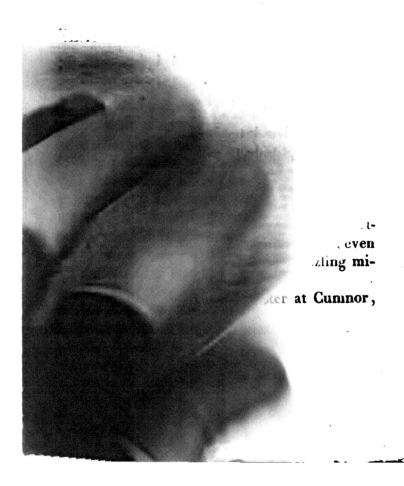

t-
, even
zling mi-

ter at Cumnor,

CHAPTER XXII.

Say that my beauty was but small,
  Among court ladies all despised;
Why didst thou rend it from that hall,
  Where, scornful Earl, 'twas dearly prized?

No more thou comest with wonted speed,
  Thy once beloved bride to see;
But be she alive or be she dead,
  I fear, stern Earl, 's the same to thee.
            Cumnor-Hall, by William Julius Mickle.

THE ladies of fashion of the present, or of any other period, must have allowed, that the young and lovely Countess of Leicester had, besides her youth and beauty, two qualities which entitled her to a place amongst women of rank and distinction. She displayed, as we have seen in her interview with the pedlar, a liberal promptitude to make unnecessary purchases, solely for the pleasure of acquiring useless and showy trifles which ceased to please as soon as they were possessed; and she was, besides, apt to spend a considerable space of time every day in adorning her person, although the varied splendour of her attire could only attract the half satirical praise of the precise Janet, or an approving glance from the bright eyes which witnessed their own beams of triumph reflected from the mirror.

The Countess Amy had, indeed, to plead for indulgence in those frivolous tastes, that the education of the times had done little or nothing for a mind naturally gay and averse to study. If she had not loved to collect finery and to wear it, she might have woven tapestry or sewed embroidery, till her labours spread in gay profusion all over the walls and seats at Lidcote-Hall; or she might have varied Minerva's labours with the task of preparing a mighty pudding against the time that Sir Hugh Robsart returned from the greenwood. But Amy had no natural genius either for the loom, the needle, or the receipt-book. Her mother had died in infancy; her father contradicted her in nothing; and Tressilian, the only one who approached her, that was able or desirous to attend to the cultivation of her mind, had much hurt his interest with her, by assuming too eagerly the task of a preceptor; so that he was regarded by the lively, indulged, and idle girl, with some fear and much respect; but with little or nothing of that softer emotion which it had been his hope and his ambition to inspire. And thus her heart lay readily open, and her fancy became easily captivated by the noble exterior and graceful deportment, and complacent flattery of Leicester, even before he was known to her as the dazzling minion of wealth and power.

The frequent visits of Leicester at Cumnor,

during the earlier part of their union, had reconciled the Countess to the solitude and privacy
to which she was condemned; but when these
visits became rarer and more rare, and when
the void was filled up with letters of excuse,
not always very warmly expressed, and generally
extremely brief, discontent and suspicion began
to haunt those splendid apartments which love
had fitted up for beauty. Her answers to Leicester conveyed these feelings too bluntly, and
pressed more naturally than prudently that she
might be relieved from this obscure and secluded residence, by the Earl's acknowledgment
of their marriage; and in arranging her argu-
ments with all the skill she was mistress of, she
trusted chiefly to the warmth of the entreaties
with which she urged them. Sometimes she
even ventured to mingle reproaches, of which
Leicester conceived he had good reason to complain.

« I have made her Countess, » he said to Varney, « surely she might wait till it consisted
with my pleasure that she should put on a
coronet. »

The Countess Amy viewed the subject in directly an opposite light.

« What signifies, » she said, « that I have rank
and honour in reality, if I am to live an obscure
prisoner, without either society or observance,
and suffering in my character, as one of dubious
or disgraced reputation ? I care not for all those
strings of pearl, which you fret me by warping

into my tresses, Janet. I tell you, that at Lidcote-Hall, if I put but a fresh rose-bud among my hair, my good father would call me to him, that he might see it more closely; and the kind old curate would smile, and Master Mumblazen would say something about roses gules; and now I sit here, decked out like an image with gold and gems, and no one to see my finery but you, Janet. There was the poor Tressilian too — but it avails not speaking of him. »

« It doth not, indeed, madam, said her prudent attendant; « and verily you make me sometimes wish you would not speak of him so often, or so rashly. »

« It signifies nothing to warn me, Janet — I was born free, though I am now mewed up like some fine foreign slave, rather than the wife of an English noble. I bore it all with pleasure while I was sure he loved me; but now, my tongue and heart shall be free, let them fetter my limbs as they will. — I tell thee, Janet, I love my husband — I will love him till my latest breath — I cannot cease to love him, even if I would, or if he — which, God knows, may chance — should cease to love me. But I will say, and loudly, I would have been happier than I now am, to have remained in Lidcote-Hall; even although I must have married poor Tressilian, with his melancholy look, and his head full of learning, which I cared not for. He said if I would read his favourite volumes, there would come a time that I should be glad of it — I think it is come now. »

. · « I bought you some books, madam , » said Janet, · « from a lame fellow who sold them in the Market-place — and who stared something boldly at me, I promise you. »

« Let me see them, Janet, » said the Countess; « but let them not be of your own precise cast. How is this, most righteous damsel? — *A Pair of Snuffers for the Golden Candlestick — A Handful of Myrrh and Hissop to put a Sick Soul to Purgation — A Draught of Water from the Valley of Baca — Foxes and Firebrands —* What gear call you this, maiden? »

« Nay, madam , » said Janet, « it was but fitting and seemly to put grace in your ladyship's way; but an you will none of it, there are play-books, and poet-books, I trow. »

The Countess proceeded carelessly in her examination, turning over such rare volumes as would now make the fortune of twenty retail booksellers. Here was a « *Boke of Cookery, imprinted by Richard Lant,* » and « *Skelton's Books* » — « *The Passtime of the People* » — « *The Castle of Knowledge,* etc. But neither to this lore did the Countess's heart incline, and joyfully did she start up from the listless task of turning over the leaves of the pamphlets, and hastily did she scatter them through the floor, when the hasty clatter of horse's feet, heard in the court-yard, · called her to the window, exclaiming, « It is

Leicester ! — it is my noble Earl ! — it is my
Dudley ! — Every stroke of his horse's hoof
sounds like a note of lordly music! »

There was a brief bustle in the mansion, and
Foster, with his downward look and sullen manner, entered the apartment to say, « That Master
Richard Varney was arrived from my lord, having ridden all night, and craved to speak with
her ladyship instantly. »

« Varney? — and to speak with me? — pshaw!
— But he comes with news from Leicester —
so admit him instantly. »

Varney entered her dressing apartment, where
she sat arrayed in her native loveliness, adorned
with all that Janet's art, and a rich and tasteful
undress, could bestow. But the most beautiful
part of her attire was her beautiful and luxu-
riant light-brown locks, which floated in such
rich abundance around a neck that resembled a
swan's, and over a bosom heaving with anxious
expectation, which communicated a hurried
tinge of red to her whole countenance.

Varney entered the room in the dress in which
he had waited on his master that morning to
court, the splendour of which made a strange
contrast with the disorder arising from hasty
riding, during a dark night and foul ways. His
brow bore an anxious and hurried expression,
as one who has that to say of which he doubts
the reception, and who hath yet posted on from
the necessity of communicating his tidings. The
Countess's anxious eye at once caught the alarm,

as she exclaimed, « You bring news from my
lord, Master Varney — Gracious Heaven, is he
ill ? »

« No, Madam, thank Heaven ! » said Varney.
« Compose yourself, and permit me to take
breath ere I communicate my tidings. »

« No breath, sir, » replied the lady, impatiently; « I know your theatrical arts. Since
your breath hath sufficed to bring you hither,
it may suffice to tell your tale, as least briefly,
and in the gross. »

« Madam, » answered Varney, « we are not
alone, and my lord's message was for your ear
only. »

« Leave us, Janet, and Master Foster, » said
the lady; « but remain in the next apartment,
and within call. »

Foster and his daughter retired, agreeably
to the Lady Leicester's commands, into the
next apartment, which was the withdrawing-
room. The door which led from the sleeping-
chamber was then carefully shut and bolted,
and the father and daughter remained both in a
posture of anxious attention; the first with a
stern, suspicious, anxious cast of countenance,
and Janet with folded hands, and looks which
seemed divided betwixt her desire to know the
fortunes of her mistress, and her prayers to
Heaven for her safety. Anthony Foster seemed
himself to have some idea of what was passing
through his daughter's mind, for he crossed the
apartment and took her anxiously by the hand,

saying, « That is right—pray, Janet, pray—
we have all need of prayers, and some of us
more than others. Pray, Janet—I would pray
myself, but I must listen to what goes on within
— evil has been brewing, love — evil has been
brewing. God forgive our sins, but Varney's
sudden and strange arrival bodes us no good. »

Janet had never before heard her father excite
or even permit her attention to any thing which
passed in their mysterious family, and now that
he did so, his voice sounded in her ear—she
knew not why—like that of a screech-owl de-
nouncing some deed of terror and of woe. She
turned her eyes fearfully towards the door, almost as if she expected some sounds of horror
to be heard, or some sight of fear to display
itself.

All, however, was as still as death, and the
voices of those who spoke in the inner-chamber,
were, if they spoke at all, carefully subdued to a
tone which could not be heard in the next. At
once, however, they were heard to speak fast,
thick, and hastily; and presently after the voice
of the Countess was heard exclaiming, at the
highest pitch to which indignation could raise
it, « Undo the door, sir, I command you!—
Undo the door!—I will have no other reply! »
she continued, drowning with her vehement
accents the low and muttered sounds which Varney was heard to utter betwixt whiles. « What ho!
without there! » she persisted, accompanying
her words with shrieks, « Janet, alarm the house,

—Foster, break open the door—I am detained
here by a traitor! —Use axe and lever, Master
Foster—I will be your warrant! »

« It shall not need, madam, » Varney was at
length distinctly heard to say. « If you please to
expose my lord's important concerns and your
own to the general ear, I will not be your hin-
derance. »

The door was unlocked and thrown open,
and Janet and her father rushed in, anxious
to learn the cause of these reiterated exclamations.

When they entered the apartment, Varney
stood by the door grinding his teeth, with an
expression in which rage, and shame, and fear,
had each their share. The Countess stood in the
midst of her apartment like a juvenile Pytho-
ness, under the influence of the prophetic fury.
The veins in her beautiful forehead started into
swoln blue lines through the hurried impulse of
her articulation — her cheek and neck glowed
like scarlet—her eyes were like those of an imprisoned eagle, flashing red lightning on the foes
whom it cannot reach with its talons. Were
it possible for one of the Graces to have been
animated by a Fury, the countenance could not
have united such beauty with so much hatred,
scorn, defiance, and resentment. The gesture
and attitude corresponded with the voice and
looks, and altogether presented a spectacle which
was at once beautiful and fearful; so much of
the sublime had the energy of passion united

with the Countess Amy's natural loveliness. Janet, as soon as the door was open, ran to her mistress; and more slowly, yet with more haste than he was wont, Anthony Foster went to Richard Varney.

« In the Truth's name, what ails your ladyship? » said the former.

« What, in the name of Satan, have you done to her? » said Foster to his friend.

« Who, I?—nothing, » answered Varney, but with sunken head and sullen voice; « nothing but communicated to her her lord's commands, which, if the lady list not to obey, she knows better how to answer it than I may pretend to do. »

« Now, by Heaven, Janet, » said the Countess, « the false traitor lies in his throat! He must needs lie, for he speaks to the dishonour of my noble lord — he must needs lie doubly, for he speaks to gain ends of his own, equally execrable and unattainable. »

« You have misapprehended me, lady, » said Varney, with a sulky species of submission and apology; « let this matter rest till your passion be abated, and I will explain all. »

« Thou shalt never have an opportunity to do so; » said the Countess.—« Look at him, Janet. He is fairly dressed, hath the outside of a gentleman, and hither he came to persuade me it was my lord's pleasure—nay, more, my wedded lord's commands, that I should go with him to

Kenilworth, and before the Queen and nobles, and in presence of my own wedded lord, that I should acknowledge him—*him* there—that very cloak-brushing, shoe-cleaning fellow—*him* there, my lord's lacquey, for my liege lord and husband; furnishing against myself, great God! whenever I was to claim my right and my rank, such weapons as would hew my just claim from the root, and destroy my character to be regarded as an honourable matron of the English nobility! »

« You hear her, Foster, and you, young maiden, hear this lady, » answered Varney, taking advantage of the pause which the Countess had made in her charge, more for lack of breath than for lack of matter — « You hear that her heat only objects to me the coursé which our good lord, for the purpose to keep certain matters secret, suggests in the very letter which she holds in her hands. »

Foster here attempted to interfere with a face of authority, which he thought became the charge entrusted to him, « Nay, lady, I must needs say you are hasty in this — Such deceit is not utterly to be condemned when practised for a righteous end; and thus even the patriarch Abraham feigned Sarah to be his sister when they went down to Egypt. »

« Ay, sir, » answered the Countess; « but God rebuked that deceit even in the father of his chosen people, by the mouth of the heathen

Pharaoh. Out upon you, that will read Scripture only to copy those things, which are held out to us as warnings, not as examples ! »

« But Sarah disputed not the will of her husband, an it be your pleasure, » said Foster, in reply; « but did as Abraham commanded, calling herself his sister, that it might be well with her husband for her sake, and that his soul might live because of her beauty. »

« Now, so Heaven pardon me my useless anger, » answered the Countess, « thou art as daring a hypocrite as yonder fellow is an impudent deceiver. Never will I believe that the noble Dudley gave countenance to so dastardly, so dishonourable a plan. Thus I tread on his infamy, if his indeed it be, and thus destroy its remembrance for ever ! »

So saying, she tore in pieces Leicester's letter, and stamped, in the extremity of impatience, as if she would have annihilated the minute fragments into which she had rent it.

« Bear witness, » said Varney, collecting himself, « she has torn my lord's letter, in order to burthen me with the scheme of his devising; and although it promises nought but danger and trouble to me, she would lay it to my charge, as if I had any purpose of mine own in it. »

« Thou liest, thou treacherous slave ! » said Countess Amy, in spite of Janet's attempts to keep her silent, in the sad foresight that her vehemence might only furnish arms against herself. « Thou liest, » she continued — « Let me go,

Janet — Were it the last word I have to speak,
he lies.— he had his own foul ends to seek; and
broader he would have displayed them, had my
passion permitted me to preserve the silence
which at first encouraged him to unfold his vile
projects. »

« Madam, » said Varney, overwhelmed in spite
of his effrontery, « I entreat you to believe yourself mistaken. »

« As soon will I believe light darkness. Have
I drank of oblivion? Do I not remember former
passages, which, known to Leicester, had given
thee the preferment of a gallows, instead of the
honour of his intimacy. — I would I were a man
but for five minutes! It were space enough to
make a craven like thee confess his villainy. But
go—begone—Tell thy master, that when I take
the foul course to which such scandalous de-
ceits as thou hast recommended on his behalf
must necessarily lead me, I will give him a rival
something worthy of the name. He shall not be
supplanted by an ignominious lacquey, whose
best fortune is to catch his master's last suit of
clothes ere it is thread-bare, and who is only
fit to seduce a suburb-wench by the bravery of
new roses in his master's old pantofles. Go, begone, sir — I scorn thee so much, that I am
ashamed to have been angry with thee. »

Varney left the room with a mute expression
of rage, and was followed by Foster, whose apprehension, naturally slow, was overpowered
by the eager and abundant discharge of indigna-

tion, which, for the first time, he had heard
burst from the lips of a being, who had seemed
till that moment too languid, and too gentle, to
nurse an angry thought, or utter an intemperate
expression. Foster, therefore, pursued Varney
from place to place, persecuting him with in-
terrogatories, to which the other replied not,
until they were in the opposite side of the quadrangle, and in the old library; with which the
reader has already been made acquainted. Here
he turned round on his persevering follower,
and thus addressed him, in a tone tolerably
equal; that brief walk having been sufficient
to give one so habituated to command his temper, time to rally and recover his presence of
mind.

« Tony, » he said, with his usual sneering
laugh, « it avails not to deny it. The Woman and
the Devil, who, as thine oracle Holdforth will
confirm to thee, cheated man at the beginning,
have this day proved more powerful than my
discretion. Yon termagant looked so tempting,
and had the art to preserve her countenance so
naturally, while I communicated my lord's message, that, by my faith, I thought I might say
some little thing for myself. She thinks she hath
my head under her girdle now, but she is deceived.—Where is Doctor Alasco ? »

« In his laboratory, » answered Foster; « it is
the hour he is not spoken withal—we must wait
till noon is past, or spoil his important —What

said I important ?—I would say interrupt his divine studies?

« Ay, he studies the devil's divinity, » said Varney,—« but when I want him, one hour must suffice as well as another. Lead the way to his pandæmonium. »

So spoke Varney, and with hasty and perturbed steps followed Foster, who conducted him through private passages, many of which were well nigh ruinous, to the opposite side of the quadrangle, where, in a subterranean apartment, now occupied by the chemist Alasco, one of the Abbots of Abingdon, who had a turn for the occult sciences, had, much to the scandal of his convent, established a laboratory, in which, like other fools of the time, he spent much precious time, and money besides, in the pursuit of the grand arcanum.

Anthony Foster paused before the door, which was scrupulously secured within, and again shewed a marked hesitation to disturb the sage in his operations. But Varney, less scrupulous, roused him, by knocking and voice, until at length, slowly and reluctantly, the inmate of the apartment undid the door. The chemist appeared, with his eyes bleared with the heat and vapours of the stove or alembic over which he brooded, and the interior of his cell displayed the confused assemblage of heterogeneous substances, and extraordinary implements, belonging to his profession. The old man was muttering, with spiteful impatience, « Am I for ever to be recalled to the affairs of earth from those of heaven ? »

« To the affairs of hell, » answered Varney, « for that is thy proper element. — Foster, we need thee at our conference. »

Foster slowly entered the room. Varney, following, barred the door, and they betook themselves to secret council.

In the meanwhile, the Countess traversed the apartment, with shame and anger contending on her lovely cheek.

« The villain, » she said, « the cold-blooded calculating slave ! — But I unmasked him, Janet — I made the snake uncoil all his folds before me, and crawl abroad in his naked deformity — I suspended my resentment, at the danger of suffocating under the effort, until he had let me see the very bottom of a heart more foul than hell's darkest corner. — And thou, Leicester, is it possible thou couldst bid me for a moment deny my wedded right in thee, or thyself yield it to another ? But it is impossible — the villain has lied in all. — Janet, I will not remain here longer — I fear him — I fear thy father — I grieve to say it, Janet — but I fear thy father, and, worst of all, this odious Varney. I will escape from Cumnor. »

« Alas ! madam, whither would you fly, or by what means will you escape from these walls ? »

« I know not, Janet, » said the unfortunate young lady, looking upwards, and clasping her hands together, « I know not where I shall fly, or by what means; but I am certain the God I have served will not abandon me in this dreadful crisis, for I am in the hands of wicked men. »

« Do not think so, dear lady, » said Janet; « my father is stern and strict in his temper, and severely true to his trust — but yet » ——

At this moment, Anthony Foster entered the apartment, bearing in his hand a glass cup, and a small flask. His manner was singular; for, while approaching the Countess with the respect due to her rank, he had till this time suffered to become visible, or had been unable to suppress, the obdurate sulkiness of his natural disposition, which, as is usual with those of his unhappy temper, was chiefly exerted towards those over whom circumstances gave him controul. But at present he shewed nothing of that sullen consciousness of authority which he was wont to conceal under a clumsy affectation of civility and deference, as a ruffian hides his pistols and bludgeon under his ill-fashioned gaberdine. And yet it seemed as if his smile was more in fear than in courtesy, and as if, while he pressed the Countess to taste of the choice cordial, which should refresh her spirits after her late alarm, he was conscious of meditating some farther injury. His hand trembled also, his voice faultered, and his whole outward behaviour exhibited so much that was suspicious, that his daughter Janet, after she had stood looking at him in astonishment for some seconds, seemed at once to collect herself to execute some hardy resolution, raised her head, assumed an attitude and gait of determination and authority, and walking slowly betwixt her father and her mistress, took the salver from the hand of the former, and said in a low, but marked and decided tone. « Father, I will fill for my noble mistress, when such is her pleasure. »

« Thou, my child? » said Foster, eagerly and apprehensively; « no, my child—it is not thou shalt render the lady this service. »

« And why, I pray you, » said Janet, « if it be fitting that the noble lady should partake of the cup at all? »

« Why—why, » said the seneschal, hesitating, and then bursting into passion, as the readiest mode of supplying the lack of all other reason—« Why, because it is my pleasure, minion, that you should not—Get you gone to the evening lecture. »

« Now, as I hope to hear lecture again, » replied Janet, « I will not go thither this night, unless I am better assured of my mistress's safety. Give me that flask, father; »—and she took it from his reluctant hand, while he resigned it as if conscience-struck — « And now, » she said, « father, that which shall benefit my mistress, cannot do *me* prejudice. Father, I drink to you. »

Foster, without speaking a word, rushed on his daughter and wrested the flask from her hand; then, as if embarrassed by what he had

done, and totally unable to resolve what he
should do next, he stood with it in his hand,
one foot advanced and the other drawn back,
glaring on his daughter with a countenance, in
which rage, fear, and convicted villainy, formed
a hideous combination.

« This is strange, my father, » said Janet,
keeping her eye fixed on his, in the manner in
which those who have the charge of lunatics
are said to overawe their unhappy patients;
« will you neither let me serve my lady, nor
drink to her myself? »

The courage of the Countess sustained her
through this dreadful scene, of which the import was not the less obvious that it was not
even hinted at. She preserved even the rash
carelessness of her temper, and though her cheek
had grown pale at the first alarm, her eye was
calm and almost scornful. « Will *you* taste this
rare cordial, Master Foster? Perhaps you will
not yourself refuse to pledge us, though you
permit not Janet to do so — Drink, sir, I pray
you. »

« I will not, » answered Foster.

« And for whom, then, is the precious bever-
age reserved, sir? » said the Countess.

« For the devil, who brewed it, » answered
Foster; and, turning on his heel, he left the
chamber.

Janet looked at her mistress with a countenance expressive in the highest degree of shame,
dismay, and sorrow.

« Do not weep for me, Janet, » said the Countess, kindly.

« No, madam, » replied her attendant, in a voice broken by sobs, it is not for you I weep, it. is, for myself — it is for that unhappy man. Those who are dishonoured before man—those who are condemned by God, have cause to mourn — not those who are innocent! Farewell, madam! she said, hastily assuming the mantle in which she was wont to go abroad.

. . « Do you leave me, Janet? » said her mistress — « desert me in such an evil strait? »

« Desert you, madam! » exclaimed Janet ; and, running back to her mistress, she imprinted a thousand kisses on her hand — . « desert you! — may the Hope of my trust desert me when I do so! — No, madam; well you said the God you serve will open you a path for deliverance. There is a way of escape; I have prayed night and day for light, that I might see how to act betwixt my duty to yonder unhappy man, and that which I owe to you. Sternly and fearfully that light has now dawned, and I must not. shut the door, which God opens. — Ask me no more. I will return in brief space. »

So speaking, she wrapped herself in her mantle, and saying to the old woman whom she passed in the outer room, that she was going to evening prayer, she left the house.

Meanwhile her father had reached once more the laboratory, where he found the accomplices of his intended guilt.

« Has the sweet bird sipped ? » said Varney,
with half a smile; while the astrologer put the
same question with his eyes, but spoke not a
word.

« She has not, nor she shall not from my
hands, » replied Foster; « would you have me
do murther in my daughter's presence ? »

« Wert thou not told, thou sullen and yet
faint-hearted slave, » answered Varney with bitterness, « that no *murther*, as thou call'st it,
with that staring look and stammering tone, is
designed in the matter ? Wert thou not told,
that a brief illness, such as woman puts on in
very wantonness, that she may wear her night-
gear at noon, and lie on a settle when she should
mind her domestic business, is all here aimed
at ? Here is a learned man will swear it to thee
by the key of the Castle of Wisdom. »

« I swear it, » said Alasco, « that the elixir
thou hast there in the flask will not prejudice
life! I swear it by that immortal and indestruc-
tible quintessence of gold, which pervades every
substance in nature, though its secret existence
can be traced by him only, to whom Tresmi-
gistus renders the key of the Cabala. »

« An oath of force, » said Varney. « Foster,
thou wert worse than a pagan to disbelieve it.
Believe me, moreover, who swear by nothing
but my own word, that if you be not conchor-
mable, there is no hope, no, not a glimpse of
hope, that this thy leasehold may be transmuted
into a copy-hold. Thus, Alasco will leave your

pewter artillery untransmigrated, and I, honest Anthony, will still have thee for my tenant. »

« I know not, gentlemen, » said Foster, « where your designs tend to; but in one thing I am bound up,—that, fall back fall edge, I will have one in this place that may pray for me, and that one shall be my daughter. I have lived ill, and the world has been too weighty with me; but she is as innocent as ever she was when on her mother's lap, and she, at least, shall have her portion in that happy City, whose walls are of pure gold, and the foundations garnished with all manner of precious stones »

« Ay, Tony, » said Varney, « that were a paradise to thy heart's content.—Debate the matter with him, Doctor Alasco; I will be with you anon. »

So speaking, Varney arose, and, taking the flask from the table, he left the room.

« I tell thee, my son, » said Alasco to Foster, as soon as Varney had left them, « that whatever this bold and profligate railer may say of the mighty science, in which, by heaven's blessing, I have advanced so far, that I would not call the wisest of living artists my better or my teacher — I say, howsoever yonder reprobate may scoff at things too holy to be apprehended by men merely of carnal and evil thoughts, yet believe, that the city beheld by St John, in that bright vision of the Christian Apocalypse, that New Jerusalem, of which all Christian men hope to partake, sets

3*

forth typically the discovery of the GRAND SE-
CRET, whereby the most precious and perfect of
nature's works are elicited out of her basest and
most crude productions; just as the light and
gaudy butterfly, the most beautiful child of the
summer's breeze, breaks forth from the dungeon
of a sordid chrysalis. »

« Master Holdforth said nought of this exposition, » said Foster, doubtfully; « and moreover,
Doctor Alasco, the Holy Writ says, that the
gold and precious stones of the Holy City are in
no sort for those who work abomination, or who
frame lies. »

« Well, my son, » said the Doctor, « and what
is your inference from thence ? »

« That those, » said Foster, » who distil poi-
sons, and administer them in secrecy, can have
no portion in those unspeakable riches. »

« You are to distinguish, my son, » replied the
alchemist, « betwixt that which is necessarily evil
in its progress and in its end also, and that which
being evil, is, nevertheless, capable of working
forth good. If, by the death of one person, the
happy period shall be brought nearer to us, in
which all that is good shall be attained, by wishing its presence—all that is evil escaped, by desiring its absence—in which sickness, and pain,
and sorrow, shall be the obedient servants of
human wisdom, and made to fly at the slightest
signal of a sage,—in which that which is now
richest and rarest shall be within the compass of
every one who shall be obedient to the voice of

wisdom,—when the art of healing shall be lost
and absorbed in the one universal medicine,—
when sages shall become monarchs of the earth,
and death itself retreat before their crown,—if
this blessed consummation of all things can be
hastened by the slight circumstance, that a frail
earthly body, which must needs partake cor-
ruption, shall be consigned to the grave a short
space earlier than in the course of nature, what
is such a sacrifice to the advancement of the holy
Millenium ? »

« Millenium is the reign of the Saints, » said
Foster, somewhat doubtfully.

« Say it is the reign of the Sages, my son, » answered Alasco; « or rather the reign of Wisdom
itself. »

« I touched on the question with Master Holdforth last exercising night, » said Foster; « but he
says your doctrine is heterodox, and a damnable
and false exposition. »

« He is in the bonds of ignorance, my son, »
answered Alasco, « and as yet burning bricks in
Egypt; or, at best, wandering in the dry desert
of Sinai. Thou didst ill to speak to such a man
of such matters. I will, however, give thee proof,
and that shortly, which I will defy that peevish
divine to confute, though he should strive with
me as the magicians strove with Moses before
King Pharaoh. I will do projection in thy presence, my son,— in thy very presence, — and
thine eyes shall witness the truth. »

« Stick to that, learned sage, » said Varney,

who at this moment entered the apartment ; « if
he refuse the testimony of thy tongue, yet how
shall he deny that of his own eyes ? »

« Varney ! » said the adept — « Varney already
returned ! Hast thou » —— he stopped short.

« Have I done mine errand , thou wouldst
say, » replied Varney — « I have ! — And thou, »
he added , shewing more symptoms of interest
than he had hitherto exhibited , « art thou sure
thou hast poured forth neither more nor less
than the just measure ? »

« Ay , » replied the alchemist , « as sure as men
can be in these nice proportions ; for there is
diversity of constitutions. »

« Nay , then , » said Varney , « I fear nothing.
I know thou wilt not go a step farther to the devil than thou art justly considered for. Thou wert
paid to create illness, and would esteem it thrift-
less prodigality to do murther at the same price.
Come , let us each to our chamber — We shall
see the event to-morrow. »

« What didst thou do to make her swallow it ? »
said Foster , shuddering.

« Nothing , » answered Varney , « but looked
on her with that aspect which governs madmen ,
women and children. They told me, in Saint
Luke's Hospital , that I have the right look for
overpowering a refractory patient. The keepers
made me their compliments on't; so I know how
to win my bread, when my court-favour fails me.»

« And art thou not afraid , » said Foster , « lest
the dose be disproportioned ? »

« If so , » replied Varney , « she will but sleep the sounder, and the fear of that shall not break my rest. Good night , my masters. »

Anthony Foster groaned heavily , and lifted up his hands and eyes. The alchemist intimated his purpose to continue some experiment of high import during the greater part of the night, and the others separated to their places of repose.

....

CHAPTER XXIII.

Now God be good to me in this wild pilgrimage!
All hope in human aid I cast behind me.
Oh, who would be a woman? — who that fool,
A weeping, pining, faithful, loving woman?
She hath hard measure still where she hopes kindest,
And all her bounties only make ingrates.
Love's Pilgrimage.

THE summer evening was closed, and Janet, just when her longer stay might have occasioned suspicion and inquiry in that jealous household, returned to Cumnor-Place, and hastened to the apartment in which she had left her lady. She found her with her head resting on her arms, and these crossed upon a table which stood before her. As Janet came in, she neither looked up nor stirred.

Her faithful attendant ran to her mistress with the speed of lightning, and rousing her at the same time with her hand, conjured the Countess in the most earnest manner to look up, and say what thus affected her. The unhappy lady raised her head accordingly, and looking on her attendant with a ghastly eye, and cheek as pale as clay, « Janet, » she said, « I have drank it. »

« God be praised! said Janet, hastily — « I mean God be praised that it is no worse — the potion will not harm you. — Rise, shake this lethargy from your limbs, and this despair from your mind. »

· « Janet, » repeated the Countess again, « disturb me not — leave me at peace — let life pass quietly — I am poisoned. »

« You are not, my dearest lady, » answered the maiden eagerly — « What you have swallowed cannot injure you, and I hastened hither to tell you that the means of escape are open to you. »

« Escape ! » exclaimed the lady, as she raised herself hastily in her chair, while light returned to her eye and life to her cheek ; « but ah ! Janet, it comes too late. »

« Not so, dearest lady — Rise, take mine arm, walk through the apartment — Let not fancy do the work of poison ! — So; feel you not now that you are possessed of the full use of your limbs ? »

« The torpor seems to diminish, » said the Countess, as, supported by Janet, she walked to and fro in the apartment; « but is it then so, and have I not swallowed a deadly draught ? Varney was here since thou wert gone, and commanded me, with eyes in which I read my fate, to swallow yon horrible drug. O, Janet ! it must be fatal; never was harmless draught served by such a cup-bearer ! »

« He did not deem it harmless, I fear, » replied the maiden; « but God confounds the devices of the wicked. Believe me, as I swear

by the dear Gospel in which we trust, your life
is safe from his practice. Did you not debate with
him ? »

« The house was silent, » answered the lady
— « thou gone — no other but he in the chamber — and he capable of every crime. I did
but stipulate he would remove his hateful presence, and I drank whatever he offered. —
But you spoke of escape, Janet; can I be so
happy ? »

« Are you strong enough to bear the tidings,
and make the effort ? »

« Strong ! » answered the Countess — « Ask
the hind, when the fangs of the deer-hound are
stretched to gripe her, if she is strong enough
to spring the chasm. I am equal to every effort
that may relieve me from this place. »

« Hear me then, » said Janet, « One, whom I
deem an assured friend of yours, has shewn himself to me in various disguises, and sought speech
of me, which, — for my mind was not clear on
the matter until this evening, — I have ever de-
clined. He was the pedlar who brought you
goods—the itinerant hawker who sold me books
— whenever I stirred abroad I was sure to see
him. The event of this night determined me to
speak with him. He waits even now at the postern-gate of the park with means for your flight.
— But have you strength of body ? — Have you
courage of mind ? — Can you undertake the
enterprize ? »

« She that flies from death, » said the lady,

« finds strength of body — she that would escape from shame, lacks no. strength of mind. The thoughts of leaving behind me the villain who menaces both my life and honour, would give me strength to rise from my death-bed. »

« In God's name then, lady, » said Janet, « I must bid you adieu, and to God's charge I must commit you. »

« Will you not fly with me then, Janet? » said the Countess, anxiously — « Am I to lose thee? Is this thy faithful service? »

« Lady, I would fly with you as willingly as bird ever fled from cage, but my doing so would occasion instant discovery and pursuit. I must remain, and use means to disguise the truth for some time — May heaven pardon the falsehood, because of the necessity! »

« And am I then to travel alone with this stranger? » said the lady — « Bethink thee, Janet, may not this prove some deeper and darker scheme to separate me perhaps from you, who are my only friend? »

« No, madam, do not suppose it, » answered Janet, readily; « the youth is an honest youth in his purpose to you; and a friend to Master Tressilian, under whose direction he is come hither. »

« If he be a friend of Tressilian, » said the Countess, « I will commit myself to his charge, as to that of an angel sent from heaven; for than Tressilian, never breathed mortal man more free of whatever was base, false, or selfish. He forgot

himself whenever he could be of use to others
— Alas! and how was he requited ! »

With eager haste they collected the few neces-
saries which it was thought proper the Countess
should take with her, and which Janet, with
speed and dexterity, formed into a small bundle,
not forgetting to add such ornaments of intrinsic
value as came most readily in her way, and particularly a casket of jewels, which she wisely
judged might prove of service in some future
emergency. The Countess of Leicester next changed her dress for one which Janet usually wore
upon any brief journey, for they judged it necessary to avoid every external distinction which
might attract attention, Ere these preparations
were fully made, the moon had arisen in the
summer heaven, and all in the retired mansion
had betaken themselves to rest, or at least to the
silence and retirement of their chambers.

There was no difficulty anticipated in escaping,
whether from the house or garden, providing
only they could elude observation. Anthony Foster had accustomed himself to consider his daughter as a conscious sinner might regard a visible
guardian angel, which, notwithstanding his guilt,
continued to hover around him, and therefore
his trust in her knew no bounds. Janet commanded her own motions during the day-time, and
had a master-key which opened the postern-
door of the park, so that she could go to the
village at pleasure, either upon the household
affairs, which were entirely confided to her

management, or to attend her devotions at the
meeting-house of her sect. It is true the daughter
of Foster was thus liberally entrusted, under the
solemn condition that she should not avail herself of these privileges, to do any thing inconsistent with the safe-keeping of the Countess;
for so her residence at Cumnor-Place had been
termed, since she began of late to exhibit impatience of the restrictions to which she was
subjected. Nor is there reason to suppose, that
any thing short of the dreadful suspicions which
the scene of that evening had excited, could
have induced Janet to have violated her word,
or deceived her father's confidence. But from
what she had witnessed, she now conceived
herself not only justified, but imperatively called
upon to make her lady's safety the principal object of her care, setting all other considerations
aside.

The fugitive Countess with her guide were
traversing with hasty steps the broken and interrupted path, which had once been an avenue,
now totally darkened by the boughs of spread-
ing trees which met above their head, and
now receiving a doubtful and deceiving light
from the beams of the moon, which penetrated
where the axe had made openings in the wood.
Their path was repeatedly interrupted by felled
trees, or the large boughs which had been left
on the ground till time served to make them
into faggots and billets. The inconvenience and
difficulty attending these interruptions, the

breathless haste of the first part of their route,
the exhausting sensations of hope and fear, so
much affected the Countess's strength, that Janet
was forced to propose that they should pause
for a few minutes to recover breath and spirits.
Both therefore stood still beneath the shadow of
a huge old gnarled oak-tree, and both naturally
looked back to the mansion which they had
left behind them, whose long dark front was
seen in the gloomy distance, with its huge stalks
of chimnies, turrets, and clock-house, rising
above the line of the roof, and definedly visible
against the pure azure blue of the summer sky.
One light only twinkled from the extended and
shadowy mass, and it was placed so low that
it rather seemed to glimmer from the ground
in front of the mansion, than from one of the
windows. The Countess's terror was awakened.
— « They follow us! » she said, pointing out to
Janet the light which thus alarmed her.

Less agitated than her mistress, Janet perceived that the gleam was stationary, and informed the Countess in a whisper, that the light
proceeded from the solitary cell in which the
alchemist pursued his occult experiments. —
« He is of those, » she added, « who sit up and
watch by night that they may commit iniquity.
Evil was the chance which sent hither a man,
whose mixed speech of earthly wealth and un-
earthly or superhuman knowledge, has in it what
does so especially captivate my poor father. Well
spoke the good Master Holdforth — and, me-

thought, not without meaning that those of our
household should find therein a practical use.
« There be those, » he said, « and their number
is legion, who will rather, like the wicked
Ahab, listen to the dreams of the false prophet
Zedechias, than to the words of him by whom
the Lord has spoken. » And he further insisted
—« Ah, my brethren, there be many Zedechiases
among you — men that promise you the light
of their carnal knowledge, so you will sur-
render to them that of your heavenly understanding. What are they better than the tyrant
Naas, who demanded the right eye of those
who were subjected to him ? » and farther he
insisted » ——

. It is uncertain how long the fair puritan's
memory might have supported her in the re-
capitulation of Master Holdforth's discourse;
but the Countess now interrupted her, and
assured her she was so much recovered that she
could now reach the postern without the necessity of a second delay.

They set out accordingly, and performed the
second part of their journey with more deliberation, and of course more easily, than the first
hasty commencement. This gave them leisure
for reflection; and Janet now, for the first time,
ventured to ask her lady, which way she proposed
to direct her flight. Receiving no immediate
answer, — for perhaps, in the confusion of
her mind, this very obvious subject of deliberation had not occurred to the Countess, —

Janet ventured to add , « Probably to your
father's house, where you are sure of safety and
protection? »

« No, Janet, » said the lady, mournfully, « I
left Lidcote-Hall while my heart was light and
my name was honourable, and I will not return
thither till my lord's permission and public acknowledgment of our marriage restore me to my
native home, with all the rank and honour which
he has bestowed on me. »

« And whither will you then, madam? » said
Janet.

« To Kenilworth, girl, » said the Countess,
boldly and freely. « I will see these revels —
these princely revels — the preparation for
which makes the land ring from side to side.
Methinks, when the Queen of England feasts
within my husband's halls , the Countess of
Leicester should be no unbeseeming guest. »

« I pray God you may be a welcome one, »
said Janet hastily.

« You abuse my situation, Janet, » said the
Countess angrily, « and you forget your own. »

« I do neither, dearest madam, » said the
sorrowful maiden ; « but have you forgotten
that the noble Earl has given such strict charges
to keep your marriage secret, that he may preserve his court-favour? and can you think that
your sudden appearance at his castle, at such a
juncture, and in such a presence, will be ac-
ceptable to him? »

« Thou thinkest I would disgrace him, » said

the Countess; — « nay, let go my arm, I can walk without aid, and work without counsel. »

« Be not angry with me, lady, » said Janet meekly, « and let me still support you; the road is rough, and you are little accustomed to walk in darkness. »

« If you deem me not so mean as may disgrace my husband, » said the Countess in the same resentful tone, « you suppose my Lord of Leicester capable of abetting, perhaps of giving aim and authority to the base proceedings of your father and Varney, whose errand I will do to the good Earl. »

« For God's sake, madam, spare my father in your report, » said Janet; « let my services, however poor, be some atonement for his errors. »

« I were most unjust, dearest Janet, were it otherwise, » said the Countess, resuming at once the fondness and confidence of her manner towards her faithful attendant. « Yes, Janet, not a word of mine shall do your father prejudice. But thou seest, my love, I have no desire but to throw myself on my husband's protection. I have left the abode he assigned for me, because of the villainy of the persons by whom I was surrounded — but I will disobey his commands in no other particular. I will appeal to him alone — I will be protected by him alone — To no other, than at his pleasure, have I or will I communicate the secret union which combines our hearts and our destinies. I will see him, and receive from his own lips the directions for my

future conduct. Do not argue against my resolution, Janet; you will only confirm me in it —
And to own the truth, I am resolved to know
my fate at once, and from my husband's own
mouth, and to seek him at Kenilworth is the
surest way to attain my purpose. »

While Janet hastily revolved in her mind the
difficulties and uncertainties attendant on the
unfortunate lady's situation, she was inclined to
alter her first opinion, and to think, upon the
whole, that since the Countess had withdrawn
herself from the retreat in which she had been
placed by her husband, it was her first duty to
repair to his presence, and possess him with the
reasons of such conduct. She knew what importance the Earl attached to the concealment
of their marriage, and could not but own, that
by taking any step to make it public without
his permission, the Countess would incur, in a
high degree, the indignation of her husband.
If she retired to her father's house without an
explicit avowal of her rank, her situation was
likely greatly to prejudice her character, and
if she made such an avowal, it might occasion
an irreconcileable breach with her husband. At
Kenilworth, again, she might plead her cause
with her husband himself, whom Janet, though
distrusting him more than the Countess did,
believed incapable of being accessary to the base
and desperate means which his dependants,
from whose power the lady was now escaping,
might resort to, in order to stifle her complaints

of the treatment she had received at their hands. But at the worst, and were the Earl himself to deny her justice and protection, still at Kenilworth, if she chose to make her wrongs public, The Countess might have Tressilian for her advocate, and the Queen for her judge, for so much Janet had learned in her short conference with Wayland. She was, therefore, on the whole, reconciled to her lady's proposal of going towards Kenilworth, and so expressed herself; recommending, however, to the Countess the utmost caution in making her arrival known to her husband.

« Hast thou thyself been cautious, Janet ? » said the Countess ; « this guide, in whom I must put my confidence, hast thou not entrusted to him the secret of my condition ? »

« From me he has learned nothing, » said Janet, « nor do I believe that he knows more than what the public in general believe of your situation. »

« And what is that ? » said the lady.

« That you left your father's house — but I shall offend you again if I go on, » said Janet, interrupting herself.

« Nay, go on, » said the Countess ; « I must learn to endure the evil report which my folly has brought upon me. They think, I suppose, that I have left my father's house to follow lawless pleasure — It is an error which will soon be removed, — indeed it shall, for I will live with spotless fame, or I shall cease to live. — I

am accounted, then, the paramour of my Leicester ? »

« Most men say of Varney, » said Janet ; « yet
some call him only the convenient cloak of his
master's pleasures ; for reports of the profuse
expence in garnishing yonder apartments have
secretly gone abroad , and such doings far sur-
pass the means of Varney. But this latter opinion
is little prevalent ; for men dare hardly even
hint suspicion when so high a name is concerned , lest the Star-chamber should punish them
for scandal of the nobility. »

« They do well to speak low, » said the Countess, « who would mention the illustrious Dudley
as the accomplice of such a wretch as Varney.—
We have reached the postern—Ah ! Janet ; I must
bid thee farewell?—Weep not, my good girl, «
said she, endeavouring to cover her own reluctance to part with her faithful attendant under
an attempt at playfulness, « and against we meet
again, reform me, Janet, that precise ruff of
thine for an open rabatine of lace and cut work,
that will let men see thou hast a fair neck ; and
that kirtle of Philippine chency , with that bugle
lace which befits only a chamber-maid, into
three-piled velvet and cloth of gold—thou wilt
find plenty of stuffs in my chamber, and I freely
bestow them on you. Thou must be brave, Janet ; for though thou art now but the attendant
of a distressed and errant lady, who is both nameless and fameless, yet, when we meet again,
thou must be dressed as becomes the gentlewo-

man nearest in love and in service to the first Countess in England. »

« Now, may God grant it, dear lady!—not that I may go with gayer apparel, but that we may both wear our kirtles over lighter hearts. »

By this time the lock of the postern-door had, after some hard wrenching, yielded to the master-key; and the Countess, not without internal shuddering, saw herself beyond the walls which her husband's strict commands had assigned to her as the boundary of her walks. Waiting with much anxiety for their appearance, Wayland Smith stood at some distance, shrouding himself behind a hedge which bordered the highroad.

« Is all safe ? » said Janet to him, anxiously, as he approached them with caution.

« All, » he replied; « but I have been unable to procure a horse for the lady. Giles Gosling, the cowardly hilding, refused me one on any terms; lest, forsooth, he should suffer—but no matter. She must ride on my palfrey, and I must walk by her side until I come by another horse. There will be no pursuit, if you, pretty Mistress Janet, forget not thy lesson. »

« No more than the wise widow of Tekoa forgot the words which Joab put into her mouth, » answered Janet. « To-morrow, I say that my lady is unable to rise. »

« Ay, and that she hath aching and heaviness of the head—a throbbing at the heart, and lists not to be disturbed.—Fear not, they will take

the hint, and trouble thee with few questions—
they understand the disease. »

» But, » said the lady, « my absence must be
soon discovered, and they will murther her in
revenge.—I will rather return than expose her
to such danger. »

» Be at ease on my account, madam, » said
Janet; « I would you were as sure of receiving
the favour you desire from those to whom you
must make appeal, as I am that my father,
however angry, will suffer no harm to befal me. »

The Countess was now placed by Wayland
upon his horse, around the saddle of which he
had placed his cloak, so folded as to make her a
commodious seat.

« Adieu, and may the blessing of God wend
with you! » said Janet, again kissing her mistress's
hand, who returned her benediction with a mute
caress. They then tore themselves asunder, and
Janet, addressing Wayland, exclaimed, « May
Heaven deal with you at your need, as you are
true or false to this most injured and most helpless lady! »

« Amen! pretty Janet, » replied Wayland; —
« and believe me, I will so acquit myself of my
trust, as may tempt even your pretty eyes, saint-
like as they are, to look less scornfully on me
when we next meet. »

The latter part of this adieu was whispered into Janet's ear; and, although she made no reply
to it directly, yet her manner, influenced no doubt
by her desire to leave every motive in force which

could operate towards her mistress's safety, did not discourage the hope which Wayland's words expressed. She re-entered the postern-door, and locked it behind her, while Wayland, taking the horse's bridle in his hand, and walking close by its head, they began in silence their dubious and moonlight journey.

Although Wayland Smith used the utmost dispatch which he could make, yet this mode of travelling was so slow, that when morning began to dawn through the eastern mist, he found himself not farther than about ten miles distant from Cumnor. « Now, a plague upon all smooth-spoken hosts! » said Wayland, unable longer to suppress his mortification and uneasiness. « Had the false loon, Giles Gosling, but told me plainly two days since, that I was to reckon nought upon him, I had shifted better for myself. But they have such a custom of promising whatever is called for, that it is not till the steed is to be shod you find they are out of iron. Had I but known, I could have made twenty shifts; nay, for that matter, and in so good a cause, I would have thought little to have prigged a prancer from the next common — it had but been sending back the brute to the Headborough. The farcy and the founders confound every horse in the stables of the Black Bear! »

The lady endeavoured to comfort her guide, observing, that the dawn would enable him to make more speed.

« True, madam, » replied he; « but then it

will enable other folks to take note of us , and
that may prove an ill beginning of our journey.
I had not cared a spark from anvil about the
matter, had we been farther advanced on our
way. But this Berkshire has been notoriously
haunted e'er since I knew the country, with
that sort of malicious elves, who sit up late and
rise early, for no other purpose than to pry into
other folks affairs. I have been endangered by
them ere now. But do not fear, » he added,
« good madam; for wit, meeting with opportunity, will not miss to find a salve for every sore. »

The alarms of her guide made more impres-
sion on the Countess's mind than the comfort
which he judged fit to administer along with it.
She looked anxiously around her, and as the
shadows withdrew from the landscape, and the
heightening glow of the eastern sky promised
the speedy rise of the sun, expected at every
turn that the increasing light would expose
them to the view of the vengeful pursuers, or
present some dangerous and insurmontable obstacle to the prosecution of their journey.Way-
land Smith perceived her uneasiness, and , displeased with himself for having given her cause
of alarm, strode on with affected alacrity, now
talking to the horse as one expert in the language
of the stable, now whistling to himself low and
interrupted snatches of tunes, and now assuring
the lady there was no danger, while at the same
time he looked sharply around to see that there
was nothing in sight, which might give the lie

to his words while they were issuing from his mouth. Thus did they journey on, until an unexpected incident gave them the means of continuing their pilgrimage with more speed and convenience.

....

CHAPTER XXIV.

Richard. A horse!—a horse!—my kingdom for a horse!
Catesby. ——— My lord, I'll help you to a horse.
                                        Richard III.

OUR travellers were in the act of passing a small
thicket of trees close by the road-side, when the
first living being presented himself whom they
had seen since their departure from Cumnor-
Place. This was a stupid lout, seemingly a farm-
er's boy, in a grey jerkin, with his head bare,
his hose about his heels, and huge startups upon
his feet. He held by the bridle what of all things
they most wanted, a palfrey, namely, with a
side-saddle, and all other garniture for a woman's mounting; and he hailed Wayland Smith
with, « Zur, be ye zure the party? »

« Ay, that I be, my lad, » answered Wayland,
without an instant's hesitation; and it must be
owned that consciences, trained in a stricter
school of morality, might have given way to
an occasion so tempting. While he spoke he
caught the rein out of the boy's hand, and almost at the same time helped down the Countess
from his own horse, and aided her to mount on
that which chance had thus presented for her

acceptance. Indeed, so naturally did the whole take place, that the Countess, as it afterwards appeared, never suspected but what the horse had been placed there to meet them by the precaution of the guide or some of his friends.

The lad, however, who was thus hastily dispossessed of his charge, began to stare hard, and scratch his head, as if seized with some qualms of conscience for delivering up the animal on such brief explanation. — « I be right zure thou be'st the party, » said he, muttering to himself, but thou shouldst ha zaid *Beans*, thou knaw'st. »

« Ay, ay, » said Wayland, speaking at a venture; « and thou *Bacon*, thou know'st. »

« Noa, noa, » said the lad; « bide ye — bide ye — it was *Pease* ye should ha said. »

« Well, well, » answered Wayland, pease be it, a' God's name, though bacon were the better password. »

And, being by this time mounted on his own horse, he caught the rein of the palfrey from the uncertain hold of the hesitating young boor, flung him a small piece of money, and made amends for lost time by riding briskly off without farther parley. The lad was still visible from the hill up which they were riding, and Wayland, as he looked back, beheld him standing with his fingers in his hair as immoveable as a guide-post, and his head turned in the direction in which they were escaping from him. At length, just as they topped the hill, he saw the

clown stoop to lift up the silver groat which his
benevolence had imparted.—« Now this is what
I call a Godsend, » said Wayland; « this is a
bonny well-ridden bit of a going thing, and it
will carry us so far till we get you as well
mounted, and then we will send it back to satisfy the Hue and Cry. »

But he was deceived in his expectations; and
fate, which seemed at first to promise so fairly,
soon threatened to turn the incident, which
he thus gloried in, into the cause of their utter
ruin.

They had not ridden a short mile from the
place where they left the lad, before they heard
a man's voice shouting on the wind behind
them, « Robbery! robbery! — Stop thief! »
and similar exclamations, which Wayland's
conscience readily assured him must arise out
of the transaction to which he had been just
accessary.

« I had better have gone barefoot all my
life, he said; « it is the Hue and Cry, and I am
a lost man. Ah! Wayland, Wayland, many a
time thy father said horse-flesh would be the
death of thee. Were I once safe among the
horse-coursers in Smithfield, or Turnball Street,
they should have leave to hang me as high as
St Paul's, if I e'er meddled more with nobles,
knights, or gentlewomen. »

Amidst these dismal reflections, he turned
his head repeatedly to see by whom he was
chased, and was much comforted when he could

only discover a single rider, who was, however, well mounted, and came after them at a speed which left them no chance of escaping, even had the lady's strength permitted her to ride as fast as her palfrey might have been able to gallop.

« There may be fair play betwixt us sure, » thought Wayland, « where there is but one man on each side, and yonder fellow sits on his horse more like a monkey than a cavalier. Pshaw! if it come to the worst, it will be easy unhorsing him. Nay, 'snails! I think his horse will take the matter in ᴗhis own hand, for he has the bridle betwixt his teeth. Oons, what care I for him? » said he, as the pursuer drew yet nearer; « it is but the little animal of a mercer from Abingdon, when all is over. »

Even so it was, as the experienced eye of Wayland had descried at a distance. For the valiant mercer's horse, which was a beast of mettle, feeling himself put to his speed, and discerning a couple of horses riding fast, at some hundred yards distance before him, betook himself to the road with such alacrity, as totally deranged the seat of his rider, who not only came up with, but passed, at full gallop, those whom he had been pursuing, pulling the reins with all his might, and ejaculating, « Stop! stop! » an interjection which seemed rather to regard his own palfrey, than what seamen call « the chase. » With the same involuntary speed, he shot a-head, (to use another nautical phrase) about a furlong, ere he was able to stop and turn his horse, and then rode back towards our travellers, adjusting, as well as he could, his disordered dress, resettling himself in the saddle, and endeavouring to substitute a bold and martial frown, for the confusion and dismay which sate upon his visage during his involuntary career.

Wayland had just time to caution the lady not to be alarmed, adding, « this fellow is a gull, and I will use him as such. »

When the mercer had recovered breath and audacity enough to confront them, he ordered Wayland, in a menacing tone, to deliver up his palfrey.

« How » said the smith, in King Cambyses' vein, « are we commanded to stand and deliver on the King's high-way? Then out, Excalibar, and tell this knight of prowess, that dire blows must decide between us. »

« Haro and help, and hue and cry, every true man! said the mercer, « I am withstood in seeking to recover mine own. »

« Thou swearest thy Gods in vain, foul paynim, » said Wayland, » for I will through with my purpose, were death at the end on't. Nevertheless, know, thou false man of frail cambric and ferrateen, that I am he, even the pedlar, whom thou didst boast to meet on Maidencastle-moor, and despoil of his pack; wherefore betake thee to thy weapons presently. »

« I spoke but in jest, man » said Goldthred;

« I am an honest shopkeeper and citizen, who scorn to leap forth on any man from behind a hedge.

« Then, by my faith, most puissant mercer, I am sorry for my vow, which was, that wherever I met thee, I would despoil thee of thy palfrey, and bestow it upon my leman, unless thou couldst defend it by blows of force. But the vow is passed and registred — and all I can do for thee, is to leave the horse at Donnington, in the nearest hostelrie. »

« But I tell thee friend, » said the mercer, « it is the very horse on which I was this day to carry Jane Thackham, of Shottesbrok, as far as the parish-church yonder, to become Dame Goldthred. She hath jumped out of the shot-window of old Gaffer Thackham's grange; and lo ye, yonder she stands, at the place where she should have met the palfrey, with her camlet riding-cloak, and ivory-handled whip, like a picture of Lot's wife. I pray you, in good terms, let me have back the palfrey. »

« Grieved am I, » said Wayland, « as much for the fair damsel, as for thee, most noble imp of muslin. But vows must have their course — thou wilt find the palfrey at the Angel yonder at Donnington. It is all I may do for thee, with a safe conscience. »

« To the devil with thy conscience! » said the dismayed mercer — « Would'st thou have a bride walk to church on foot? »

« Thou may'st take her on thy crupper, Sir

Goldthred, » answered Wayland; « it will take
down thy steed's mettle. »

« And how if you — if you forget to leave
my horse, as you propose? » said Goldthred,
not without hesitation, for his soul was afraid
within him.

« My pack shall be pledged for it — yonder
it lies with Giles Gosling, in his chamber with
the damask'd leathern hangings, stuffed full
with velvet, single, double, treble-piled—rash-
taffeta, and parapa—shag, damask, and mocka-
do, plush, and grogram » ——

« Hold! hold! » exclaimed the mercer; « nay,
if there be, in truth and sincerity, but the half
of these wares — but if ever I trust bumpkin
with bonny Bayard again! »

« As you list for that, good Master Goldthred,
and so good morrow to you — and well parted, »
he added, riding on cheerfully with the lady,
while the discountenanced mercer rode back
much slower than he came, pondering what
excuse he should make to the disappointed bride, who stood waiting for her gallant groom in
the midst of the king's high-way.

« Methought, » said the lady, « as they rode
on, yonder fool stared at me, as if he had some
remembrance of me; yet I kept my muffler as
high as I might. »

« If I thought so, » said Wayland, « I would
ride back, and cut him over the pate — there
would be no fear of harming his brains, for he
never had so much as would make pap to a

sucking gosling. We must now push on, however, and at Donnington we will leave the oaf's horse, that he may have no farther temptation to pursue us, and endeavour to assume such a change of shape as may baffle his pursuit, if he should persevere in it. »

The travellers reached Donnington without farther alarm, where it became matter of necessity that the Countess should enjoy two or three hours repose, during which Wayland disposed himself, with equal address and alacrity, to carry through those measures on which the safety of their future journey seemed to depend.

Exchanging his pedlar's gaberdine for a smock-frock, he carried the palfrey of Goldthred to the Angel Inn, which was at the other end of the village from that where our travellers had taken up their quarters. In the progress of the morning, as he travelled about his other business, he saw the steed brought forth, and delivered to the cutting mercer himself, who, at the head of a valorous poss of the Hue and Cry, came to rescue by force of arms what was delivered to him without any other ransom than the price of a huge quantity of ale, drunk out by his assistants, thirsty, it would seem, with their walk, and concerning the price of which Master Goldthred had a fierce dispute with the Headborough, whom he had summoned to aid him in raising the country.

Having made this act of prudent, as well as just restitution, Wayland procured such change

of apparel for the lady, as well as himself, as
gave them both the appearance of country people of the better class; it being farther resolved,
that, in order to attract the less observation,
she should pass upon the road for the sister of
her guide. A good, but not a gay horse, fit to
keep pace with his own, and gentle enough for
a lady's use, completed the preparations for the
journey; for making which, he had been furnished with sufficient funds by Tressilian. And
thus, about noon, after the Countess had been
refreshed by the sound repose of several hours,
they resumed their journey, with the purpose
of making the best of their way to Kenilworth,
by Coventry and Warwick. They were not,
however, destined to travel far, without meeting some cause of apprehension.

It is necessary to premise, that the landlord
of the inn had informed them, a jovial party,
intended, as he understood, to present some of
the masques or mummeries, which made a part
of the entertainment with which the Queen was
usually welcomed on the royal Progresses, had
left the village of Donnington an hour or two
before them, in order to proceed to Kenilworth.
Now it had occurred to Wayland, that, by at-
taching themselves in some sort to this groupe,
as soon as they should overtake them on the
road, they would be less likely to attract notice,
than if they continued to travel entirely by
themselves. He communicated his idea to the
Countess, who, only anxious to arrive at Kenil-

worth without interruption, left him free to chuse the manner in which this was to be accomplished. They pressed forward their horses, therefore, with the purpose of overtaking the party of intended revellers, and making the journey in their company; and had just seen the little party, consisting partly of riders, partly of people on foot, crossing the summit of a gentle hill, at about half a mile's distance, and disappearing on the other side, when Wayland, who maintained the most circumspect observation of all that met his eye in every direction, was aware that a rider was coming up behind them on a horse of uncommon action, accompanied by a serving man, whose utmost efforts were unable to keep up with his master's trotting hackney, and who, therefore, was fain to follow him at a hand gallop. Wayland looked anxiously back at these horsemen, became considerably disturbed in his manner, looked back again, and became pale, as he said to the lady—« That is Richard Varney's trotting gelding — I would know him among a thousand nags — this is a worse business than meeting the mercer. »

« Draw your sword, » answered the lady, « and pierce my bosom with it, rather than I should fall into his hands. »

« I would rather by a thousand times, » answered Wayland, « pass it through his body, or even mine own. But to say truth, fighting is not my best point, though I can look on cold iron like another, when needs must be. And indeed,

as for my sword — (put on I pray you) — it is
a poor provant rapier, and I warrant you he has
a special Toledo. He has a serving man too, and
I think it is the drunken ruffian Lambourne,
upon the horse on which men say — (I pray
you heartily to put on) — he did the great robbery of the west-country grazier. It is not that
I fear either Varney or Lambourne in a good
cause — (your palfrey will go yet faster if you
urge him) — But yet — (nay, I pray you let
him not break off into the gallop, lest they
should see we fear them, and give chace — keep
him only at the full trot,) — But yet, though I
fear them not, I would we were well rid of
them, and that rather by policy than by violence.
Could we once reach the party before us, we
may herd among them, and pass unobserved,
unless Varney be really come in express pursuit
of us, and then, happy man be his dole. »

While he thus spoke, he alternately urged
and restrained his horse, desirous to maintain
the fleetest pace that was consistent with the idea
of an ordinary journey on the road, but to avoid
such rapidity of movement as might give rise to
suspicion that they were flying.

At such a pace, they ascended the gentle hill
we have mentioned, and, looking from the top,
had the pleasure to see that the party which had
left Donnington before them, were in the little
valley or bottom on the other side, where the
road was traversed by a rivulet, beside which
was a cottage or two. In this place they seemed

to have made a pause, which gave Wayland the hope of joining them, and becoming a part of their company, ere Varney should overtake them. He was the more anxious, as his companion, though she made no complaints, and expressed no fear, began to look so deadly pale, that he was afraid she might drop from her horse. Notwithstanding this symptom of decaying strength, she pushed on her palfrey so briskly, that they joined the party in the bottom of the valley, ere Varney appeared on the top of the gentle eminence which they descended.

They found the company to which they meant to associate themselves in great disorder. The women with dishevelled locks, and looks of great importance, ran in and out of one of the cottages, and the men stood around holding the horses, and looking silly enough, as is usual in cases where their assistance is not wanted.

Wayland and his charge paused, as if out of curiosity, and then gradually, without making any inquiries, or being asked any questions, they mingled with the groupe, as if they had always made part of it.

They had not stood there above five minutes, anxiously keeping as much to the side of the road as possible, so as to place the other travellers betwixt them and Varney, when Lord Leicester's master of the horse, followed by Lambourne, came riding fiercely down the hill, their horses' flanks and the rowels of their spurs shewing bloody tokens of the rate at which they tra-

velled. The appearance of the stationary groupe
around the cottages, wearing their buckram suits
in order to protect their masquing dresses, having their light cart for transporting their sce-
nery, and carrying various fantastic properties
in their hands for the more easy conveyance, let
the riders at once into the character and purpose
of the company.

« You are revellers, » said Varney, « designing
for Kenilworth ? »

« *Rectè quidem, Domine spectatissime*, » answered one of the party.

« And why the devil stand you here, » said
Varney, « when your utmost dispatch will but
bring you to Kenilworth in time? The Queen
dines at Warwick to-morrow; and you loiter
here, ye knaves. »

« In very truth, sir, » said a little diminutive
urchin, wearing a vizard with a couple of sprout-
ing horns of an elegant scarlet hue, having moreover a black serge jerkin drawn close to his body by lacing, garnished with red stockings, and
shoes so shaped as to resemble cloven feet, —
« in very truth, sir, and you are in the right on't.
It is my father the Devil, who, being taken in
labour, has delayed our present purpose, by increasing our company with an imp too many. »

« The devil he has! » answered Varney, whose
laugh, however, never exceeded a sarcastic
smile.

« It is even as the juvenal hath said, » added
the masquer who spoke first; « our major devil,

for this is but our minor one, is even now at *Lucina fer opem*, within that very *tugurium.* »

« By Saint George, or rather by the Dragon, who may be a kinsman of the fiend in the straw, a most comical chance! » said Varney. « How sayest thou, Lambourne, wilt thou stand godfather for the nonce? — if the devil were to chuse a gossip, I know no one more fit for the office. »

« Saving always when my betters are in presence, » said Lambourne, with the civil impudence of a servant who knows his services to be so indispensable, that his jest will be permitted to pass muster.

« And what is the name of this devil or devil's dam, who has timed her turns so strangely? » said Varney. « We can ill afford to spare any of our actors. »

« *Gaudet nomine Sybillæ*, » said the first speaker, « she is called Sybill Laneham, wife of Master Richard Laneham »————

« Clerk to the Council-chamber door, » said Varney; « why she is inexcusable, having had experience how to have ordered her matters better. But who were those, a man and a woman I think, who rode so hastily up the hill before me even now? — do they belong to your company? »

Wayland was about to hazard a reply to this alarming inquiry, when the little diablotin again thrust in his oar.

« So please you, » he said, coming close up to

Varney, and speaking so as not to be overheard
by his companions, « the man was our devil major, who has tricks enough to supply the lack of
a hundred such as Dame Laneham ; and the woman — if you please — is the sage person whose
assistance is most particularly necessary to our
distressed comrade. »

« Oh , what, you have got the wise woman
then ? » said Varney. « Why truly, she rode like
one bound to a place where she was needed —
And you have a spare limb of Satan, besides, to
supply the place of Mistress Laneham ? »

« Ay, sir, » said the boy, they are not so
scarce in this world as your honour's virtuous
eminence would suppose — This master-fiend
shall spit a few flashes of fire, and eruct a volume or two of smoke on the spot , if it will do
you pleasure—you would think he had Ætna
in his abdomen. »

« I lack time just now , most hopeful imp of
darkness, to witness his performance, » said Varney ; « but here is something for you all to drink
the lucky hour — and so, as the play says, God
be with your labour ! »

Thus speaking, he struck his horse with the
spurs, and rode on his way.

Lambourne tarried a moment or two behind
his master, and rummaged his pouch for a piece
of silver, which he bestowed on the communi-
cative imp, as he said, for his encouragement
on his path to the infernal regions, some sparks
of whose fire, he said , he could discover flashing

from him already. Then having received the
boy's thanks for his generosity, he also spurred
his horse, and rode after his master as fast as
the fire flashes from flint.

« And now, » said the wily imp, sideling close
up to Wayland's horse, and cutting a gambol
in the air, which seemed to vindicate his title
to relationship with the prince of that element,
« I have told them who *you* are, do you in
return tell me who *I* am? »

« Either Flibbertigibbet, » answered Wayland
Smith, « or else an imp of the devil in good
earnest. »

« Thou hast hit it, » answered Dickie Sludge;
« I am thine own Flibbertigibbet, man; and I
have broken forth of bounds, along with my
learned preceptor, as I told thee I would do,
whether he would or not. — But what lady hast
thou got with thee? I saw thou wert at fault
the first question was asked, and so I drew up
for thy assistance. But I must know all who she
is, dear Wayland. »

« Thou shalt know fifty finer things, my dear
ingle, » said Wayland; « but a truce to thine
inquiries just now; and since you are bound
for Kenilworth, thither will I too, even for
the love of thy sweet face and waggish company. »

« Thou should'st have said my waggish face
and sweet company, » said Dickie; « but how
wilt thou travel with us — I mean in what
character? »

« E'en in that thou hast assigned me, to be
sure — as a juggler; thou know'st I am used to
the craft, » answered Wayland.

« Ay, but the lady? » answered Flibbertigibbet; « credit me, I think she *is* one, and thou
art in a sea of troubles about her at this moment,
as I can perceive by thy fidgetting. »

« O, she, man! — she is a poor sister of
mine, said Wayland — « she can sing and play
o' the lute, would win the fish out o' the
stream. »

« Let me hear her instantly, » said the boy;
« I love the lute rarely; I love it of all things,
though I never heard it. »

« Then how canst thou love it, Flibbertigibbet? » said Wayland.

« As knights love ladies in old tales, » answered
Dickie — « on hearsay. »

« Then love it on hearsay a little longer, till
my sister is recovered from the fatigue of her
journey, » said Wayland; — muttering afterwards betwixt his teeth, « The devil take the
imp's curiosity! — I must keep fair weather with
him, or we shall fare the worse. »

He then proceeded to state to Master Holiday
his own talents as a juggler, with those of his
sister as a musician. Some proof of his dexterity
was demanded, which he readily gave in such a
style of excellence, that, delighted at obtaining
such an accession to their party, they readily
acquiesced in the apology which he offered,
when a display of his sister's talents was required.

The new-comers were invited to partake of the refreshments with which the party were provided; and it was with some difficulty that Wayland Smith obtained an opportunity of being apart with his supposed sister during the meal, of which interval he availed himself to entreat her to forget for the present both her rank and her sorrows, and condescend, as the most probable chance of remaining concealed, to mix in the society of those with whom she was to travel.

The Countess allowed the necessity of the case, and when they resumed their journey, endeavoured to comply with her guide's advice, by addressing herself to a female near her, and expressing her concern for the woman whom they were thus obliged to leave behind them.

« O, she is well attended, madam, » replied the dame whom she addressed, who, from her jolly and laughter-loving demeanour, might have been the very emblem of the Wife of Bath; « and my gossip Laneham thinks as little of these matters as any one. By the ninth day, an the revels last so long, we shall have her with us at Kenilworth, even if she should travel with her bantling on her back. »

There was something in this speech which took away all desire on the Countess of Leicester's part to continue the conversation; but having broken the charm by speaking to her fellow-traveller first, the good dame, who was to play Rare Gillian of Croydon, in one of the interlu-

des, took care that silence did not again settle
on the journey, but entertained her silent companion with a thousand anecdotes of revels,
from the days of King Harry downwards, with
the reception given them by the great folks,
and all the names of those who played the
principal characters; but ever concluding with
« they would be nothing to the princely pleasures
of Kenilworth. »

« And when shall we reach Kenilworth ? »
said the Countess, with an agitation which she
in vain attempted to conceal.

« We that have horses may, with late riding,
get to Warwick to-night, and Kenilworth may
be distant some four or five miles, — but then
we must wait till the foot-people come up;
although it is like my good Lord of Leicester
will have horses or light carriages to meet them,
and bring them up without being travel-toiled,
which last is no good preparation, as you may
suppose, for dancing before your betters— And
yet, Lord help me, I have seen the day I would
have tramped five leagues of lea-land, and turned on my toe the whole evening after, as a
juggler spins a pewter platter on the point of a
needle. But age has clawed me somewhat in his
clutch, as the song says; though, if I like the
tune and like my partner, I'll dance the heys
yet with any merry lass in Warwickshire, that
writes that unhappy figure four with a round O
after it. »

If the Countess was overwhelmed with the

garrulity of this good dame, Wayland Smith, on his part, had enough to do to sustain and parry the constant attacks made upon him by the indefatigable curiosity of his old acquaintance Richard Sludge. Nature had given that arch youngster a prying cast of disposition, which matched admirably with his sharp wit; the former inducing him to plant himself as a spy on other people's affairs, and the latter quality leading him perpetually to interfere, after he had made himself master of that which concerned him not. He spent the live-long day in attempting to peer under the Countess's muffler, and apparently what he could there discern greatly sharpened his curiosity.

« That sister of thine, Wayland, » he said, « has a fair neck to have been born in a smithy, and a pretty taper hand to have been used for twirling a spindle — faith, I'll believe in your relationship when the crow's egg is hatched into a cygnet. »

« Go to, » said Wayland, « thou art a prating boy, and should be breeched for thine assurance. »

« Well, » said the imp, drawing off, « all I say is, — remember you have kept a secret from me! and if I give thee not a Rowland for thine Oliver, my name is not Dickon Sludge. »

This threat, and the distance at which Hob-goblin kept from him for the rest of the way, alarmed Wayland very much, and he suggested to his pretended sister, that, on pretext of weari-

ness, she should express a desire to stop two or
three miles short of the fair town of Warwick,
promising to rejoin the troop in the morning.
A small village inn afforded them a resting-
place; and it was with secret pleasure that Wayland saw the whole party, including Dickon,
pass on, after a courteous farewell, and leave
them behind.

« To-morrow, madam, » he said to his charge;
« we will, with your leave, again start early,
and reach Kenilworth before the rout which are
to assemble there. »

The Countess gave assent to the proposal of
her faithful guide; but, somewhat to his surprise, said nothing farther on the subject, which
left Wayland under the disagreeable uncertainty
whether or no she had formed any plan for her
own future proceedings, as he knew her situation
demanded circumspection, although he was but
imperfectly acquainted with all its peculiarities.
Concluding, however, that she must have friends
within the castle, whose advice and assistance
she could safely trust, he supposed his task
would be best accomplished by conducting her
thither in safety, agreeably to her repeated
commands.

CHAPTER XXV.

Hark, the bells summon, and the bugle calls,
But she the fairest answers not— the tide
Of nobles and of ladies throngs the halls,
But she the loveliest must in secret hide.
What eyes were thine, proud Prince, which in the gleam
Of yon gay meteors lost that better sense,
That o'er the glow-worm doth the star esteem,
And merit's modest blush o'er courtly insolence?
                                        The Glass Slipper.

THE unfortunate Countess of Leicester had, from her infancy upwards, been treated by those around her with indulgence as unbounded as injudicious. The natural sweetness of her disposition had saved her from becoming insolent and ill-humoured; but the caprice which preferred the handsome and insinuating Leicester before Tressilian, of whose high honour and unalterable affection she herself entertained so firm an opinion — that fatal error, which ruined the happiness of her life, had its origin in the mistaken kindness that had spared her childhood the painful, but most necessary lesson, of submission and self-command. From the same indulgence, it followed that she had only been accustomed to form and to express her wishes, leaving to others the task of fulfilling them; and thus, at the most momentous period of her life, she was alike destitute of presence of mind, and of ability to form for herself any reasonable or prudent plan of conduct.

These difficulties pressed on the unfortunate lady with overwhelming force, on the morning which seemed to be the crisis of her fate. Overlooking every intermediate consideration, she had only desired to be at Kenilworth, and to approach her husband's presence; and now, when she was in the vicinity of both, a thousand considerations arose at once upon her mind, startling her with accumulated doubts and dangers, some real, some imaginary, and all exalted and exaggerated by a situation alike helpless, and destitute of aid and counsel.

A sleepless night rendered her so weak in the morning, that she was altogether unable to attend Wayland's early summons. The trusty guide became extremely distressed on the lady's account, and somewhat alarmed on his own, and was on the point of going alone to Kenilworth, in the hope of discovering Tressilian, and intimating to him the lady's approach, when about nine in the morning he was summoned to attend her. He found her dressed, and ready for resuming her journey, but with a paleness of countenance which alarmed him for her health. She intimated her desire that the horses might be got instantly ready, and resisted with impatience her guide's request, that she would take some refreshment before setting forward. « I have had, » she said,

« a cup of water—the wretch who is dragged to execution needs no stronger cordial, and that may serve me which suffices for him—do as I command you. » Wayland Smith still hesitated. « What would you have? » said she — « Have I not spoken plainly? »

« Yes, madam, » answered Wayland ; « but may I ask what is your farther purpose ? — I only wish to know, that I may guide myself by your wishes. The whole country is afloat, and streaming towards the Castle of Kenilworth. It will be difficult travelling thither , even if we had the necessary passports for safe-conduct and free-admittance — Unknown and unfriended , we may come by mishap. — Your ladyship will forgive my speaking my poor mind — Were we not better try to find out the masquers, and again join ourselves with them ? » — The Countess shook her head , and her guide proceeded , « Then I see but one other remedy. »

« Speak out , then , » said the lady , not displeased , perhaps , that he should thus offer the advice which she was ashamed to ask ; « I believe thee faithful — what wouldst thou counsel? »

« That I should warn Master Tressilian, » said Wayland , « that you are in this place. I am right certain he would get to horse with a few of Lord Sussex's followers , and ensure your personal safety. »

« And is it to *me* you advise , » said the Countess, « to put myself under the protection of Sussex , the unworthy rival of the noble Leicester ? »

Then , seeing the surprise with which Wayland
stared upon her , and afraid of having too strongly intimated her interest in Leicester, she added,
« And for Tressilian , it must not be — mention
not to him , I charge you , my unhappy name ;
it would but double *my* misfortunes, and involve
him in dangers beyond the power of rescue. »
She paused ; but when she observed that Wayland continued to look on her with that anxious
and uncertain gaze , which indicated a doubt
whether her brain was settled , she assumed an
air of composure , and added , « Do thou but
guide me to Kenilworth Castle, good fellow,
and thy task is ended , since I will then judge
what farther is to be done. Thou hast yet been
true to me — here is something that will make
thee rich amends. »

She offered the artist a ring , containing a va-
luable stone. Wayland looked at it, hesitated a
moment , and then returned it. « Not , » he said ,
« that I am above your kindness , madam , being
but a poor fellow , who have been forced , God
help me ! to live by worse shifts than the bounty
of such a person as you. But as my old master
the farrier used to say to his customers, « No cure
no pay. » We are not yet in Kenilworth Castle ,
and it is time enough to discharge your guide,
as they say, when you take your boots off. I trust
in God your ladyship is as well assured of fitting reception when you arrive , as you may
hold yourself certain of my best endeavours to
conduct you thither safely. I go to get the horses ;

meantime let me pray you once more, as your poor physician as well as guide, to take some sustenance. »

« I will — I will, » said the lady, hastily. « Begone, begone instantly! — It is in vain I assume audacity, » said she when he left the room; even this poor groom sees through my affectation of courage, and fathoms the very ground of my fears. »

She then attempted to follow her guide's advice by taking some food, but was compelled to desist, as the effort to swallow even a single morsel gave her so much uneasiness as amounted well nigh to suffocation. A moment afterwards the horses appeared at the latticed window. the lady mounted, and found that relief from the free air and change of place, which is frequently experienced in similar circumstances.

It chanced well for the Countess's purpose that Wayland Smith, whose previous wandering and unsettled life had made him acquainted with almost all England, was intimate with all the bye-roads, as well as direct communications, through the beautiful county of Warwick. For such and so great was the throng which flocked in all directions towards Kenilworth, to see the entry of Elizabeth into that splendid mansion of her prime favourite, that the principal roads were actually blockaded and interrupted, and it was only by circuitous bye-paths that the travellers could proceed on their journey.

5*

The Queen's purveyors had been abroad,
sweeping the farms and villages of those articles
usually exacted during a royal Progress, and
for which the owners were afterwards to obtain
a tardy payment from the Board of Green Cloth.
The Earl of Leicester's household officers had
been scouring the country for the same purpose; and many of his friends and allies, both
near and remote, took this opportunity of
ingratiating themselves, by sending large quantities of provisions and delicacies of all kinds,
with game in huge quantities, and whole tons
of the best liquors, foreign and domestic. Thus
the high roads were filled with droves of bul-
locks, sheep, and calves and hogs, and choked
with loaded wains, whose axle-trees cracked
under their burdens of wine-casks and hogsheads
of ale, and huge hampers of grocery goods, and
slaughtered game, and salted provision, and
sacks of flour. Perpetual stoppages took place as
these wains became entangled; and their rude
drivers, swearing and brawling till their wild
passions were fully raised, began to debate
precedence with their waggon-whips and quar-
ter-staves, which occasional riots were usually quieted by a purveyor, deputy-marshal's-
man, or some other person in authority, breaking the heads of both parties.

Here were, besides, players and mummers,
jugglers and showmen of every description,
traversing in joyous bands the paths which led
to the Palace of Princely Pleasure; for so the

travelling minstrels had termed Kenilworth in
the songs which already had come forth in
anticipation of the revels which were there
expected. In the midst of this motley show,
mendicants were exhibiting their real or pretended miseries, forming a strange, though
common, contrast betwixt the vanities and the
sorrows of human existence. All these floated
along with the immense tide of population,
whom mere curiosity had drawn together; and
where the mechanic, in his leathern apron,
elbowed the dink and dainty dame, his city
mistress; where clowns, with hob-nailed shoes,
were treading on the kibes of substantial burghers and gentlemen of worship; and where
Joan of the dairy, with robust pace, and red
sturdy arms, rowed her way onward, amongst
those prim and pretty moppets, whose sires
were knights and squires.

The throng and confusion was, however, of a
gay and cheerful character. All came forth to see
and to enjoy, and all laughed at the trifling in-
conveniencies which at another time might have
chafed their temper. Excepting the occasional
brawls which we have mentioned amongst that
irritable race the carmen, the mingled sounds
which arose from the multitude were those of
light-hearted mirth, and tiptoe jollity. The
musicians preluded on their instruments — the
minstrels hummed their songs — the licensed
jester whooped betwixt mirth and madness, as
he brandished his bauble—the morrice-dancers

jangled their bells — the rustics halloo'd and whistled—men laughed loud, and maidens giggled shrill; while many a broad jest flew like a shuttle-cock from one party to be caught in the air and returned from the opposite side of the road by another, at which it was aimed.

No infliction can be so distressing to a mind absorbed in melancholy, as being plunged into a scene of mirth and revelry, forming an accompaniment so dissonant from its own feelings. Yet, in the case of the Countess of Leicester, the noise and tumult of this giddy scene distracted her thoughts, and rendered her this sad service, that it became impossible for her to brood on her own misery, or to form terrible anticipations of her approaching fate. She travelled on, like one in a dream, following implicitly the guidance of Wayland, who, with great address, now threaded his way through the general throng of passengers, now stood still until a favourable opportunity occurred of again moving forward, and frequently turning altogether out of the direct road, followed some circuitous by-path, which brought them into the high road again, after having given them the opportunity of traversing a considerable way with greater ease and rapidity.

It was thus he avoided Warwick, within whose Castle (that fairest monument of ancient and chivalrous splendour which yet remains uninjured by time) Elizabeth had passed the previous night, and where she was to tarry until past noon, at that time the general hour of dinner throughout England, after which repast she was to proceed to Kenilworth. In the meanwhile, each passing groupe had something to say in the Sovereign's praise, though not absolutely without the usual mixture of satire which qualifies more or less our estimate of our neighbours, especially if they chance to be also our betters.

« Heard you, » said one, « how graciously she spoke to Master Bailiff and the Recorder, and to good Master Griffin the preacher, as they kneeled down at her coach-window? »

« Ay, and how she said to little Aglionby, ' master Recorder, men would have persuaded me that you were afraid of me, but truly I think, so well did you reckon up to me the virtues of a sovereign, that I have more reason to be afraid of you'—And then with what grace she took the fair-wrought purse with the twenty gold sovereigns, seeming as though she would not willingly handle it, and yet taking it withal. »

« Ay, ay, » said another, « her fingers closed on it pretty willingly methought, when all was done; and methought, too, she weighed them for a second in her hand, as she would say, I hope they be avoirdupois. »

« She needed not, neighbour, » said a third ; « it is only when the corporation pay the accounts of a poor handicraft like me, that they put him off with clipt coin.—Well, there is a God above all — Little Master Recorder, since that is the word, will be greater now than ever. »

« Come, good neighbour, » said the first speaker, « be not envious—She is a good Queen, and
a generous — She gave the purse to the Earl of
Leicester. »

« I envious?—beshrew thy heart for the word!»
replied the handicraft—« But she will give all to
the Earl of Leicester anon, methinks. »

« You are turning ill, lady, » said Wayland
Smith to the Countess of Leicester, and proposed that she should draw off from the road, and
halt till she recovered. But, subduing her feelings
at this, and different speeches to the same purpose, which caught her ear as they passed on,
she insisted that her guide should proceed to
Kenilworth with all the haste which the numerous impediments of their journey permitted.
Meanwhile, Wayland's anxiety at her repeated
fits of indisposition, and her obvious distraction
of mind, was hourly increasing, and he became
extremely desirous, that, according to her reiterated requests, she should be safely introduced
into the Castle, where, he doubted not, she
was secure of a kind reception, though she
seemed unwilling to reveal on whom she reposed
her hopes.

« An I were once rid of this peril, » thought
he, « and if any man shall find me playing squire
of the body to a damosel-errant, he shall have
leave to beat my brains out with my own sledge-
hammer. »

At length the princely Castle appeared, upon
improving which, and the domains around, the

Earl of Leicester had; it is said, expended sixty thousand pounds sterling, a sum equal to half a million of our present money.

The outer wall of this splendid and gigantic structure enclosed seven acres, a part of which was occupied by extensive stables, and by a pleasure garden, with its trim arbours and parterres, and the rest formed the large base-court, or outer yard, of the noble Castle. The lordly structure itself, which rose near the centre of this spacious enclosure, was composed of a huge pile of magnificent castellated buildings, apparently of different ages, surrounding an inner court, and bearing in the names attached to each portion of the magnificent mass, and in the armorial bearings which were there blazoned, the emblems of mighty chiefs who had long passed away, and whose history, could Ambition have lent ear to it, might have read a lesson to the haughty favourite, who had now acquired and was augmenting the fair domain. A large and massive Keep, which formed the citadel of the Castle, was of uncertain though great antiquity. It bore the name of Cæsar, perhaps from its resemblance to that in the Tower of London so called. Some antiquaries ascribed its foundation to the time of Kenelph, from whom the Castle had its name, a Saxon King of Mercia, and others to an early æra after the Norman Conquest. On the exterior walls frowned the scutcheon of the Clintons, by whom they were founded in the reign of Henry I, and

of the yet more redoubted Simon de Montfort,
by whom, during the Barons' Wars, Kenilworth
was long held out against Henry III. Here Mortimer, Earl of March, famous alike for his rise
and his fall, had once gaily revelled, while his
dethroned sovereign, Edward II, languished in
its dungeons. Old John of Gaunt, « time-ho-
noured Lancaster, » had widely extended the Castle, erecting that noble and massive pile which
yet bears the name of Lancaster's Buildings ; and
Leicester himself had outdone the former pos-
sessors, princely and powerful as they were, by
erecting another immense structure, which now
lies crushed under its own ruins, the monument
of its owner's ambition. The external wall of this
royal Castle was, on the south and west sides,
adorned and defended by a lake partly artificial,
across which Leicester had constructed a stately
bridge, that Elizabeth might enter the Castle
by a path hitherto untrodden, instead of the
usual entrance to the northward, over which he
had erected a gate-house or barbican, which still
exists; and is equal in extent and superior in architecture, to the baronial castle of many a northern chief.

Beyond the lake lay an extensive chase, full
of red deer, fallow deer, roes, and every species of game, and abounding with lofty trees,
from amongst which the extended front and
massive towers of the castle were seen to rise
in majesty and beauty. We cannot but add, that
of this lordly palace, where princes feasted and

heroes fought, now in the bloody earnest of storm and siege, and now in the games of chivalry, where beauty dealt the prize which valour won, all is now desolate. The bed of the lake is but a rushy swamp; and the massive ruins of the Castle only serve to shew what their splendour once was, and to impress on the musing visitor the transitory value of human possessions, and the happiness of those who enjoy an humble lot in virtuous contentment.

It was with far different feelings that the unfortunate Countess of Leicester viewed those grey and massive towers, when she first beheld them rise above the embowering and richly shaded woods, over which they seemed to preside. She, the undoubted wife of the great Earl, of Elizabeth's minion, and England's mighty favourite, was approaching the presence of her husband, and that husband's sovereign, under the protection, rather than the guidance, of a poor juggler; and though unquestioned Mistress of that proud Castle, whose lightest word ought to have had force sufficient to make its gates leap from their massive hinges to receive her, yet she could not conceal from herself the difficulty and peril which she must experience in gaining admission into her own halls.

The risk and difficulty, indeed, seemed to increase every moment, and at length threatened altogether to put a stop to her farther progress, at the great gate leading to a broad and fair road, which, traversing the breadth of the Chase for

the space of two miles , and commanding several
most beautiful views of the Castle and lake ,
terminated at the newly constructed bridge , to
which it was an appendage , and which was destined to form the Queen's approach to the Castle
on that memorable occasion.

Here the Countess and Wayland found the
gate at the end of this avenue , which opened on
the Warwick road , guarded by a body of the
Queen's mounted yeomen of the guard , armed
in corslets richly carved and gilded , and wearing
morions instead of bonnets , having their carabines resting with the butt-end on their thighs.
These guards, who did duty wherever the Queen
went in person , were here stationed under the
direction of a pursuivant , graced with the Bear
and Ragged Staff on his arm , as belonging to
the Earl of Leicester, and peremptorily refused
all admittance, excepting to such as were guests
invited to the festival , or persons who were to
perform some part in the mirthful exhibitions
which were proposed.

The press was of consequence great around
the entrance , and persons of all kinds presented
every sort of plea for admittance ; to which the
guards turned an inexorable ear , pleading , in
return to fair words and even to fair offers , the
strictness of their orders, founded on the Queen's
well-known dislike to the rude pressing of a multitude. With those whom such reasons did not
serve , they dealt more rudely , repelling them
without ceremony by the pressure of their po-

werful barbed horses, and good round blows from the stock of their carabines. These last manœuvres produced undulations amongst the crowd, which rendered Wayland much afraid that he might perforce be separated from his charge in the throng. Neither did he know what excuse to make in order to obtain admittance, and he was debating the matter in his head with great uncertainty, when the Earl's pursuivant having cast an eye upon him, exclaimed, to his no small surprise, « Yeomen, make room for the fellow in the orange-tawny cloak — Come forward, Sir Coxcomb, and make haste. What, in the fiend's name, has kept you waiting? Come forward with your bale of woman's gear. »

While the pursuivant gave Wayland this pressing yet uncourteous invitation, which, for a minute or two, he could not imagine was applied to him, the yeomen speedily made a free passage for him, while only cautioning his companion to keep the muffler close around her face, he entered the gate leading her palfrey; but with such a drooping crest, and such a look of conscious fear and anxiety, that the crowd, not greatly pleased at any rate with the preference bestowed upon them, accompanied their admission with hooting, and a loud laugh of derision.

Admitted thus within the chace, though with no very flattering notice or distinction, Wayland and his charge rode forward, musing what difficulties it would be next their lot to encounter,

through the broad avenue, which was centinelled
on either side by a long line of retainers, armed
with swords and partizans, richly dressed in the
Earl of Leicester's liveries, and bearing his cog-
nizance of thee Bear and Ragged Staff, each
placed within three paces of each other, so as to
line the whole road from the entrance into the
park to the bridge. And, indeed, when the lady
obtained the first commanding view of the
Castle, with its stately towers rising from within
a long sweeping line of outward walls, ornamented with battlements, and turrets, and plat-
forms, at every point of defence, with many a
banner streaming from its walls, and such a
bustle of gay crests, and waving plumes, disposed on the terraces and battlements, and all
the gay and gorgeous scene, her heart, unaccus-
tomed to such splendour, sank as if it died
within her, and for a moment she asked herself,
what she had offered up to Leicester to deserve
to become the partner of this princely splendour. But her pride and generous spirit resisted
the whisper which bade her despair.

« I have given him, » she said, « all that woman has to give. Name and fame, heart and
hand, have I given the lord of all this magnificence at the altar, and England's Queen could
give him no more. He is my husband — I am
his wife — Whom God hath joined, man cannot
sunder. I will be bold in claiming my right;
even the bolder, that I come thus unexpected,
and thus forlorn. I know my noble Dudley well!

He will be something impatient at my disobey-
ing him, but Amy will weep, and Dudley will
forgive her. ».

These meditations were interrupted by a cry
of surprise from her guide Wayland, who suddenly felt himself grasped firmly round the body
by a pair of long thin black arms, belonging to
some one who had dropped himself out of an
oak tree, upon the croupe of his horse, amidst
the shouts of laughter which burst from the
centinels.

« This must be the devil, or Flibbertigibbet
again ! » said Wayland, after a vain struggle to
disengage himself, and unhorse the urchin who
clung to him ; « Do Kenilworth oaks bear such
acorns ? »

« In sooth do they, Master Wayland, » said
his unexpected adjunct, « and many others, too
hard for you to crack, for as old as you are,
without my teaching you. How would you have
passed the pursuivant at the upper gate yonder,
had not I warned him our principal juggler was
to follow us? and here have I waited for you,
having clambered up into the tree from the top
of our wain, and I suppose they are all mad for
want of me by this time. »

« Nay, then, thou art a limb of the devil in
good earnest, » said Wayland. « I give thee way,
good imp, and will walk by thy counsel ; only
as thou art powerful be merciful. »

As he spoke, they approached a strong tower,
at the south extremity of the long bridge we have

mentioned, which served to protect the outer gateway of the castle of Kenilworth.

Under such disastrous circumstances, and in such singular company, did the unfortunate Countess of Leicester approach, for the first time, the magnificent abode of her almost princely husband.

———

CHAPTER XXVI.

Snug. Have you the lion's part written? pray, if it be, give it
me, for I am slow of study.

Quince. You may do it extempore, for it is nothing but roaring.
Midsummer-Night's Dream.

WHEN the Countess of Leicester arrived at
the outer gate of the Castle of Kenilworth, she
found the tower, beneath which its ample portal
arch opened, guarded in a singular manner. Upon
the battlements were placed gigantic warders,
with clubs, battle-axes, and other implements
of ancient warfare, designed to represent the
soldiers of King Arthur; those primitive Britons, by whom, according to romantic tradition,
the Castle had been first tenanted, though history carried back its antiquity only to the times
of the Heptarchy. Some of these tremendous
figures were real men, dressed up with vizards
and buskins; others were mere pageants composed of paste-board and buckram, which,
viewed from beneath, formed a sufficiently
striking representation of what was intended.
But the gigantic porter who waited at the gate
beneath, and actually discharged the duties of
warder, owed none of his terrors to fictitious

means. He was a man whose huge stature, thewes, sinews, and bulk in proportion, would have enabled him to enact Colbrand, Ascapart, or any other giant of romance, without raising himself nearer to heaven even by the altitude of a chopin. The legs and knees of this son of Anak were bare, as were his arms from a span below the shoulder; but his feet were defended with sandals, fastened with cross straps of scarlet leather, studded with brazen knobs. A close jerkin of scarlet velvet, looped with gold, with short breeches of the same, covered his body and a part of his limbs; and he wore on his shoulders, instead of a cloak, the skin of a black bear. The head of this formidable person was uncovered, excepting by his shaggy black hair, which descended on either side around features of that huge, lumpish, and heavy cast, which are often annexed to men of very uncommon size, and which, notwithstanding some distinguished exceptions, have created a general prejudice against giants, as being a dull and sullen kind of persons. This tremendous warder was appropriately armed with a heavy club, spiked with steel. In fine, he represented excellently one of those giants of popular romance, who figure in every fairy tale, or legend of knight-errantry.

The demeanour of this modern Titan, when Wayland Smith bent his attention to him, had in it something arguing much mental embarrassment and vexation; for sometimes he sat down for an instant on a massive stone bench, which

seemed placed for his accommodation beside the
gate-way, and then ever and anon he started up,
scratching his huge head, and striding to and fro
on his post, like one under a fit of impatience and
anxiety. It was while the porter was pacing before the gate in this agitated manner, that Wayland, modestly, yet as a matter of course, (not
however without some mental misgiving,) was
about to pass him, and enter the portal arch. The
porter, however, stopped his progress, bidding
him, in a thundering voice, « Stand back! » and
enforcing his injunction by heaving up his steel-
shod mace, and dashing it on the ground before
Wayland's horse's nose with such vehemence,
that the pavement flashed fire, and the arch-way
rang to the clamour. Wayland, availing himself
of Dickie's hint, began to state that he belonged
to a band of performers to which his presence
was indispensible, that he had been accidentally
detained behind, and much to the same purpose.
But the warder was inexorable, and kept muttering and murmuring something betwixt his
teeth, which Wayland could make little of; and
addressing betwixt whiles a refusal of admittance, couched in language which was but too
intelligible. A specimen of his speech might run
thus.—« What, how now; my masters?(to himself) — Here's a stir—here's a coil. — (Then to
Wayland) — You are a loitering knave, and
shall have no entrance—(Again to himself,)—
Here's a throng — here's a thrusting. — I shall
ne'er get through with it—Here's a—humph—

ha — (To Wayland)— Back from the gate, or I'll break the pate of thee —(Once more to himself) — Here's a — no — I shall never get through it. »

« Stand still, » whispered Flibbertigibbet into Wayland's ear, « I know where the shoe pinches, and will tame him in an instant. »

He dropped down from the horse, and skipping up to the porter, plucked him by the tail of the bear-skin, so as to induce him to decline his huge head, and whispered something in his ear. Not at the command of the lord of some eastern talisman did ever Afrite change his horrid frown into a look of smooth submission, more suddenly than the gigantic porter of Kenilworth relaxed the terrors of his look, at the instant Flibbertigibbet's whisper reached his ears. He flung his club upon the ground, and caught up Dickie Sludge, raising him to such a distance from the earth, as might have proved perilous had he chanced to let him slip.

« It is even so, » he said, with a thundering sound of exultation—« it is even so, my little dandieprat — But who the devil could teach it thee ? »

« Do not thou care about that, » said Flibbertigibbet; « but —— he looked at Wayland and the lady, and then sunk what he had to say in a whisper, which needed not be a loud one, as the giant held him for his convenience close to his ear. The porter then gave Dickie a warm caress, and set him on the ground with the same care which a careful housewife uses in replacing a cracked china cup upon her mantle-piece, calling out at the same time to Wayland and the lady, « In with you—in with you—and take heed how you come too late another day when I chance to be porter. »

« Ay, ay, in with you, » added Flibbertigibbet; « I must stay a short space with mine honest Philistine, my Goliath of Gath here; but I will be with you anon, and at the bottom of all your secrets, were they as deep and dark as the Castle dungeon. »

« I do believe thou would'st, » said Wayland; « but I trust the secret will be soon out of my keeping, and then I shall care the less whether thou or any one knows it. »

« They now crossed the entrance tower, which obtained the name of the Gallery-tower, from the following circumstance:—The whole bridge, extending from the entrance to another tower on the opposite side of the lake, called Mortimer's Tower, was so disposed as to make a spacious tilt-yard, about one hundred and thirty yards in length, and ten in breadth, strewed with the finest sand, and defended on either side by strong and high palisades. The broad and fair gallery, destined for the ladies who were to witness the feats of chivalry presented on this area, was erected on the northern side of the outer tower, to which it gave name. Our travellers passed slowly along the bridge or tilt-yard, and arrived at Mortimer's Tower,

at its farthest extremity, through which the
approach led into the outer, or base court of the
Castle. Mortimer's Tower bore on its front the
scutcheon of the Earl of March, whose daring
ambition overthrew the throne of Edward II, and
aspired to share his power with the « She-wolf of
France, » to whom the unhappy monarch was
wedded. The gate, which opened under this
ominous memorial, was guarded by many warders in rich liveries; but they offered no opposition to the entrance of the Countess and her
guide, who, having passed by license of the
principal porter at the Gallery-tower, were not,
it may be supposed, liable to interruption from
his deputies. They entered accordingly, in silence, the great outward court of the Castle;
having then full before them that vast and
lordly pile, with all its stately towers, each
gate open, as if in sign of unlimited hospitality,
and the apartments filled with noble guests of
every degree, besides dependants, retainers,
domestics of every description, and all the
appendages and promoters of mirth and revelry.

Amid this stately and busy scene, Wayland
halted his horse, and looked upon the lady, as
if waiting her commands what was next to be
done, since they had safely reached the place of
destination. As she remained silent, Wayland,
after waiting a minute or two, ventured to ask
her in direct terms, what were her next commands. She raised her hand to her forehead, as if
in the act of collecting her thoughts and resolution,

whileshe answered him in a low and suppressed voice, like the murmurs of one who speaks in a dream—« Commands ? I may indeed claim right to command, but who is there will obey me. »

Then suddenly raising her head like one who has formed a decisive resolution, she addressed a gaily dressed domestic, who was crossing the court with importance and bustle in his countenance. — « Stop, sir, » she said, « I desire to speak with the Earl of Leicester. »

« With whom, an it please you ? » said the man, surprised at the demand; and then looking upon the mean equipage of her who used towards him such a tone of authority, he added with insolence, « Why, what Bess of Bedlam is this, would ask to see my lord on such a day as the present ? »

« Friend, » said the Countess, « be not insolent—my business with the Earl is most urgent. »

« You must get some one else to do it, were it thrice as urgent, » said the fellow. — « I should summon my lord from the Queen's royal presence to do *your* business, should I ? — I were like to be thanked with a horse-whip. I marvel our old porter took not measure of such ware with his club, instead of giving them passage; but his brain is addled with getting his speech by heart. »

Two or three persons stopped, attracted by the fleering way in which the serving-man expressed himself; and Wayland, alarmed both for himself and the lady, hastily addressed himself to one who appeared the most civil, and thrusting a piece of money into his hand, held a moment's counsel with him, on the subject of finding a place. of temporary retreat for the lady. The person to whom he spoke, being one in some authority, rebuked the others for their incivility, and commanding one fellow to take care of the strangers' horses, he desired them to follow him. The Countess retained presence of mind sufficient to see that it was absolutely necessary she should comply with his request; and, leaving the rude lacqueys and grooms to crack their brutal jests about light heads, light heels, and so forth, Wayland and she followed in silence the deputy usher, who undertook to be their conductor.

They entered the inner court of the Castle by the great gateway, which extended betwixt the principal Keep or Donjon, called Cæsar's Tower, and a stately building which passed by the name of King Henry's Lodging, and were thus placed in the centre of the noble pile, which presented on its different fronts magnificent specimens of every species of castellated architecture, from the Conquest to the reign of Elizabeth, with the appropriate style and ornaments of each.

Across this inner court also they were conducted by their guide to a small but strong tower, occupying the north-east angle of the building, adjacent to the great hall, and filling up a space betwixt the immense range of kitchens and the end of the great hall itself. The lower part of this tower was occupied by some of the household officers of Leicester, owing to its convenient vicinity to the places where their duty lay; but in the upper storey, which was reached by a narrow winding stair, was a small chamber, which, in the great demand for lodgings, had been on the present occasion fitted up for the reception of guests, though generally said to have been used as a place of confinement for some unhappy person who had been there murdered. Tradition called this prisoner Mervyn, and transferred his name to the tower. That it had been used as a prison was not improbable; for the floor of each storey was arched, the walls of tremendous thickness, while the space of the chamber did not exceed fifteen feet square. The window, however, was pleasant, though narrow, and commanded a delightful view of what was called the *Pleasance;* a space of ground enclosed and decorated with arches, trophies, statues, fountains, and other architectural monuments, which formed one access from the castle itself to the garden. There was a bed in the apartment, and other preparations for the reception of a guest, to which the Countess paid but slight attention, her notice being instantly arrested by the sight of writing materials placed on the table, (not very commonly to be found in the bed-rooms of those days) which instantly suggested the idea of writing to

Leicester ; and remaining private until she had
received his answer.

The deputy-usher having introduced them
into this commodious apartment ; courteously
asked Wayland, whose generosity he had experienced , whether he could do any thing
farther for his service. Upon receiving a gentle
hint , that some refreshment would not be
unacceptable, he presently conveyed the smith
to the buttery-hatch , where dressed provisions
of all sorts were distributed , with hospitable
profusion , to all who asked for them. Wayland
was readily supplied with some light provisions ,
such as he thought would best suit the faded
appetite of the lady ; and did not omit the opportunity of himself making a hasty but hearty
meal on more substantial fare. He then returned
to the apartment in the turret, where he found
the Countess, who had finished her letter to
Leicester ; and, in lieu of a seal and silken thread,
had secured it with a braid of her own beautiful
tresses , secured by what is called a true-love
knot.

« Good friend, » said she to Wayland, « whom
God hath sent to aid me at my utmost need , I
do beseech thee, as the last trouble you shall
take for an unfortunate lady , to deliver this
letter to the noble Earl of Leicester. Be it received as it may, » she said , with features agitated betwixt hope and fear, « thou, good fellow,
shalt have no more cumber with me. But I hope

the best; and if ever lady made a poor man
rich, thou hast surely deserved it at my hand,
should my happy days ever come round again.
Give it, I pray you, into Lord Leicester's own
hand, and mark how he looks on receiving it. »

Wayland, on his part, readily undertook the
commission, but anxiously prayed the lady, in
his turn, to partake of some refreshment; in
which he at length prevailed, more through im-
portunity, and her desire to see him begone on
his errand, than from any inclination the Countess felt to comply with his request. He then left
her, advising her to lock her door on the inside,
and not to stir from her little apartment — and
went to seek an opportunity of discharging her
errand, as well as of carrying into effect a purpose of his own, which circumstances had induced him to form.

In fact, from the conduct of the lady during
the journey — her long fits of profound silence
— the irresolution and uncertainty which
seemed to pervade all her movements, and the
obvious incapacity of thinking and acting for
herself, under which she seemed to labour,
Wayland had formed the not improbable opinion, that the difficulties of her situation had
in some degree affected her understanding.

When she had escaped from the seclusion of
Cumnor Place, and the dangers to which she
was there exposed, it would have seemed her
most rational course to retire to her father's,
or elsewhere, at a distance from the power of

6*

those by whom these dangers had been created. When, instead of doing so, she demanded to be conveyed to Kenilworth, Wayland had been only able to account for her conduct, by supposing that she meant to put herself under the tutelage of Tressilian, and to appeal to the protection of the Queen. But now, instead of following this natural course, she entrusted him with a letter to Leicester, the patron of Varney, and within whose jurisdiction at least, if not under his express authority, all the evils she had already suffered were inflicted upon her. This seemed an unsafe, and even a desperate measure, and Wayland felt anxiety for his own safety, as well as that of the lady, should he execute her commission, before he had secured the advice and countenance of a protector. He therefore resolved, before delivering the letter to Leicester, that he would seek out Tressilian, and communicate to him the arrival of the lady at Kenilworth, and thus at once rid himself of all further responsibility, and devolve the task of guiding and protecting this unfortunate lady upon the patron who had at first employed him in her service.

« He will be a better judge than I am, » said Wayland, « whether she is to be gratified in this humour of appeal to my Lord of Leicester, which seems like an act of insanity; and, therefore, I will turn the matter over on his hands, deliver him the letter, receive what they list to give me by way of guerdon, and then shew the

Castle of Kenilworth a pair of light heels; for, after the work I have been engaged in, it will be, I fear, neither a safe nor wholesome place of residence; and I would rather shoe colts on the coldest common in England, than share in their gayest revels. »

———

CHAPTER XXVII.

In my time I have seen a boy do wonders.
Robin, the red tinker, had a boy
Would ha' run through a cat-hole
The Coxcomb.

AMID the universal bustle which filled the Castle and its environs, it was no easy matter to find out any individual; and Wayland was still less likely to light upon Tressilian, whom he sought so anxiously, because, sensible of the danger of attracting attention, in the circumstances in which he was placed, he dared not make general inquiries among the retainers or domestics of Leicester. He learned, however, by indirect questions, that, in all probability, Tressilian must have been one of a large party of gentlemen in attendance on the Earl of Sussex, who had accompanied their patron that morning to Kenilworth, when Leicester had received them with marks of the most formal respect and distinction. He farther learned, that both Earls, with their followers, and many other nobles, knights, and gentlemen, had taken horse, and gone towards Warwick several hours since, for the purpose of escorting the Queen to Kenilworth.

Her Majesty's arrival, like other great events, was delayed from hour to hour; and it was now announced by a breathless post, that her Majesty being detained by her gracious desire, to receive the homage of her lieges who had thronged to wait upon her at Warwick, it would be the hour of twilight ere she entered the Castle. The intelligence released for a time those who were upon duty, in the immediate expectation of the Queen's appearance, and ready to play their part in the solemnities with which it was to be accompanied; and Wayland, seeing several horsemen enter the Castle, was not without hopes that Tressilian might be of the number. That he might not lose an opportunity of meeting his patron in case this should be the case, Wayland placed himself in the base-court of the Castle, near Mortimer's Tower, and watched every one who went or came by the bridge, the extremity of which was protected by that building. Thus stationed, nobody could enter or leave the Castle without his observation, and most anxiously did he study the garb and countenance of every horseman, as, passing from under the opposite Gallery-tower, they paced slowly, or curvetted, along the tilt-yard, and approached the entrance of the base-court.

But while Wayland gazed thus eagerly to discover him whom he saw not, he was pulled by the sleeve by one by whom he himself would not willingly have been seen.

This was Dickie Sludge, or Flibbertigibbet, who, like the imp whose name he bore, and whom he had been accoutred in order to resemble, seemed to be ever at the ear of those who thought least of him. Whatever were Wayland's internal feelings, he judged it necessary to express pleasure at their unexpected meeting.

« Ha ! is it thou, my minikin — my millar's thumb—my prince of caco-dæmons — my little mouse ? »

« Ay, » said Dickie, « the mouse which gnawed asunder the toils, just when the lion who was caught in them began to look wonderfully like an ass. »

« Why, thou little hop-the-gutter, thou art as sharp as vinegar this afternoon. But tell me, how did'st thou come off with yonder jolter-headed giant, whom I left thee with ?—I was afraid he would have stripped thy clothes, and so swallowed thee as men peel and eat a roasted chesnut. »

« Had he done so, replied the boy, « he would have had more brains in his guts than ever he had in his noddle. But the giant is a courteous monster, and more grateful than many other folks whom I have helped at a pinch, Master Wayland Smith. »

« Beshrew me, Flibbertigibbet, » replied Wayland, « but thou art sharper than a Sheffield whittle ! I would I knew by what charm you muzzled yonder old bear ? »

« Ay, that is in your own manner, » answered

Dickie;« you think fine speeches will pass muster instead of good will. However, as to this honest porter, you must know, that when we presented ourselves at the gate yonder, his brain was over-burthened with a speech that had been penned for him, and which proved rather an overmatch for his gigantic faculties. Now this same pithy oration had been indited, like sundry others, by my learned magister, Erasmus Holiday, so I had heard it often enough to remember every line. As soon as I heard him blundering, and floundering like a fish upon dry land, through the first verse, and perceived him at a stand, I knew where the shoe pinched, and helped him to the next word, when he caught me up in an ecstacy, even as you saw but now. I promised, as the price of your admission, to hide me under his bearish gaberdine, and prompt him in the hour of need. I have just now been getting some food in the Castle, and am about to return to him. »

« That's right—that's right, my dear Dickie, » replied Wayland; « haste thee, for Heaven's sake! else the poor giant will be utterly disconsolate for want of his dwarfish auxiliary—Away with thee, Dickie. »

« Ay, ay! » answered the boy—« Away with Dickie, when we have got what good of him we can.—You will not let me know the story of this lady, then, who is as much sister of thine as I am? »

« Why, what good would it do thee, thou silly elf? » said Wayland.

« O, stand ye on these terms? said the boy ; « well, I care not greatly about the matter, — only, I never smell out a secret, but I try to be either at the right or the wrong end of it, and so good evening to ye. »

« Nay, but Dickie, » said Wayland, who knew the boy's restless and intriguing disposition too well not to fear his enmity — « stay, my dear Dickie—part not with old friends so shortly !— Thou shalt know all I know of the lady one day. »

« Ay ! » said Dickie ; « and that day may prove a nigh one.—Fare thee well, Wayland—I will to my large-limbed friend, who, if he have not so sharp a wit as some folks, is at least more grateful for the service which other folks render him. And so again, good evening to ye.»

So saying, he cast a somerset through the gateway, and, lighting on the bridge, ran with the extraordinary agility, which was one of his distinguished attributes, towards the Gallery-tower, and was out of sight in an instant.

« I would to God I were safe out of this Castle again ! » prayed Wayland, internally; « for now that this mischievous imp has put his finger in the pye, it cannot but prove a mess fit for the devil's eating. I would to Heaven Master Tressilian would appear. »

Tressilian, whom he was thus anxiously expecting in one direction, had returned to Kenilworth by another access. It was indeed true, as Wayland had conjectured, that, in the earlier

part of the day, he had accompanied the Earls
on their cavalcade towards Warwick, not without hope that he might in that town hear some
tidings of his emissary. Being disappointed in this
expectation, and observing Varney amongst
Leicester's attendants, seeming as if he had some
purpose of advancing to and addressing him,
he conceived, in the present circumstances, it
was wisest to avoid the interview. He, therefore,
left the presence-chamber when the High-She-
riff of the county was in the very midst of his
dutiful address to her Majesty; and, mounting
his horse, rode back to Kenilworth by a remote
and circuitous road, and entered the Castle by
a small sally-port in the western wall, at which
he was readily admitted as one of the followers
of the Earl of Sussex, towards whom Leicester
had commanded the utmost courtesy to be exercised. It was thus that he met not Wayland, who
was impatiently watching his arrival, and whom
he himself would have been, at least, equally
desirous to have seen.

Having delivered his horse to the charge of
his attendant, he walked for a space in the Pleasance and in the garden, rather to indulge in
comparative solitude his own reflexions, than
to admire those singular beauties of nature and
art which the magnificence of Leicester had
there assembled. The greater part of the persons of condition had left the Castle for the
present, to form part of the Earl's cavalcade;
others, who remained behind, were on the bat-

tlements, outer walls, and towers, eager to
view the splendid spectacle of the royal entry.
The garden, therefore, while every other part
of the Castle resounded with the human voice,
was silent, but for the whispering of the leaves,
the emulous warbling of the tenants of a large
aviary, with their happier companions who remained denizens of the free air, and the plash-
ing of the fountains, which, forced into the
air from sculptures of fantastic and grotesque
forms, fell down with ceaseless sound into the
great basins of Italian marble.

The melancholy thoughts of Tressilian cast a
gloomy shade on all the objects with which he
was surrounded. He compared the magnificent
scenes which he here traversed, with the deep
woodland and wild moorland which surrounded
Lidcote-Hall, and the image of Amy Robsart
glided like a phantom through every landscape
which his imagination summoned up. Nothing
is perhaps more dangerous to the future happiness of men of deep thought and retired habits,
than the entertaining an early, long, and unfortunate attachment. It frequently sinks so deep
into the mind, that it becomes their dream by
night and their vision by day — mixes itself
with every source of interest and enjoyment;
and when blighted and withered by final disappointment, it seems as if the springs of the heart
were dried up along with it. This aching of the
heart, this languishing after a shadow which has
lost all the gaiety of its colouring, this dwelling

on the remembrance of a dream from which we have been long roughly awakened , is the weakness of a gentle and generous heart, and it was that of Tressilian.

He himself at length became sensible of the necessity of forcing other objects upon his mind; and for this purpose he left the Pleasance , in order to mingle with the noisy crowd upon the walls , and view the preparation for the pageants. But as he left the garden , and heard the busy hum mixed with music and laughter, which floated around him , he felt an uncontroulable reluctance to mix with society , whose feelings were in a tone so different from his own , and resolved, instead of doing so , to retire to the chamber assigned him , and employ himself in study until the tolling of the great castle-bell should announce the arrival of Elizabeth.

Tressilian crossed accordingly by the passage betwixt the immense range of kitchens and the great hall , and ascended to the third storey of Mervyn's Tower , and applying himself to the door of the small apartment which had been allotted to him, was surprised to find it was locked. He then recollected that the deputy-chamberlain had given him a master-key , advising him , in the present confused state of the Castle , to keep his door as much shut as possible. He applied this key to the lock , the bolt revolved , he entered , and in the same instant saw a female form seated in the apartment , and recognized that form to be Amy Bobsart. His first idea was, that a heated imagination had raised the image on which it doated into visible existence; his second, that he beheld an apparition — the third and abiding conviction, that it was Amy herself; paler, indeed, and thinner than in the days of heedless happiness, when she possessed the form and hue of a wood-nymph, with the beauty of a sylph; but still Amy, unequalled in loveliness by aught which had ever visited his eyes.

The astonishment of the Countess was scarce less than that of Tressilian, although it was of shorter duration, because she had heard from Wayland that he was in the Castle. She had started up at first entrance, and now stood facing him, the paleness of her cheeks having given way to a deep blush.

« Tressilian, » she said, at length, « why come you here? »

« Nay, why come *you* here, Amy, » returned Tressilian, « unless it be at length to claim that aid, which, as far as one man's heart and arm can extend, shall instantly be rendered to you? »

She was silent a moment, and then answered in a sorrowful, rather than an angry tone, — « I require no aid, Tressilian, and would rather be injured than benefited by any which your kindness can offer me. Believe me, I am near one whom law and love oblige to protect me. »

« The villain then hath done you the poor justice which remained in his power, » said

Tressilian ; « and I behold before me the wife of
Varney ! »

« The wife of Varney ! » she replied, with all
the emphasis of scorn ; « With what base
name , sir , does your boldness stigmatize the
— the — the » — She hesitated, dropped her
tone of scorn, looked down, and was confused
and silent , for she recollected what fatal consequences might attend her completing the sentence with « the Countess of Leicester , » which
were the words that had naturally suggested
themselves. It would have been a betrayal of the
secret, on which her husband had assured her
that his fortunes depended, to Tressilian, to
Sussex, to the Queen, and to the whole assembled court. « Never, » she thought, « will I break
my promised silence. I will submit to every
suspicion rather than that. »

The tears rose to her eyes, as she stood silent
before Tressilian ; while, looking on her with
mingled grief and pity, he said, « Alas ! Amy,
your eyes contradict your tongue. That speaks
of a protector, willing and able to watch over
you ; but these tell me you are ruined and deserted by the wretch to whom you have attached
yourself. »

She looked on him , with eyes in which
anger sparkled through her tears, but only repeated the word « wretch ! » with a scornful
emphasis.

« Yes, *wretch !* » said Tressilian ; « for were
he aught better, why are you here, and alone

in my apartment? why was not fitting provision made for your honourable reception ? »

« In your apartment? » repeated Amy; « in *your* apartment? It shall instantly be relieved of my presence. » She hastened towards the door; but the sad recollection of her deserted state at once pressed on her mind, and, pausing on the threshold, she added, in a tone unutterably pathetic, « Alas! I had forgot — I know not where to go » ——

« I see — I see it all, » said Tressilian, springing to her side, and leading her back to the seat, on which she sunk down — « You *do* need aid — you *do* need protection, though you will not own it; and you shall not need it in vain. Leaning on my arm, as the representative of your excellent and broken-hearted father, on the very threshold of the Castle-gate, you shall meet Elizabeth; and the first deed she shall do in the halls of Kenilworth, shall be an act of justice to her sex and her subjects. Strong in my good cause, and in the Queen's justice, the power of her minion shall not shake my resolution. I will instantly seek Sussex. »

« Not for all that is under heaven ! » said the Countess, much alarmed, and feeling the absolute necessity of obtaining time, at least, for consideration. « Tressilian, you were wont to be generous — Grant me one request, and believe, if it be your wish to save me from misery, and from madness, you will do more by making me the promise I ask of you, than Elizabeth can do for me with all her power. »

« Ask me any thing for which you can allege reason, » said Tressilian ; « but demand not of me » ——

« O, limit not your boon, dear Edmund! » exclaimed the Countess — « you once loved that I should call you so — Limit not your boon to reason! for my case is all madness, and phrenzy must guide the counsels which alone can aid me. »

« If you speak thus wildly, » said Tressilian, astonishment again overpowering both his grief and his resolution, « I must believe you indeed incapable of thinking or acting for yourself. »

« Oh no! » she exclaimed, sinking on one knee before him, « I am not mad—I am but a creature unutterably miserable, and, from circumstances the most singular, dragged on to a precipice by the arm of him who thinks he is keeping me from it—even by yours, Tressilian—by yours, whom I have honoured, respected — all but loved—and yet loved too—loved too, Tressilian —though not as you wished me. »

There was an energy—a self-possession—an abandonment in her voice and manner—a total resignation of herself to his generosity, which, together with the kindness of her expressions to himself, moved him deeply. He raised her, and, in broken accents, entreated her to be comforted.

« I cannot, » she said, « I will not be comforted, till you grant me my request! I will speak as
plainly as I dare—I am now awaiting the commands of one who has a right to issue them—The
interference of a third person—of you in especial, Tressilian, will be ruin—utter ruin to me.
Wait but four-and-twenty hours, and it may be
that the poor Amy may have the means to shew
that she values, and can reward, your disinterested friendship — that she is happy herself,
and has the means to make you so—It is surely
worth your patience, for so short a space ? »

Tressilian paused, and weighing in his mind
the various probabilities which might render a
violent interference on his part more prejudicial
than advantageous, both to the happiness and
reputation of Amy; considering also that she
was within the walls of Kenilworth, and could
suffer no injury in a castle honoured with the
Queen's residence, and filled with her guards
and attendants,—he conceived, upon the whole,
that he might render her more evil than good service, by intruding upon her his appeal to Elizabeth in her behalf. He expressed his resolution
cautiously however, doubting naturally whether
Amy's hopes of extricating herself from her difficulties rested on any thing stronger than a blinded attachment to Varney, whom he supposed to
be her seducer.

« Amy, » he said, while he fixed his sad and
expressive eyes on her's, which, in her ecstacy
of doubt, terror, and perplexity, she cast up

towards him, « I have ever remarked, that when others called thee girlish and wilful, there lay under that external semblance of youthful and self-willed folly, deep feeling and strong sense. In this I will confide, trusting your own fate in your own hands for the space of twenty-four hours, without my interference by word' or act »

« Do you promise me this, Tressilian? » said the Countess. « Is it possible you can yet repose so much confidence in me? Do you promise, as you are a gentleman and man of honour, to intrude in my matters, neither by speech nor action, whatever you may see or hear that seems to you to demand your interference ?—Will you so far trust me? »

« I will, upon my honour, » said Tressilian ; « but when that space is expired »———

« When that space is expired, » she said, interrupting him, « you are free to act as your judgment shall determine. »

« Is there nought besides which I can do for you, Amy? » said Tressilian.

« Nothing, « said she, « save to leave me—that is, if—I blush to acknowledge my helplessness by asking it—if you can spare me the use of this apartment for the next twenty-four hours. »

« This is most wonderful! » said Tressilian ; « what hope or interest can you have in a Castle, where you cannot command even an apartment? »

« Argue not, but leave me, » she said; and

added, as he slowly and unwillingly retired,
« Generous Edmund! the time may come, when
Amy may shew she deserved thy noble attach-
ment. »

———

CHAPTER XXVIII.

What, man, ne'er lack a draught, when the full can
Stands at thine elbow, and craves emptying!—
Nay, fear not me, for I have no delight
To watch men's vices, since I have myself
Of virtue nought to boast of.—I'm a striker,
Would have the world strike with me, pell-mell, all.
Pandæmonium.

TRESSILIAN, in strange agitation of mind, had hardly stepped down the first two or three steps of the winding stair-case, when, greatly to his surprise and displeasure, he met Michael Lambourne, wearing an impudent familiarity of visage, for which Tressilian felt much disposed to throw him down stairs; until he remembered the prejudice which Amy, the only object of his solicitude, was likely to receive from his engaging in any act of violence at that time, and in that place.

He therefore contented himself with looking sternly upon Lambourne, as upon one whom he deemed unworthy of notice, and attempted to pass him in his way down stairs, without any symptom of recognition. But Lambourne, who, amidst the profusion of that day's hospitality, had not failed to take a deep, though not an overpowering cup of sack, was not in the humour of

humbling himself before any man's looks. He
stopped Tressilian upon the stair-case without
the least bashfulness or embarrassment, and addressed him as if he had been on kind and intimate terms : — « What, no grudge between us
I hope upon old scores, Master Tressilian ? —
nay, I am one who remember former kindness
rather than later feud — I'll convince you that
I meant honestly and kindly, ay, and comfor-
tably by you. »

« I desire none of your intimacy, » said Tressilian — « keep company with your mates. »

« Now see how hasty he is ! » said Lambourne;
« and how these gentles, that are made questionless out of the porcelain clay of the earth,
look down upon poor Michael Lambourne ! You
would take Master Tressilian now for the most
maid-like, modest, simpering squire of dames,
that ever made love when candles were long i'
the stuff — snuff — call you it ? — Why you
would play the saint on us, Master Tressilian,
and forget that even now thou hast a commo-
dity in thy very bed-chamber, to the shame of
my lord's Castle, ha ! ha ! ha ! Have I touched
you, Master Tressilian ? »

« I know not what you mean, » said Tressilian, inferring, however, too surely, that this
licentious ruffian must have been sensible of
Amy's presence in his apartment; « but if, » he
continued, « thou art varlet of the chambers,
and lackest a fee, there is one to leave mine
unmolested. »

Lambourne looked at the piece of gold, and put it in his pocket, saying — « Now, I know not but you might have done more with me by a kind word, than by this chiming rogue. But after all he pays well that pays with gold — and Mike Lambourne was never a make-bate, or a spoil-sport, or the like. E'en live and let others live, that is my motto — only, I would not let some folks cock their beaver at me neither, as if they were made of silver ore, and I of Dutch pewter. So if I keep your secret, Master Tressilian, you may look sweet on me at least; and were I to want a little backing or countenance, being caught, as you see the best of us may be, in a sort of peccadillo—why, you owe it me — and so e'en make your chamber serve you and that same bird in bower beside — it's all one to Mike Lambourne. »

« Make way, sir, » said Tressilian, unable to bridle his indignation, « you have had your fee. »

« Um ! » said Lambourne, giving place, however, while he sulkily muttered between his teeth, repeating Tressilian's words — « Make way — and you have had your fee — but it matters not, I will spoil no sport, as I said before ; I am no dog in the manger — mind that. »

He spoke louder and louder, as Tressilian, by whom he felt himself overawed, got farther and farther out of hearing.

« I am no dog in the manger — but I will not carry coals neither — mind that, my Master Tressilian; and I will have a peep at this wench,

whom you have quartered so commodiously in
your old haunted room — afraid of ghosts belike, and not too willing to sleep alone. If *I* had
done this now in a strange lord's castle, the word
had been, — The porter's lodge for the knave !
and, — Have him flogged — trundle him down
stairs like a turnip ! — Ay but your virtuous
gentlemen take strange privileges over us, who
are downright servants of our senses. Well — I
have my Master Tressilian's head under my belt
by this lucky discovery, that is one thing certain; and I will try to get a sight of this Linda-
brides of his, that is another. »

CHAPTER XXIX.

Now fare thee well, my master — if true service
Be guerdon'd with hard e'e, uncut the tow-line,
And let our barks across the pathless flood
Hold several courses ——
                                        Shipwreck.

TRESSILIAN walked into the outer yard of the Castle, scarce knowing what to think of his late strange and most unexpected interview with Amy Robsart, and dubious if he had done well, being intrusted with the delegated authority of her father, to pass his word so solemnly to leave her to her own guidance for so many hours. Yet how could he have denied her request, — dependant as she had too probably rendered herself upon Varney? Such was his natural reasoning. The happiness of her future life might depend upon his not driving her to extremities, and since no power of Tressilian's could extricate her from the power of Varney, supposing he was to acknowledge Amy to be his wife, what title had he to destroy the hope of domestic peace, which might yet remain to her, by setting enmity betwixt them? Tressilian resolved, therefore, scrupulously to observe his word pledged to Amy, both because it had been given, and because,

as he still thought, while he considered and re-
considered that extraordinary interview, it could
not with justice or propriety have been refused.

In one respect, he had gained much towards
securing effectual protection for this unhappy
and still beloved object of his early affection.
Amy was no longer mewed up in a distant and
solitary retreat, under the charge of persons of
doubtful reputation. She was in the Castle of
Kenilworth, within the verge of the Royal Court
for the time, free from all risk of violence, and
liable to be produced before Elizabeth on the
first summons. These were circumstances which
could not but assist greatly the efforts which
he might have occasion to use in her behalf.

While he was thus balancing the advantages
and perils which attended her unexpected presence in Kenilworth, Tressilian was hastily and
anxiously accosted by Wayland, who, after
hastily ejaculating, « Thank God, your worship
is found at last! » proceeded with breathless caution to pour into his ear the intelligence, that
the lady had escaped from Cumnor Place.

« And is at present in this Castle, » said
Tressilian; « I know it, and I have seen her —
Was it by her own choice she found refuge in
my apartment? »

« No, » answered Wayland; « but I could
think of no other way of safely bestowing her,
.and was but too happy to find a deputy-usher
who knew where you were quartered; — in

jolly society truly, the hall on the one hand, and the kitchen on the other!

« Peace, this no time for jesting, » answered Tressilian, sternly.

« I wot that but too well, » said the artist, « for I have felt these three days as if I had an halter round my neck. This lady knows not her own mind — she will have none of your aid — commands you not to be named to her— and is about to put herself into the hands of my Lord Leicester. I had never got her safe under your chamber, had she known the owner of it. »

« Is it possible? » said Tressilian. « But she may have hopes the Earl will exert his influence in her favour over his villainous dependant. »

« I know nothing of that, » said Wayland — « but I believe, if she is to reconcile herself with either Leicester or Varney, the side of the Castle of Kenilworth, which will be safest for us, will be the outside from which we can fastest fly away. It is not my purpose to abide an instant after delivery of the letter to Leicester, which waits but your commands to find its way to him. See, here it is—but no—a plague on it—I must have left it in my dog-hole, in the hay-loft yonder, where I am to sleep. »

« Death and fury! » said Tressilian, transported beyond his usual patience; « thou hast not lost that on which may depend a stake more important than a thousand such lives as thine? »

7*

« Lost it ! » answered Wayland, readily; « that were a jest indeed! No, sir, I have it carefully put up with my night-sack, and some matters I have occasion to use—I will fetch it in an instant. »

« Do so, said Tressilian; » be faithful, and thou shalt be well rewarded. But if I have reason to suspect thee, a dead dog were in better case than thou. »

Wayland bowed, and took his leave with seeming confidence and alacrity; but, in fact, filled with the utmost dread and confusion. The letter was lost, that was certain, notwithstanding the apology which he had made to appease the impatient displeasure of Tressilian. It was lost—it might fall into wrong hands—it would then, certainly, occasion a discovery of the whole intrigue in which he had been engaged; nor, indeed, did Wayland see much prospect of its remaining concealed, in any event. He felt much hurt, besides, at Tressilian's burst of impatience.

« Nay, if I am to be paid in this coin, for services where my neck is concerned, it is time I should look to myself. Here have I offended, for aught I know, to the death, the lord of this stately Castle, whose word were as powerful to take away my life, as the breath which speaks it to blow out a farthing candle. And all this for a mad lady, and a melancholy gallant; who, on the loss of a four-nooked bit of paper, has his hand on his poignardo, and swears death and fury ! — Then there is the Doctor and Varney—I will save myself from the whole mess of them—Life is dearer than gold—I will fly this instant, though I leave my reward behind me. »

These reflections naturally enough occurred to a mind like Wayland's, who found himself engaged far deeper than he had expected in a train of mysterious and unintelligible intrigues, in which the actors seemed hardly to know their own course. And yet, to do him justice, his personal fears were, in some degree, counterbalanced by his compassion for the deserted state of the lady.

« I care not a groat for Master Tressilian, » he said; « I have done more than bargain by him, and I have brought his errant-damozel within his reach, so that he may look after her himself; but I fear the poor thing is in much danger amongst these stormy spirits. I will to her chamber, and tell her the fate which has befallen her letter, that she may write another if she list. She cannot lack a messenger, I trow, where there are so many lacqueys that can carry a letter to their lord. And I will tell her also that I leave the Castle, trusting her to God, her own guidance, and Master Tressilian's care and looking after.—Perhaps she may remember the ring she offered me — it was well earned, I trow; but she is a lovely creature, and — marry hang the ring! I will not bear a base mind for the matter. If I fare ill in this world for my good nature, I will have better chance in the next.— So now for the lady, and then for the road. »

. With the stealthy step and jealous eye of the cat that steals on her prey, Wayland resumed the way to the Countess's chamber, sliding along by the side of the courts and passages, alike observant of all around him, and studious himself to escape observation. In this manner he crossed the outward and inward castle-yard, and the great arched passage, which, running betwixt the range of kitchen offices and the hall, led to the bottom of the little winding-stair that gave access to the chambers of Mervyn's Tower.

The artist congratulated himself on having escaped the various perils of his journey, and was in the act of ascending by two steps at once, when he observed that the shadow of a man, thrown from a door which stood a-jar, darkened the opposite wall of the stair-case. Wayland drew back cautiously, went down to the inner court-yard, spent about a quarter of an hour, which seemed at least quadruple its usual duration, *in* walking from place to place, and then returned to the tower, in hopes to find that the lurker had disappeared. He ascended as high as the suspicious spot—there was no shadow on the wall—he ascended a few yards farther—the door was still a-jar, and he was doubtful whether to advance or retreat, when it was suddenly thrown wide open, and Michael Lambourne bolted out upon the astonished Wayland. « Who the devil art thou? and what seek'st thou in this part of the Castle? March into that chamber, and be hanged to thee! »

« I am no dog, to go at every man's whistle, » said the artist, affecting a confidence which was belied by a timid shake in his voice.

« Say'st thou me so?—Come hither, Lawrence Staples. »

A huge ill-made and ill-looked fellow, upwards of six feet high, appeared at the door, and Lambourne proceeded : « If thou be'st so fond of this tower, my friend, thou shalt see its foundations, good twelve feet below the bed of the lake, and tenanted by certain jolly toads, snakes, and so forth, which thou wilt find mighty good company. Therefore, once more I ask you in fair play, who thou art, and what thou seek'st here ? »

If the dungeon-grate once clashes behind me, thought Wayland, I am a gone man.—He therefore answered submissively, « He was the poor juggler whom his honour had met yesterday in Weatherly-bottom. »

« And what juggling trick art thou playing in this tower ? Thy gang, » said Lambourne, « lie over against Clinton's buildings. »

« I came here to see my sister, » said the jug gler, who is in Master Tressilian's chamber, just above. »

« Aha! » said Lambourne, smiling, « here be truths — upon my honour, for a stranger, this same Master Tressilian makes himself at home among us, and furnishes out his cell handsomely, with all sort of commodities. — Hark thee, sirrah — This will be a precious tale of the

sainted Master Tressilian, and will be welcome
to some folks, as a purse of broad pieces to
me — Hark ye, fellow, " he continued, addressing Wayland, " thou shalt not give Puss a hint
to steal away — we must catch her in her form.
So, back with that pitiful sheep-biting visage
of thine, or I will fling thee from the window of
the tower, and try if your juggling skill can
save your bones. "

" Your worship will not be so hard-hearted,
I trust, said Wayland; " poor folks must live.
I trust your honour will allow me to speak with
my sister ? "

" Sister on Adam's side, I warrant, said Lambourne; " or, if otherwise, the more knave
thou. But sister or no sister, thou diest on point
of fox, if thou comest a prying to this tower
once more. And now I think of it, uds daggers
and death! I will see thee out of the Castle, for
this is a more main concern than thy jugglery. "

" But, please your worship, " said Wayland,
" I am to enact Arion in the pageant upon the
lake this very evening. "

" I will act it myself, by Saint Christopher, "
said Lambourne — " Orion, call'st thou him?
— I will act Orion, his belt and his seven stars
to boot. Come along, for a rascal knave as thou
art — follow me! — Or stay — Lawrence, do
thou bring him along. "

Lawrence seized by the collar of the cloak
the unresisting juggler, while Lambourne, with
hasty steps, led the way to that same sally-port,

or secret postern, by which Tressilian had returned to the Castle, and which opened in the western wall, at no great distance from Mervyn's Tower.

While traversing with a rapid foot the space betwixt the tower and the sally-port, Wayland in vain racked his brain for some device which might avail the poor lady, for whom, notwithstanding his own imminent danger, he felt deep interest. But when he was thrust out of the Castle, and informed by Lambourne, with a tremendous oath, that instant death would be the consequence of his again approaching it, he cast up his hands and eyes to heaven, as if to call God to witness he had stood to the uttermost in defence of the oppressed; then turned his back on the proud towers of Kenilworth, and went his way to seek a humbler and safer place of refuge.

Lawrence and Lambourne gazed a little while after Wayland, and then turned to go back to their tower, when the former thus addressed his companion: « Never credit me, Master Lambourne, if I can guess why thou hast driven this poor caitiff from the Castle, just when he was to bear a part in the show that was beginning, and all this about a wench. »

« Ah, Lawrence, » replied Lambourne, « thou art thinking of Black Joan Jugges of Slingdon, and hast sympathy with human frailty. But couragio, most noble Duke of the Dungeon and Lord of Limbo, for thou art as dark in this matter as

thine own dominions of little-ease. My most reverend Seignor of the Low Countries of Kenilworth, know that our most notable master, Richard Varney, would give as much to have a
hole in this same Tressilian's coat, as would
make us some fifty midnight carousals, with the
full leave of bidding the steward go snick up, if
he came to startle us too soon from our goblets.»

« Nay, an that be the case, thou hast right,»
said Lawrence Staples, the upper-warder, or in
common phrase, the first jailor of Kenilworth
Castle, and of the Liberty and Honour belonging
thereto; « but how will you manage when you
are absent at the Queen's entrance, Master Lambourne; for methinks thou must attend thy
master there? »

« Why thou, mine honest prince of prisons,
must keep ward in my absence—Let Tressilian
enter if he will, but see thou let no one come
out. If the damsel herself would make a break,
as 'tis not unlike she may, scare her back with
rough words—she is but a paltry player's wench
after all. »

« Nay, for that matter, » said Lawrence, « I
might shut the iron wicket upon her, that stands
without the double door, and so force per force
she will be bound to her answer without more
trouble. »

« Then Tressilian will not get access to her,»
said Lambourne, reflecting a moment. But 'tis
no matter—she will be detected in his chamber, and that is all one. — But confess, thou

old bat's-eyed dungeon-keeper, that you fear to keep awake by yourself in that Mervyn's Tower of thine ? »

« Why , as to fear , Master Lambourne , » said the fellow , « I mind it not the turning of a key ; but strange things have been heard and seen in that tower. — You have heard , for as short time as you have been in Kenilworth , that it is haunted by the spirit of Arthur ap Mervyn , a wild chief taken by fierce Lord Mortimer , when he was one of the Lords Marchers of Wales , and murthered , as they say , in that same tower which bears his name ? »

« O , I have heard the tale five hundred times, » said Lambourne, « and how the ghost is always most vociferous when they boil leeks and stir about, or fry toasted cheese in the culinary regions. Santo Diavolo , man, hold thy tongue , I know all about it. »

« Ay, but thou dost not though , » said the turnkey, « for. as wise as thou wouldst make thyself. Ah, it is an awful thing to murder a prisoner in his ward! — You, that may have given a man a stab in a dark street, know nothing of it. To give a mutinous fellow a knock on the head with the keys, and bid him be quiet , that's what I call keeping order in the ward ; but to draw weapon and slay him, as was done to this Welsh lord, *that* raises you a ghost that will render your prison-house untenantable by any decent captive for some hundred years. And I have that regard for my prisoners, poor

II. 8

things, that I have put good squires and men of worship, that have taken a ride on the highway, or slandered my Lord of Leicester, or the like, fifty feet under ground, rather than I would put them into that upper chamber yonder that they call Mervyn's Bower. Indeed, by good Saint Peter of the Fetters, I marvel my noble lord, or Master Varney, would think of lodging guests there; and if this Master Tressilian could get any one to keep him company, and in especial a pretty wench, why truly I think he was in the right on't. »

« I tell thee, » said Lambourne, leading the way into the turnkey's apartment, « thou art an ass — Go bolt the wicket on the stair, and trouble not thy noddle about ghosts. — Give me the wine-stoup, man; I am somewhat heated with chafing with yonder rascal. »

While Lambourne drew a long draught from a pitcher of claret, which he made use of without any cup, the warder went on, vindicating his own belief in the supernatural.

« Thou hast been few hours in this Castle, and hast been for the whole space so drunk, Lambourne, that thou art deaf, dumb, and blind. But we should hear less of your bragging, were you to pass a night with us at full moon, for then the ghost is busiest; and more especially when a rattling wind sets in from the north-west, with some sprinkling of rain, and now and then a growl of thunder. Body o' me, what crackings and clashings, what groanings and what howlings will there be at such times in Mervyn's Bower, right as it were over our heads, till the matter of two quarts of distilled waters has not been enough to keep my lads and me together. »

« Pshaw, man! » replied Lambourne, on whom his last draught, joined to repeated visitation of the pitcher upon former occasions, began to make some innovation, « thou speak'st thou know'st not what about spirits. No one knows justly what to say about them; and, in short, least said may in that matter be soonest amended. Some men believe in one thing, some in another—it is all matter of fancy. I have known them of all sorts, my dear Lawrence Lock-the-Door, and sensible men too. There's a great lord — we'll pass his name, Lawrence—he believes in the stars and the moon, the planets and their courses, and so forth, and that they twinkle exclusively for his benefit; when in sober, or rather in drunken truth, Lawrence, they are only shining to keep honest fellows like me out of the kennel. Well, sir, let his humour pass, he is great enough to indulge it.—Then look ye, there is another — a very learned man, I promise you, and can vent Greek and Hebrew as I can Thieves'-latin — he has an humour of sympathies and antipathies— of changing lead into gold and the like—why, via, let that pass too, and let him pay those in transmigrated coin, who are fools enough to let it be current with them. — Then here comest thou thyself, another great man, though neither learned nor noble, yet full six feet high,

and thou, like a purblind mole, must needs believe in ghosts and goblins, and such like.—
Now, there is, besides, a great man—that is, a
great little man, or a little great man, my dear
Lawrence — and his name begins with V. and
what believes he ? Why nothing, honest Lawrence — nothing in earth, heaven, or hell; and
for my part, if I believe there is a devil, it is only
because I think there must be some one to catch
our friend by the back « when soul and body
sever.,»as the ballad says—for your antecedent
will have a consequent—*raro antecedentem*, as
Doctor Bricham was wont to say—But this is
Greek to you now, honest Lawrence, and in
sooth learning is dry work— Hand me the pitcher once more. »

« In faith, if you drink more, Michael, » said
the Warder, you will be in sorry case either to
play Arion or to wait on your master on such a
solemn night ; and I expect each moment to hear
the great bell toll for the muster at Mortimer's
Tower, to receive the Queen. »

- While Staples remonstrated, Lambourne
drank; and then setting down the pitcher, which
was nearly emptied, with a deep sigh, he said,
in an under tone, which soon rose to a high one
as his speech proceeded ; « Never mind, Lawrence — if I be drunk, I know that shall make
Varney uphold me sober. But, as I said, never
mind, I can carry my drink discreetly. Moreover, I am to go on the water as Orion, and
shall take cold unless I take something comfor-

table before-hand. Not play Orion! Let us see
the best roarer that ever strained his lungs for
twelve pence outmouth me. What if they see me
a little disguised?—Wherefore should any man
be sober to-night? answer me that—It is matter
of loyalty to be merry—and I tell thee, there are
those in the castle, who if they are not merry
when drunk, have little chance to be merry when
sober—I name no names, Lawrence. But your
pottle of sack is a fine shoeing-horn to pull on
a loyal humour, and a merry one. Huzza for
Queen Elizabeth!—for the noble Leicester!—
for the worshipful Master Varney!—and for
Michael Lambourne, that can turn them all
round his finger!»

So saying, he walked down stairs, and across
the inner court.

The Warder looked after him, shook his head,
and, while he drew close and locked a wicket,
which, crossing the stair-case, rendered it impossible for any one to ascend higher than the
storey immediately beneath Mervyn's Bower, as
Tressilian's chamber was named, he thus soli-
loquized with himself — « It's a good thing to
be a favourite—I well nigh lost mine office, because one frosty morning Master Varney thought
I smelled of aquavitæ; and this fellow can appear
before him drunk as a wine-skin, and yet meet
no rebuke. But then he is a pestilent clever fellow withal, and no one can understand above
one half of what he says.»

CHAPTER XXX.

Now bid the steeple rock—she comes , she comes ! —
Speak for us, bells — speak for us, shrill-tongued tuckets.
Stand to thy linstock, gunner; let thy cannon
Play such a peal, as if a paynim foe
Came stretch'd in turban'd ranks to storm the ramparts.
We will have pageants too—but that craves wit,
And I'm a rough-hewn soldier.
The Virgin Queen—a Tragi-Comedy.

TRESSILIAN, when Wayland had left him, as mentioned in the last chapter, remained uncertain what he ought next to do, when Raleigh and Blount came up to him arm in arm, yet, according to their wont, very eagerly disputing together. Tressilian had no great desire for their society in the present state of his feelings, but there was no possibility of avoiding them; and indeed he felt that, bound by his promise not to approach Amy, or take any step in her behalf, it would be his best course at once to mix with general society, and to exhibit on his brow as little as he could of the anguish and uncertainty which sat heavy at his heart. He therefore made a virtue of necessity, and hailed his comrades with, « All mirth to you, gentlemen. Whence come ye? »

« From Warwick, to be sure, » said Blount; « we must needs home to change our habits , like poor players, who are fain to multiply their persons to outward appearance by change of suits; and you had better do the like, Tressilian.»

«Blount is right,» said Raleigh; «the Queen loves such marks of deference, and notices, as wanting in respect, those who, not arriving in her immediate attendance, may appear in their soiled and ruffled riding dress. But look at Blount himself, Tressilian, for the love of laughter, and see how his villainous tailor hath apparelled him — in blue, green, and crimson, with carnation ribbons, and yellow roses in his shoes!»

«Why, what would'st thou have?»said Blount. «I told the cross-legged thief to do his best, and spare no cost; and methinks these things are gay enough — gayer than thine own — I'll be judged by Tressilian.»

«I agree — I agree,» said Walter Raleigh. «Judge betwixt us, Tressilian, for the love of heaven!»

Tressilian, thus appealed to, looked at them both, and was immediately sensible at a single glance, that honest Blount had taken upon the tailor's warrant the pied garments which he had chosen to make, and was as much embarrassed by the quantity of points and ribands which garnished his dress, as a clown is in a holiday suit; while the dress of Raleigh was a well-fancied and rich suit, which the wearer bore as a garb too well adapted to his elegant person to attract particular attention. Tressilian said, therefore, «That Blount's dress was finest, but Raleigh's the best fancied.»

Blount was satisfied with his decision. « I knew
mine was finest, » he said ; « if that knave Double-
stitch had brought me home such a simple doublet as that of Raleigh's, I would have beat his
brains out with his own pressing-iron. Nay, if
we must be fools, ever let us be fools of the first
head, say I. »

« But why gettest thou not on thy braveries,
Tressilian ? » said Raleigh.

« I am excluded from my apartment by a silly
mistake, » said Tressilian, « and separated for
the time from my baggage. I was about to seek
thee, to beseech a share of thy lodging. »

« And welcome, » said Raleigh; « it is a noble
one. My Lord of Leicester has done us that kindness, and lodged us in princely fashion. If his
courtesy be extorted reluctantly, it is at least extended far. I would advise you to tell your
streight to the Earl's chamberlain — you will
have instant redress. »

« Nay, it is not worth while, since you can
spare me room, » replied Tressilian — « I would
not be troublesome. — Has any one come hither
with you ? »

« O, ay, » said Blount ; « Varney and a whole
tribe of Leicestrians, besides about a score of
us honest Sussex folks. — We are all, it seems,
to receive the Queen at what they call the Gallery-tower, and witness some fooleries there; and
then we're to remain in attendance upon the
Queen in the Great Hall, God bless the mark,
while those who are now waiting upon her Grace

get rid of their slough, and doff their riding-suits. Heaven help me, if her Grace should speak to me, I shall never know what to answer! »

« And what has detained them so long at Warwick ? » said Tressilian, unwilling that their conversation should return to his own affairs.

« Such a succession of fooleries, » said Blount « as were never seen at Bartholomew-fair. We have had speeches and players, and dogs and bears, and men making monkies, and women moppets of themselves — I marvel the Queen could endure it. But ever and anon came in something of ' the lovely light of her gracious countenance ', or some such trash. Ah! vanity makes a fool of the wisest. But, come, let us on to this same Gallery-tower, — though I see not what thou, Tressilian, canst do with thy riding-dress and boots. »

« I will take my station behind thee, Blount, » said Tressilian, who saw that his friend's unusual finery had taken a strong hold of his imagination; « thy goodly size and gay dress will cover my defects. »

« And so thou shalt, Edmund, » said Blount. « In faith I am glad thou think'st my garb well-fancied, for all Master Wittypate here; for when one does a foolish thing, it is right to do it handsomely. »

So saying, Blount cocked his beaver, threw out his leg, and marched manfully forward, as if at the head of his brigade of pikemen, ever and anon looking with complaisance on his

crimson stockings, and the huge yellow roses
which blossomed on his shoes. Tressilian followed, wrapped in his own sad thoughts, and
scarce minding Raleigh, whose quick fancy,
amused by the awkward vanity of his respec-
table friend, vented itself in jests, which he
whispered into Tressilian's ear.

In this manner they crossed the long bridge,
or tilt-yard, and took their station, with other
gentlemen of quality, before the outer gate of the
Gallery or Entrance-tower. The whole amounted to about forty persons, all selected as of the
first rank under that of knighthood, and were
disposed in double rows on either side of the
gate, like a guard of honour, within the close
hedge of pikes and partizans, which was formed
by Leicester's retainers, wearing his liveries.
The gentlemen carried no arms, save their
swords and daggers. These gallants were as gaily
dressed as imagination could devise; and as the
garb of the time permitted a great display of ex-
pensive magnificence, nought was to be seen but
velvet and cloth of gold and silver, ribands,
feathers, gems, and golden chains. In spite of
his more serious subjects of distress, Tressilian
could not help feeling, that he, with his ri-
ding-suit, however handsome it might be, made
rather an unworthy figure among these « fierce
vanities, » and the rather because he saw that
his dishabille was the subject of wonder among
his own friends, and of scorn among the partizans of Leicester.

We could not suppress this fact, though it may seem something at variance with the gravity of Tressilian's character; but the truth is, that a regard for personal appearance is a species of self-love, from which the wisest are not exempt, and to which the mind clings so instinctively, that not only the soldier advancing to almost inevitable death, but even the doomed criminal who goes to certain execution, shews an anxiety to array his person to the best advantage. But this is a digression.

It was the twilight of a summer night, (9th July, 1575,) the sun having for some time set, and all were in anxious expectation of the Queen's immediate approach. The multitude had remained assembled for many hours, and their numbers were still rather on the increase. A profuse distribution of refreshments, together with roasted oxen, and barrels of ale set a-broach in different places of the road, had kept the populace in perfect love and loyalty towards the Queen and her favourite, which might have somewhat abated had fasting been added to watching. They passed away the time, therefore, with the usual popular amusements of whooping, hallooing, shrieking, and playing rude tricks upon each other, forming the chorus of discordant sounds usual on such occasions. These prevailed all through the crowded roads and fields, and especially beyond the gate of the Chace, where the greater number of the common sort were stationed; when, all of a sudden, single rocket was seen to shoot into the atmosphere, and, at the instant, far-heard over flood and field, the great bell of the Castle tolled.

Immediately there was a pause of dead silence, succeeded by a deep hum of expectation, the united voice of many thousands, none of whom spoke above their breath; or, to use a singular expression, the whisper of an immense multitude.

« They come now, for certain, » said Raleigh. « Tressilian, that sound is grand. We hear it from this distance, as mariners, after a long voyage, hear, upon their night-watch, the tide rush upon some distant and unknown shore. »

« Mass ! » answered Blount; « I hear it rather as I used to hear mine own kine lowing from the close of Wittens-westlowe. »

« He will assuredly graze presently, » said Raleigh to Tressilian; « his thought is all of fat oxen and fertile meadows—he grows little better than one of his own beeves, and only becomes grand when he is provoked to pushing and goring. »

« We shall have him at that presently, » said Tressilian, « if you spare not your wit. »

« Tush, I care not, » answered Raleigh; « but thou too, Tressilian, hast turned a kind of owl, that flies only by night; hast exchanged thy songs for screechings, and good oompany for an ivy-tod. »

« But what manner of animal art thou thyself, Raleigh, » said Tressilian, « that thou holdest us all so lightly ? »

« Who, I ? » replied Raleigh. « An eagle am
I, that never will think of dull earth, while
there is a heaven to soar in, and a sun to gaze
upon. »

« Well bragged, by Saint Barnaby! » said
Blount; « but, good Master Eagle, beware the
cage, and beware the fowler. Many birds have
flown as high, that I have seen stuffed with
straw, and hung up to scare kites. — But
hark, what a dead silence hath fallen on them
at once! »

« The procession pauses, » said Raleigh, « at
the gate of the Chace, where a sybil, one of
the *fatidicæ*, meets the Queen, to tell her fortune. I saw the verses; there is little savour in
them, and her Grace has been already crammed
full with such poetical compliments. She whispered to me during the Recorder's speech yonder, at Ford-mill, as she entered the liberties
of Warwick, how she was *pertæsa barbaræ
loquelæ*. »

« The Queen whispered to *him* ! » said Blount,
in a kind of soliloquy; « Good God, to what
will this world come! »

His farther meditations were interrupted by
a shout of applause from the multitude, so tre-
mendously vociferous, that the country echoed
for miles round. The guards, thickly stationed
upon the road by which the Queen was to advance, caught up the acclamation, which ran
like wild-fire to the Castle, and announced to
all within that Queen Elizabeth had entered

the Royal Chace of Kenilworth. The whole music of the Castle sounded at once, and a round of artillery, with a salvo of small arms, was discharged from the battlements; but the noise of drums and trumpets, and even of the cannon themselves, was but faintly heard, amidst the roaring and reiterated welcomes of the multitude.

As the noise began to abate, a broad glare of light was seen to appear from the gate of the Park, and, broadening and brightening as it came nearer, advanced along the open and fair avenue that led towards the Gallery-tower; and which, as we have already noticed, was lined on either hand by the retainers of the Earl of Leicester. The word was passed along the line, « The Queen! The Queen! Silence and stand fast! » Onward came the cavalcade, illuminated by two hundred thick waxen torches, in the hands of as many horsemen, which cast a light like that of broad day all around the procession, but especially on the principal groupe, of which the Queen herself, arrayed in the most splendid manner, and blazing with jewels, formed the central figure. She was mounted on a milk-white horse, which she reined with peculiar grace and dignity; and in the whole of her stately and noble carriage, you saw the daughter of an hundred kings.

The ladies of the court, who rode beside her Majesty, had taken especial care that their own external appearance should not be more glorious than their rank and the occasion altogether demanded, so that no inferior luminary might appear to approach the orbit of royalty. But their personal charms, and the magnificence by which, under every prudential restraint, they were necessarily distinguished, exhibited them as the very flower of a realm so far famed for splendour and beauty. The magnificence of the courtiers, free from such restraints as prudence imposed on the ladies, was yet more unbounded.

Leicester, who glittered like a golden image with jewels and cloth of gold, rode on her Majesty's right hand, as well in quality of her host, as of her Master of the Horse. The black steed which he mounted had not a single white hair on his body, and was one of the most renowned chargers in Europe, having been purchased by the Earl at large expence for this royal occasion. As the noble steed chafed at the slow pace of the procession, and, arching his stately neck, champed on the silver bits which restrained him, the foam flew from his mouth, and specked his well-formed limbs as if with spots of snow. The rider well became the high place which he held, and the proud animal which he bestrode; for no man in England, or perhaps in Europe, was more perfect than Dudley in horsemanship, and all other exercises belonging to his quality. He was bareheaded, as were all the courtiers in the train; and the red torch-light shone upon his long curled tresses of dark hair, and on his noble features, to the beauty of which even the severest criticism could only object the lordly fault, as it may be

termed, of a forehead somewhat too high. On
that proud evening, those features wore all the
grateful solicitude of a subject, to shew himself
sensible of the high honour which the Queen was
conferring on him, and all the pride and satisfaction which became so glorious a moment. Yet,
though neither eye nor feature betrayed aught
but feelings which suited the occasion, some of
the Earl's personal attendants remarked, that he
was unusually pale, and they expressed to each
other their fear that he was taking more fatigue
than consisted with his health.

Varney followed close behind his master, as the
principal esquire in waiting, and had charge of
his lordship's black velvet bonnet, garnished with
a clasp of diamonds, and surmounted by a white
plume. He kept his eye constantly on his master;
and, for reasons with which the reader is not
unacquainted, was, among Leicester's numerous
dependants, he who was most anxious that his
lord's strength and resolution should carry him
successfully through a day so agitating. For although Varney was one of the few — the very few
moral monsters, who contrive to lull to sleep the
remorse of their own bosoms, and are drugged
into moral insensibility by atheism, as men in extreme agony are lulled by opium, yet he knew
that in the breast of his patron there was already
awakened the fire that is never quenched, and
that his lord felt, amid all the pomp and magnificence we have described, the gnawing of the
worm that dieth not. Still, however, assured as

Lord Leicester stood, by Varney's own intelligence, that his Countess laboured under an indisposition which formed an unanswerable apology to the Queen for her not appearing at Kenilworth, there was little danger, his wily retainer thought, that a man so ambitious would betray himself by giving way to any external weakness.

. The train, male and female, who attended immediately upon the Queen's person, were of course of the bravest and the fairest, — the highest born nobles, and the wisest counsellors, of that distinguished reign, to repeat whose names were but to weary the reader. Behind came a long crowd of knights and gentlemen, whose rank and birth, however distinguished, were thrown into shade, as their persons into the rear of a procession, whose front was of such august majesty.

Thus marshalled, the cavalcade approached the Gallery-tower, which formed, as we have often observed, the extreme barrier of the Castle.

It was now the part of the huge porter to step forward; but the lubbard was so overwhelmed with confusion of spirit, — the contents of one immense black jack of double ale, which he had just drank to quicken his memory, having at the same time treacherously confused the brain it was intended to clear, — that he only groaned piteously, and remained sitting on his stone seat; and the Queen would have passed on without greeting, had not the gigantic warder's secret ally, Flibbertigibbet, who lay perdue behind

8*

him, thrust a pin into the rear of the short fe-
moral garment which we elsewhere described.

The porter uttered a sort of a yell, which
came not amiss into his part, started up with
his club, and dealt a sound douse or two on each
side of him; and then, like a coach-horse pricked
by the spur, started off at once into the full career of his address, and by dint of active prompt-
ing on the part of Dickie Sludge, delivered, in
sounds of gigantic intonation, a speech which
may be thus abridged; — the reader being to
suppose that the first lines were addressed to the
throng who approached the gateway; the conclusion, at the approach of the Queen, upon
sight of whom, as struck by some heavenly vision, the gigantic warder dropped his club,
resigned his keys, and gave open way to the
Goddess of the night, and all her magnificent
train.

« What stir, what turmoil, have we for the nones?
Stand back, my masters, or beware your bones!
Sirs, I'm a warder, and no man of straw,
My voice keeps order, and my club gives law.

Yet soft—nay stay—what vision have we here?
What dainty darling's this—what peerless peer?
What loveliest face, that loving ranks enfold,
Like brightest diamond chased in purest gold?
Dazzled and blind, mine office I forsake,
My club, my key, my knee, my homage take.
Bright paragon, pass on in joy and bliss;—
Beshrew the gate that opes not wide at such a sight as this! »

Elizabeth received most graciously the homage of the herculean porter, and, bending

her head to him in requital, passed through his
guarded tower, from the top of which was poured a clamorous blast of warlike music, which
was replied to by other bands of minstrelsy
placed at different points on the Castle walls,
and by others again stationed in the·Chace;
while the tones of the one, as they yet vibrated
on the echoes, were caught up and answered
by new harmony from different quarters.

Amidst these bursts of music, which, as if
the work of enchantment, seemed now close
at hand, now softened by distant space, now
wailing so low and sweet as if that distance was
gradually prolonged until only the last lingering
strains alone could reach the ear, Queen Elizabeth crossed the Gallery-tower, and came upon
the long bridge, which extended from thence
to Mortimer's Tower, and which was already
as light as day, so many torches had been fastened to the palisades on either side. Most of the
nobles here·alighted, and sent their horses to
the neighbouring village of Kenilworth, following the Queen on foot, as did the gentlemen
who had stood in array to receive her at the
Gallery-tower.

On this occasion, as at different times during
the evening, Raleigh addressed himself to Tressilian, and was not a little surprised at his vague
and unsatisfactory answers; which, joined to
his leaving his apartment without any assigned
reason, appearing in an undress when it was
likely to be offensive to the Queen, and some

other symptoms of irregularity which he thought
he discovered, led him to doubt whether his
friend did not labour under some temporary
derangement.

Meanwhile, the Queen had no sooner stepped
on the bridge than a new spectacle was provided; for as soon as the music gave signal that
she was so far advanced, a raft, so disposed as
to resemble a small floating island, illuminated
by a great variety of torches, and surrounded
by floating pageants formed to represent sea-
horses, on which sat Tritons, Nereids, and
other fabulous deities of the seas and rivers,
made its appearance upon the lake, and issuing
from behind a small heronry where it had been
concealed, floated gently towards the farther
end of the bridge.

On the islet appeared a beautiful woman, clad
in a watchet-coloured silken mantle, bound with
a broad girdle, inscribed with characters *like*
the phylacteries of the Hebrews. Her feet and
arms were bare, but her wrists and ancles were
adorned with gold bracelets of uncommon size.
Amidst her long silky black hair, she wore a
crown or chaplet of artificial mitletoe, and bore
in her hand a rod of ebony tipped with silver.
Two Nymphs attended on her, dressed in the
same antique and mystical guise.

The pageant was so well managed, that this
Lady of the Floating Island, having performed
her voyage with much picturesque effect, landed
at Mortimer's Tower with her two attendants,

just as Elizabeth presented herself before that outwork. The stranger then, in a well-penned speech, announced herself as that famous Lady of the Lake, renowned in the stories of King Arthur, who had nursed the youth of the redoubted Sir Lancelot, and whose beauty had proved too powerful both for the wisdom and the spells of the mighty Merlin. Since that early period she had remained possessed of her crystal dominions, she said, despite the various men of fame and might by whom Kenilworth had been successively tenanted. The Saxons, the Danes, the Normans, the Saintlowes, the Clintons, the Mountforts, the Mortimers, the Plantagenets, great though they were in arms and magnificence, had never, she said, caused her to raise her head from the waters which hid her crystal palace. But a greater than all these great names had now appeared, and she came in homage and duty to welcome the peerless Elizabeth to all sport, which the Castle and its environs, which lake or land could afford.

The Queen received this address also with great courtesy, and made answer in raillery, « We thought this lake had belonged to our own dominions, fair dame; but since so famed a lady claims it for hers, we will be glad at some other time to have further communing with you touching our joint interests. »

With this gracious answer the Lady of the Lake vanished, and Arion, who was amongst the maritime deities, appeared upon his dolphin. But

Lambourne, who had taken upon him the part
in the absence of Wayland, being chilled with
remaining immersed in an element to which he
was not friendly, having never got his speech by
heart, and not having, like the porter, the advantage of a prompter, paid if off with impudence, tearing off his vizard, and swearing,
«Cogs bones! he was none of Arion or Orion either, but honest Mike Lambourne, that had been
drinking her majesty's health from morning till
midnight, and was come to bid her heartly welcome to Kenilworth Castle.»

This unpremeditated buffoonery answered the
purpose probably better than the set speech
would have done. The Queen laughed heartily,
and swore (in her turn) that he had made the
best speech she had heard that day. Lambourne,
who instantly saw his jest had saved his bones,
jumped on shore, gave his dolphin a kick, and
declared he would never meddle with fish *again,*
except at dinner.

At the same time that the Queen was about to
enter the Castle, that memorable discharge of
fireworks by water and land took place, which
Master Laneham, formerly introduced to the
reader, has strained all his eloquence to describe.

«Such,» says the Clerk of the Council-chamber
door, «was the blaze of burning darts, the gleams
of stars coruscant, the streams and hail of fiery
sparks, lightnings of wild-fire, and flight-shot of
thunder-bolts, with continuance, terror, and
vehemency, that the heavens thundered, the

waters surged, and the earth shook, and for my part, hardy as I am, it made me very vengeably afraid. » *

---

* See Laneham's Account of the Queen's Entertainment at Killingworth Castle, in 1575, a very diverting tract, written by as great a coxcomb as ever blotted paper. The original is extremely rare, but it has been twice reprinted; once in Mr Nicholas's very curious and interesting collection of the Progresses and Public Processions of Queen Elizabeth, vol. I; and more lately in N° I. of a work termed *Kenilworth Illustrated,* beautifully printed at Chiswick, for Meridew of Coventry, and Radclyff of Birmingham, and which, if continued with the same good taste and execution, will be one of the finest antiquarian publications that has lately appeared.

CHAPTER XXXI.

Nay, this is matter for the month of March,
When hares are maddest. Either speak in reason,
Giving cold argument the wall of passion,
Or I break up the court.
                              Beaumont and Fletcher.

IT is by no means our purpose to describe mi-
nutely all the princely festivities of Kenilworth,
after the fashion of Master Robert Laneham,
whom we quoted in the conclusion of the last
Chapter. It is sufficient to say, that under discharge of the splendid fire-works, which we
have borrowed Laneham's eloquence to describe,
the Queen entered the base-court of Kenilworth,
through Mortimer's Tower, and moving on
through pageants of heathen gods and heroes
of antiquity, who offered gifts and compliments
on the bended knee, at length found her way
to the great hall of the Castle, gorgeously hung
for her reception with the richest silken tapestry, blazing with torches, misty with perfumes,
and sounding to strains of soft and delicious
music. At the upper end of the splendid apartment, was a state canopy, overshadowing a royal
throne, and beside was a door, which opened
to a long suite of apartments, decorated with

the utmost magnificence for the Queen and her ladies, whenever it should be her pleasure to be private.

The Earl of Leicester having handed the Queen up to the throne, and seated her there, knelt down before her, and kissing the hand which she held out, with an air in which romantic and respectful gallantry was happily mingled with loyal devotion, he thanked her, in terms of the deepest gratitude, for the highest honour which a sovereign could render to a subject. So handsome did he look when kneeling before her, that Elizabeth was tempted to prolong the scene a little longer than there was, strictly speaking, necessity for; and ere she raised him, she passed her hand over his head, so near, as almost to touch his long curled and perfumed hair, and with a movement of fondness, that seemed to intimate, she would, if she dared, have made the motion a slight caress.

She at length raised him, and, standing beside the throne, he explained to her the various preparations which had been made for her amusement and accommodation, all of which received her prompt and gracious approbation. The Earl then prayed her Majesty for permission, that he himself, and the nobles who had been in attendance upon her during the journey, might retire for a few minutes, and put themselves into a guise more fitting for dutiful attendance, during which space, those gentlemen of worship, (pointing to Varney, Blount, Tressilian, and others,) who had already put themselves into fresh attire, would have the honour of keeping her presence-chamber.

«Be it so, my lord,» answered the Queen; «you could manage a theatre well, who can thus command a double set of actors. For ourselves, we will receive your courtesies this evening but clownishly, since it is not our purpose to change our riding attire, being in effect something fatigued with a journey, which the concourse of our good people hath rendered slow, though the love they have shewn our person hath, at the same time, made it delightful.»

Leicester, having received this permission, retired accordingly, and was followed by those nobles who had attended the Queen to Kenilworth in person. The gentlemen who had preceded them, and were of course dressed for the solemnity, remained in attendance. But being most of them of rather inferior rank, they remained at an awful distance from the throne which Elizabeth occupied. The Queen's sharp eye soon distinguished Raleigh amongst them, with one or two others who were personally known to her, and she instantly made them a sign to approach, and accosted them very graciously. Raleigh, in particular, the adventure of whose cloak, as well as the incident of the verses, remained on her mind, was very graciously received; and to him she most frequently applied for information concerning the names and rank of those who were in presence. These he communicated concisely, and not without some traits of humorous satire, by which Elizabeth seemed much amused. « And who is yonder clownish fellow? « she said, looking at Tressilian, whose soiled dress on this occasion greatly obscured his good mien.

« A poet, if it please your Grace, » replied Raleigh.

« I might have guessed that from his careless garb, » said Elizabeth. « I have known some poets so thoughtless as to throw their cloaks into gutters. »

« It must have been when the sun dazzled both their eyes and their judgment, » answered Raleigh.

Elizabeth smiled and proceeded, « I asked that slovenly fellow's name, and you only told me his profession. »

« Tressilian is his name, » said Raleigh, with internal reluctance; for he foresaw nothing favourable to his friend from the manner in which she took notice of him.

« Tressilian! » answered Elizabeth. « O, the Menelaus of our romance. Why, he has dressed himself in a guise that will go far to exculpate his fair and false Helen. And where is Farnham, or whatever his name is—my Lord of Leicester's man, I mean — the Paris of this Devonshire tale? »

With still greater reluctance Raleigh named and pointed out to her Varney, for whom the tailor had done all that art could perform in making his exterior agreeable; and who, if he had not grace, had a sort of tact and habitual knowledge of breeding, which came in place of it.

The Queen turned her eye from the one to the other — « I doubt, » she said, « this same poetical Master Tressilian, who is too learned, I warrant me, to remember what presence he was to appear in, may be one of those of whom Geoffrey Chaucer says wittily, the wisest clerks are not the wisest men. I remember that Varney is a smooth-tongued varlet. I doubt this fair runaway had reasons for breaking her faith. »

To this Raleigh durst make no answer, aware how little he should benefit Tressilian by contradicting the Queen's sentiments, and not at all certain, on the whole, whether the best thing that could befall him, would not be that she should put an end at once by her authority to this affair, upon which it seemed to him Tressilian's thoughts were fixed with unavailing and distressing pertinacity. As these reflections *passed* through his active brain, the lower door of the hall opened, and Leicester, accompanied by several of his kinsmen, and of the nobles who had embraced his faction, re-entered the Castle-hall.

. The favourite Earl was now apparelled all in white, his shoes being of white velvet; his understocks (or stockings) of knit silk; his upper stocks of white velvet, lined with cloth of silver, which was shewn at the slashed part of the middle thigh; his doublet of cloth of silver, the close jerkin of white velvet, embroidered with silver and seed-pearl; his girdle and the scabbard of his sword of white velvet with golden buckles; his poniard and sword hilted and mounted with gold; and over all, a rich loose robe of white satin, with a border of golden embroidery a foot in breadth. The collar of the Garter, and the azure Garter itself around his knee, completed the appointments of the Earl of Leicester; which were so well matched by his fair stature., graceful gesture, fine proportion of body, and handsome countenance, that at that moment he was admitted by all who saw him, as the goodliest person whom they had ever looked upon. Sussex and the other nobles were also richly attired, but in point of splendour and gracefulness Leicester far exceeded them all.

Elizabeth received him with great complacency. « We have one piece of royal justice, » she said, « to attend to. It is a piece of justice, too, which interests us as a woman, as well as in the character of mother and guardian of the English people. »

An involuntary shudder came over Leicester, as he bowed low, expressive of his readiness to receive her royal commands; and a similar cold fit came over Varney, whose eyes (seldom during that evening removed from his patron,) instantly perceived, from the change in his looks, slight as that was, of what the Queen was speaking. But Leicester had wrought his resolution up to the point which, in his crooked policy, he judged necessary; and when Elizabeth added — « It is of the matter of Varney and

Tressilian we speak — is the lady here, my lord? » His answer was ready : — « Gracious madam, she is not. »

Elizabeth bent her brows and compressed her lips. « Our orders were strict and positive, my lord, » was her answer ——

« And should have been obeyed, good my liege, » answered Leicester., « had they been expressed in the form of the lightest wish. But — Varney, step forward — this gentleman will inform your Grace of the cause why the lady (he could not force his rebellious tongue to utter the words — *his wife*,) cannot attend on your royal presence. »

Varney advanced, and pleaded with readiness, what indeed he firmly believed, the absolute incapacity of the party, (for neither did he dare, in Leicester's presence, term her his wife,) to wait on her Grace.

« Here, » said he,. « are attestations from a most learned physician, whose skill and honour are well known to my good Lord of Leicester ; and from an honest and devout Protestant, a man of credit and substance, one Anthony Foster, the gentleman in whose house she is at present bestowed; that she now labours under an illness which altogether unfits her for such a journey as betwixt this Castle and the neighbourhood of Oxford. »

« This alters the matter, » said the Queen, taking the certificates in her hand, and glancing at their contents — « Let Tressilian come for-

ward. — Master Tressilian , we have much
sympathy for your situation , the rather that you
seem to have set your heart deeply on.this same
Amy Robsart , or Varney. Our power , thanks
to God and the willing obedience of a loving
people , is worth something , but there are some
things which it cannot compass. We cannot,
for example, command the affections of a giddy
young girl, or make her love sense and learning
better than a courtier's fine doublet; and we
cannot controul sickness, with which it seems
this lady is afflicted, who may not, by reason
of such infirmity, attend our court here, as we
had required her to do. Here are the testimonials of the physician who hath her under his
charge , and the gentleman in whose house she
resides, so setting forth. »

« Under your Majesty's favour», said Tressilian hastily, and, in his alarm for the consequence
of the imposition practised on the Queen, forgetting, in part at least, his own promise to
Amy, « these certificates speak not the truth. »

« How , sir ! » said the Queen , — « Impeach
my Lord of Leicester's veracity ! But you shall
have a fair hearing. In our presence the meanest
of our subjects shall be heard against the proudest, and the least known against the most
favoured; therefore you shall be heard fairly,
but beware you speak not without a warrant.
Look at these certificates in your own hand,
and say manfully if you impugn the truth of
them, and upon what evidence. »

As the Queen spoke, his promise and all its
consequences rushed on the mind of the unfortunate Tressilian, and while it controuled his
natural inclination to pronounce that a falsehood
which he knew from the evidence of his senses
to be untrue, gave an indecision and irresolution to his appearance and utterance, which
made strongly against him in the mind of Elizabeth, as well as of all who beheld him. He turned the papers over and over, as if he had been
an idiot, incapable of comprehending their contents. The Queen's impatience began to become
visible. — « You are a scholar, sir, » she said,
« and of some note, as I have heard; yet you
seem wondrous slow in reading text hand —
— How say you, are these certificates true
or no? »

« Madam, » said Tressilian, with obvious embarrassment and hesitation, anxious to avoid ad-
mitting evidence which he might afterwards
have reason to confute, yet equally desirous to
keep his word to Amy, and to give her, as he
had promised, space to plead her own cause in
her own way — « Madam — Madam, your Grace
calls on me to admit evidence which ought to
be proved valid by those who found their defence upon them. »

« Why, Tressilian, thou art critical as well
as poetical, » said the Queen, bending on him
a brow of displeasure; « methinks, these writings,
being produced in the presence of the noble Earl
to whom this Castle pertains, and his honour

being appealed to as the guarantee of their authenticity, might be evidence enough for thee. But since thou listst to be so fórmal —Varney, or rather my Lord of Leicester, for the affair becomes yours, « (these words, though spoken at random, thrilled through the Earl's marrow and bones) « what evidence have you as touching these certificates ? »

Varney hastened to reply, preventing Leicester, — « So please your Majesty, my young Lord of Oxford, who is here in presence, knows Master Anthony Foster's hand and his character.»

The Earl of Oxford, a young unthrift, whom Foster had more than once accommodated with loans on usurious interest, acknowledged, on this appeal, that he knew him as a wealthy and independent franklin, supposed to be worth much money, and verified the certificate produced to be his hand-writing.

« And who speaks to the Doctor's certificate? » said the Queen. « Alasco, methinks, is his name.»

Masters, her Majesty's physician (not the less willingly that he remembered his repulse from Say's Court, and thought that his present testimony might gratify Leicester, and mortify the Earl of Sussex and his faction, ») acknowledged he had more than once consulted with Doctor Alasco, and spoke of him as a man of extraordinary learning and hidden acquirements, though not altogether in the regular course of practice. The Earl of Huntingdon, Lord Leicester's brother-in-law, and the old Countess of Rutland, next sang his praises, and both remembered the thin beautiful Italian hand in which he was wont to write his receipts, and which corresponded to the certificate produced as his.

« And now, I trust, Master Tressilian, this matter is ended, » said the Queen, «. We will do something ere the night is older to reconcile old Sir Hugh Robsart to the match. You have done your duty something more than boldly ; but we were no woman had we not compassion for the wounds which true love deals ; so we forgive your audacity, and your uncleansed boots withal, which have well nigh overpowered my Lord of Leicester's perfumes. ».

So spoke Elizabeth, whose nicety of scent was one of the characteristics of her organization, as appeared long afterwards when she expelled Essex from her presence, on a charge against his boots, similar to that which she now expressed against those of Tressilian.

But Tressilian had by this time collected himself, astonished as he had at first been by the audacity of the falsehood so feasibly supported, and placed in array against the evidence of his own eyes. He rushed forward, kneeled down, and caught the Queen by the skirt of her robe. « As you are Christian woman, » he said, « Madam, as you are crowned Queen, to do equal justice among your subjects—as you hope yourself to have fair hearing (which God grant you:) at that last bar at which we must all plead, grant me one small request! Decide not this matter so hastily. Give me but twenty four hours interval, and I will, at the end of that brief space, produce evidence which will shew to demonstration, that these certificates, which state this unhappy lady to be now ill at ease in Oxfordshire, are false as hell! »

« Let go my train, sir! » said Elizabeth, who was startled at his vehemence, though she had too much of lion in her to fear; « the fellow must be distraught — that witty knave, my godson Harrington, must have him into his rhymes of Orlando Furioso!—And yet, by this light, there is something strange in the vehemence of his demand.—Speak, Tressilian; what wilt thou do if, at the end of these four-and-twenty hours, thou canst not confute a fact so solemnly proved as this lady's illness? »

« I will lay down my head on the block, » answered Tressilian.

« Pshaw! » replied the Queen. « God's light! thou speak'st like a fool. What head falls in England but by just sentence of English law? —I ask thee, man—if thou hast sense to understand me—wilt thou; if thou shalt fail in this improbable attempt of thine, render me a good and sufficient reason why thou doest undertake it? »

Tressilian paused, and again hesitated; because he felt convinced, that if, within the interval demanded, Amy should become reconciled to her husband, he would in that case do her the worst of offices, by again ripping up the

whole circumstances before Elizabeth, and show-
ing how that wise and jealous princess had
been imposed upon by false testimonials. The
consciousness of this dilemma renewed his extreme embarrassment of look, voice, and manner; he hesitated, looked down, and on the
Queen repeating her question with a stern voice
and flashing eye, he admitted with faultering
words, « That it might be—he could not posi-
tively—that is, in certain events—explain the
reasons and grounds on which he acted. »

« Now, by the soul of King Henry, » said the
Queen, « this is either moonstruck madness, or
very knavery!—Seest thou, Raleigh, thy friend
is far too Pindaric for this presence. Have him
away, and make us quit of him, or it shall be the
worse for him; for his flights are too unbridled
for aught but Parnassus, or Saint Luke's Hospital. But come back instantly thyself, when he is
placed under fitting restraint.—We wish we had
seen the beauty which could make such havoc
in a wise man's brain. »

Tressilian was again endeavouring to address
the Queen, when Raleigh, in obedience to the
orders he had received, interfered, and, with
Blount's assistance, half led half forced him out
of the presence-chamber, where he himself indeed began to perceive his presence did his cause
more harm than good.

When they had attained the anti-chamber,
Raleigh entreated Blount to see Tressilian safely conducted into the apartments allotted to

the Earl of Sussex's followers, and, if necessary, recommanded that a guard should be mounted on him.

« This extravagant passion, « he said, « and, as it would seem, the news of the lady's illness, has utterly wrecked his excellent judgment. But it will pass away if he be kept quiet. Only let him break forth again at no rate; for he is already far in her Highness's displeasure, and should she be again provoked, she will find for him a worse place of confinement, and sterner keepers. »

« I judged as much as that he was mad, » said Nicholas Blount, looking down upon his own crimson stockings and yellow roses, « whenever I saw him with these damned boots, which stunk so in her nostrils.—I will but see him stowed, and be back with you presently.—But, Walter, did the Queen ask who I was ?—methought she glanced an eye at me. »

« Twenty —twenty eye-glances she sent, and I told her all how thou wert a brave soldier, and a — But for God's sake, get off Tressilian. »

« I will—I will, » said Blount; « but methinks this court-haunting is no such bad pastime, after all. We shall rise by it, Walter, my brave lad. Thou said'st I was a good soldier, and a — What besides, dearest Walter ? »

« An all unutterable — codshead.—For God's sake begone. »

Tressilian, without farther resistance or expostulation, followed, or rather suffered himself to be conducted by Blount to Raleigh's lodging, where he was formally installed into a small truckle-bed, placed in a wardrobe, and designed for a domestic. He saw but too plainly, that no remonstrances would avail to procure the help or sympathy of his friends, until the lapse of the time for which he had pledged himself to remain inactive, should enable him either to explain the whole circumstances to them, or remove from him every pretext or desire of farther interference with the fortunes of Amy, by her having found means to place herself in a state of reconciliation with her husband.

With great difficulty, and only by the most patient and mild remonstrances with Blount, he escaped the disgrace and mortification of having two of Sussex's stoutest yeomen quartered in his apartment. At last, however, when Nicholas had seen him fairly deposited in his truckle-bed, and had bestowed one or two hearty kicks, and as hearty curses, on the boots, which, in his lately acquired spirit of foppery, he considered as a strong symptom, if not the cause, of his friend's malady, he contented himself with the modified measure of locking the door on the unfortunate Tressilian; whose gallant and disinterested efforts to save a female who had treated him with ingratitude, thus terminated, for the present, in the displeasure of his Sovereign, and the conviction of his friends, that he was little better than a madman.

••

CHAPTER XXXII.

The wisest Sovereigns err like private men,
And royal hand has sometimes laid the sword
Of chivalry upon a worthless shoulder,
Which better had been branded by the hangman.
What then? — Kings do their best—and they and we
Must answer for the intent, and not the event.

Old Play.

« IT is a melancholy matter, » said the Queen,
when Tressilian was withdrawn, to see a wise
and learned man's wit thus pitifully unsettled.
Yet this public display of his imperfection of
brain plainly shews us that his supposed injury
and accusation were fruitless ; and therefore, my
Lord of Leicester, we remember your suit formerly made to us in behalf of your faithful servant Varney, whose good gifts and fidelity, as
they are useful to you, ought to have due reward
from us, knowing well that your lordship, and
all you have, are so earnestly devoted to our service. And we render Varney the honour more especially, that we are a guest, and we fear a charge-
able and troublesome one, under your lordship's
roof ; and also for the satisfaction of the good old
Knight of Devon, Sir Hugh Robsart, whose
daughter he hath married ; and we trust the espe-

cial mark of grace which we are about to confer,
will reconcile him to his son-in-law. — Your
sword, my Lord of Leicester. »

The Earl unbuckled his sword, and, taking it
by the point, presented on bended knee the hilt
to Elizabeth.

She took is slowly, drew it from the scabbard,
and while the ladies who stood around turned
away their eyes with real or affected shuddering,
she noted with a curious eye the high polish and
rich damasked ornaments upon the glittering
blade.

« Had I been a man, » she said, « methinks,
none of my ancestors would have loved a good
sword better. As it is with me, I like to look on
one, and could, like the *fata Morgana*, of whom
I have read in some Italian rhymes — were my
godson Harrington here, he could tell me the
passage — even trim my hair, and arrange my
head-gear, in such a steel mirror as this is. —
Richard Varney, come forth and kneel down. *In
the name of God and Saint George, we dub thee
knight! Be Faithful, Brave, and Fortunate.—
Arise, Sir Richard Varney. »

Varney arose and retired, making a deep obei-
sance to the Sovereign who had done him so much
honour.

« The buckling of the spur, and what other
rites remain », said the Queen, « may be finished
to-morrow in the chapel; for we intend Sir Richard Varney a companion in his honours. And as
we must not be partial in conferring such dis-

tinction, we mean on this matter to confer with
our cousin of Sussex. »

That noble Earl, who since his arrival at Kenilworth, and indeed since the commencement of
this Progress, had found himself in a subordinate
situation to Leicester, was now wearing a heavy
cloud on his brow—a circumstance which had not
escaped the Queen, who hoped to appease his
discontent, and to follow out her system of balancing policy by a mark of peculiar favour,
the more gratifying as it was tendered at a moment when his rival's triumph appeared to be
complete.

At the summons of Queen Elizabeth, Sussex
hastily approached her person; and being asked
on which of his followers, being a gentleman and
of merit, he would wish the honour of knighthood
to be conferred, he answered, with more sincerity
than policy, that he would have ventured to speak
for Tressilian, to whom he conceived he owed
his own life, and who was a distinguished soldier
and scholar, besides a man of unstained lineage,
« only, » he said, « he feared the events of that
night »—And then he stopped.

« I am glad your lordship is thus considerate, »
said Elizabeth; « the events of this night would
make us, in the eyes of our subjects, as mad as
this poor brain-sick gentleman himself—for we
ascribe his conduct to no malice—should we
chuse this moment to do him grace. »

« In that case, » said the Earl of Sussex, somewhat discountenanced, « your Majesty will allow

2*

me to name my master of the horse, Master Nicholas Blount, a gentleman of fair estate and ancient name, who has served your majesty both in Scotland and Ireland, and brought away bloody marks on his person, all honourably taken and requited. »

The Queen could not help shrugging her shoulders slightly even at his second suggestion; and the Duchess of Rutland, who read in the Queen's manner that she had expected Sussex would have named Raleigh, and thus would have enabled her to gratify her own wish while she honoured his recommendation, only waited the Queen's assent to what he had proposed, and then said, that she hoped, since these two high nobles had been each permitted to suggest a candidate for the honours of chivalry, she, in behalf of the ladies in presence, might have a similar indulgence.

« I were no woman to refuse you such a boon, » said the Queen, smiling.

« Then, » pursued the Duchess, « in the name of these fair ladies present, I request your Majesty to confer the rank of knighthood on Walter Raleigh, whose birth, deeds of arms, and promptitude to serve our sex with sword or pen, deserve such distinction from us all. »

« Gramercy, fair ladies, » said Elizabeth, smiling, « your boon is granted; and the gentle squire Lack-Cloak shall become the good knight Lack-Cloak, at your desire. Let the two aspirants for the honour of chivalry step forward. »

Blount was not as yet returned from seeing Tressilian, as he conceived, safely disposed of; but Raleigh came forth, and, kneeling down, received at the hand of the Virgin Queen that title of honour, which was never conferred on a more distinguished or more illustrious object.

Shortly afterwards Nicholas Blount entered, and, hastily apprized by Sussex, who met him at the door of the hall, of the Queen's gracious purpose towards him, he was desired to advance towards the throne. It is a sight sometimes seen, and it is both ludicrous and pitiable, when an honest man of plain common sense is surprised, by the coquetry of a pretty woman, or any other cause, into those frivolous fopperies which only sit well upon the youthful, the gay, and those to whom long practice has rendered them a second nature. Poor Blount was in this situation. His head was already giddy from a consciousness of unusual finery, and the supposed necessity of suiting his manners to the gaiety of his dress; and now this sudden view of promotion altogether completed the conquest of the newly inhaled spirit of foppery over his natural disposition, and converted a plain, honest, awkward man into a coxcomb of a new and most ridiculous kind.

The knight-expectant advanced up the hall, the whole length of which he had unfortunately to traverse, turning out his toes with so much zeal, that he presented his leg at every

step with its broadside foremost, so that it greatly
resembled an old-fashioned knife with a curved
point, when seen sideways. The rest of his gait
was in proportion to this unhappy amble; and
the implied mixture of bashful fear, and self-
satisfaction, was so unutterably ridiculous, that
Leicester's friends did not suppress a titter, in
which many of Sussex's partisans were unable
to resist joining, though ready to eat their nails
with mortification. Sussex himself lost all patience, and could not forbear whispering into
the ear of his friend, « Curse thee! can'st thou
not walk like a man and a soldier ? » an interjection which only made honest Blount start
and stop, until a glance at his yellow roses and
crimson stockings restored his self-confidence,
when on he went at the same pace as before.

 · The Queen conferred on poor Blount the
honour of knighthood with a marked sense of
reluctance. That wise Princess was fully aware of
the propriety of using great circumspection and
economy in bestowing those titles of honour,
which the Stewarts, who succeeded to her throne,
distributed with such imprudent liberality as
greatly diminished their value. Blount had no
sooner arisen and retired, than she turned to
the Duchess of Rutland. « Our woman wit, »
she said, « dear Rutland, is sharper than that
of those pround things in doublet and hose.
See'st thou, out of these three knights, thine
is the only true metal to stamp chivalry's imprint upon ? » ·

« Sir Richard Varney, surely — the friend of
my Lord of Leicester — surely *he* has merit, »
replied the Duchess.

« Varney has a sly countenance, and a smooth
tongue, » replied the Queen. « I fear me he will
prove a knave — But the promise was of ancient
standing. My Lord of Sussex must have lost his
own wits, I think, to recommend to us first a
madman like Tressilian, and then a clownish
fool like this other fellow. I protest, Rutland,
that while he sat on his knees before me, mop-
ping and mowing as if he had scalding porridge
in his mouth, I had much to forbear cutting him
over the pate, instead of striking his shoulder.»

« Your Majesty gave him a smart *accolade*, »
said the Duchess; « we who stood behind heard
the blade clatter on his collar-bone, and the
poor man fidgetted too as if he felt it. »

« I could not help it, wench, » said the Queen,
laughing; « but we will have this same Sir Nicholas sent to Ireland or Scotland, or smewhere,
to rid our court of so antic a chevalier. »

The discourse became then more general, and
soon after there was a summons to the banquet.

In order to obey this signal, the company
were under the necessity of crossing the inner
court of the Castle, that they might reach the
new buildings, containing the large banquetting
room, in which preparations for supper were
made upon a scale of profuse magnificence, cor-
responding to the occasion.

In the course of this passage, and especially

in the court-yard, the new-made knights were
assailed by the heralds, pursuivants, minstrels,
etc. with the usual cry of *Largesse*, *largesse*,
chevaliers très hardis! an ancient invocation,
intended to awaken the bounty of the acolytes
of chivalry towards those whose business it was
to register their armorial bearings, and celebrate
the deeds by which they were illustrated. The
call was of course liberally and courteously answered by those to whom it was addressed. Varney gave his largesse with an affectation of
complaisance and humility. Raleigh bestowed
his with the graceful ease peculiar to one who
has attained his own place, and is familiar with
its dignity. Honest Blount gave what his tailor
had left him of his half-year's rent, dropping
some pieces in his hurry, then stooping down
to look for them, and then distributing them
amongst the various claimants, with the anxious
face and mien of the parish beadle dividing a
dole among paupers.

These donations were accepted with the usual
clamour and *vivats* of applause common on such
occasions; but as the parties gratified were chiefly
dependants of Lord Leicester, it was Varney
whose name was repeated with the loudest accla-
mations. Lambourne, especially, distinguished
himself by his vociferations of « Long life to Sir
Richard Varney! — Health and honour to Sir
Richard! — Never was a more worthy knight
dubbed! » — then, suddenly sinking his voice,
he added, — since the valiant Sir Pandarus of

Troy, » — a winding up of his clamorous applause, which set all men a laughing who were within hearing of it.

It is unnecessary to say any thing farther of the festivities of the evening, which were so brilliant in themselves, and received with such obvious and willing satisfaction by the Queen, that Leicester retired to his own apartment, with all the giddy raptures of successful ambition. Varney, who had changed his splendid attire, and now waited on his patron in a very modest and plain undress, attended to do the honours of the Earl's *coucher*.

« How! Sir Richard, » said Leicester, smiling, « your new rank scarce suits the humility of this attendance. »

« I would disown that rank, my lord, » said Varney, « could I think it was to remove me to a distance from your lordship's person. »

« Thou art a grateful fellow, » said Leicester; « but I must not allow you to do what would abate you in the opinion of others. »

While thus speaking, he still accepted, without hesitation, the offices about his person, which the new made knight seemed to render as eagerly as if he had really felt, in discharging the task, that pleasure which his words expressed.

« I am not afraid of men's misconstruction, » he said, in answer to Leicester's remark, « since there is not — (permit me to undo the collar) — a man within the castle, who does not expect very soon to see persons of a rank far superior to that which, by your goodness, I now hold, rendering the duties of the bed-chamber to you, and accounting it an honour. »

'« It might, indeed, so have been, » said the Earl, with an involuntary sigh; and then presently added, « My gown, Varney — I will look out on the night. Is not the moon near to the full? »

· « I think so, my lord, according to the calendar, » answered Varney.

There was an abutting window, which opened on a small projecting balcony of stone, battlemented as is usual in Gothic castles. The Earl undid the lattice, and stepped out into the open air. The station he had chosen commanded an extensive view of the lake, and woodlands beyond, where the clear moonlight rested on the clear blue waters, and the distant masses of oak and elm trees. The moon rode high in the heavens, attended by thousands and thousands of inferior luminaries. All seemed already *to be* hushed in the nether world, excepting occasionally the voice of the watch (for the yeomen of the guard performed that duty wherever the Queen was present in person,) and the distant baying of the hounds, disturbed by the preparations amongst the grooms and prickers for a magnificent hunt, which was to be the amusement of the next day.

· Leicester looked out on the blue arch of heaven, with gestures and a countenance expressive of anxious exultation, while Varney, who remained within the darkened apartment, could (himself unnoticed) with a secret satisfaction, see his patron stretch his hands with earnest gesticulation towards the heavenly bodies.

« Ye distant orbs of living fire, » so ran the muttered invocation of the ambitious Earl, « ye are silent while you wheel your mystic rounds, but Wisdom has given to you a voice. Tell me, then, to what end is my high course destined. Shall the greatness to which I have aspired be bright, pre-eminent, and stable as your own; or am I but doomed to draw a brief and glittering train along the nightly darkness, and then to sink down to earth, like the base refuse of those artificial fires with which men emulate your rays? »

He looked on the heavens in profound silence for a minute or two longer, and then again stepped into the apartment, where Varney seemed to have been engaged in putting the Earl's jewels into a casket.

« What said Alasco of my horoscope? » demanded Leicester. « You already told me, but it has escaped me, for I think but lightly of that art. »

« Many learned and great men have thought otherwise, » said Varney; « and, not to flatter your lordship, my own opinion leans that way. »

« Ay, Saul among the prophets? » said Leicester——« I thought thou wert sceptical in all such matters as thou could'st neither see, hear, smell,

taste, or touch, and that thy belief was limited
by thy senses. »

« Perhaps, my lord, » said Varney, « I may be
at present misled by my wish to find the pre-
dictions of astrology true on the present occasion.
Alasco says, that your favourite planet is culmi-
nating, and that the adverse influence—he would
not use a plainer term — though not overcome,
was evidently combust, I think he said, or re-
trograde. »

« It is even so, » said Leicester, looking at an
abstract of astrological calculations which he had
in his hand; « the stronger influence will prevail,
and, as I think, the evil hour pass away. — Lend
me your hand, Sir Richard, to doff my gown —
and remain an instant, if it is not too burthen-
some to your knighthood, while I compose myself
to sleep. I believe the bustle of this day has fe-
vered my blood, for it streams through my veins
like a current of molten lead—remain an instant,
I pray you — I would fain feel my eyes heavy ere
I closed them. »

Varney officiously assisted his lord to bed, and
placed a massive silver night-lamp, with a short
sword, on a marble table which stood close by
the head of the couch. Either in order to avoid
the light of the lamp, or to hide his countenance
from Varney, Leicester drew the curtain, heavy
with entwined silk and gold, so as completely to
shade his face. Varney took a seat near the bed,
but with his back towards his master, as if to in

timate that he was not watching him, and quietly
waited till Leicester himself led the way to the
topic by which his mind was engrossed.

« And so, Varney, » said the Earl, after waiting in vain till his dependent should commence
the conversation, « men talk of the Queen's favour towards me. »

« Ay, my good lord, » said Varney; « of what
can they else, since it is so strongly manifested.»

« She is indeed my good and gracious mistress, » said Leicester, after another pause; « but
it is written, 'Put not thy trust in Princes.' »

« A good sentence and a true, » said Varney,
« unless you can unite their interest with yours
so absolutely, that they must needs sit on your
wrist like hooded hawks. »

« I know what thou meanest, » said Leicester
impatiently, « though thou art to-night so pruden-
tially careful of what thou sayest to me. — Thou
would'st intimate, I might marry the Queen if I
would. »

« It is your speech, my lord, not mine, » answered Varney; « but whosoever be the speech,
it is the thought of ninety-nine out of an hundred
men throughout broad England. »

« Ay, but, » said Leicester, turning himself in
his bed, « the hundredth man knows better.
Thou, for example, knowest the obstacle that
cannot be overleaped. »

« It must, my lord, if the stars speak true, »
said Varney, composedly.

« What talk'st thou of them, « said Leicester,

» that believest not in them or in aught else ? »

« You mistake, my lord, under your gracious pardon, » said Varney, « I believe in many things that predict the future. I believe, if showers fall in April, that we shall have flowers in May; that if the sun shines, grain will ripen; and I believe in much natural philosophy to the same effect, which, if the stars swear to me, I will say the stars speak the truth. And in like manner, I will not disbelieve that which I see wished for and expected on earth, solely because the astrologers have read it in the heavens. »

« Thou art right, » said Leicester, again tossing himself on his couch — « Earth does wish for it. I have had advices from the reformed churches of Germany — from the Low countries — from Switzerland, urging this as a point on which Europe's safety depends. France will not oppose it — The ruling party in Scotland look to it as their best security — Spain fears it, but cannot prevent it — and yet thou knowest it is impossible. »

« I know not that, my lord, » said Varney, « the Countess is indisposed. »

« Villain ! » said Leicester, starting up on his couch, and seizing the sword which lay on the table beside him; « go thy thoughts that way? — thou wouldst not do murther! ».

« For whom, or what, do you hold me, my lord? » said Varney, assuming the superiority of an innocent man subjected to unjust suspicion. « I said nothing to deserve such a horrid impu-

tation as your violence infers. I said but that the
Countess was ill. And Countess, and lovely and
beloved as she is, surely your lordship must hold
her to be mortal? She may die, and your lordship's hand become once more your own. »

« Away! away! » said Leicester; « let me have
no more of this. »

« Good night, my lord, » said Varney, seeming
to understand this as a command to depart; but
Leicester's voice interrupted his purpose.

« Thou scapest me not thus, sir Fool, » said
he; « I think thy knighthood has addled thy
brains — Confess, thou hast talked of impossi-
bilities, as of things which may come to pass. »

« My lord, long live your fair Countess, » said
Varney; « but neither your love nor my good
wishes can make her immortal. But God grant
she live long to be happy herself, and to render
you so. I see not but you may be King of England notwithstanding. »

« Nay, now, Varney, thou art stark-mad, »
said Leicester.

« I would I were myself within the same near-
ness to a good estate of freehold, » said Varney.
« Have we not known in other countries, how a
left-handed marriage might subsist betwixt persons of differing degree? — ay, and be no hind-
rance to prevent the husband from conjoining
himself afterwards with a more suitable partner?»

« I have heard of such things in Germany, »
said Leicester.

« Ay, and the most learned doctors in foreign

universities justify the practice from the Old
Testament,» said Varney, «And after all, where
is the harm? The beautiful partner, whom you
have chosen for true love, has your secret hours
of relaxation and affection. Her fame is safe—
her conscience may slumber securely—You
have wealth to provide royally for your issue,
should Heaven bless you with offspring. Meanwhile you may give to Elizabeth ten times the
leisure, and ten thousand times the affection,
that ever Don Philip of Spain spared to her sister
Mary; yet you know how she doated on him
though so cold and neglectful. It requires but a
close mouth and an open brow, and you keep
your Eleanor and your fair Rosamond far enough
separate. — Leave me to build you a bower to
which no jealous Queen shall find a clue.»

Leicester was silent for a moment, then sighed, and said, «It is impossible. — Good night,
Sir Richard Varney — yet stay—Can you *guess*
what meant Tressilian by shewing himself in such
careless guise before the Queen to-day?—to strike
her tender heart, I should guess, with all the sympathies due to a lover, abandoned by his mistress,
and abandoning himself.»

Varney, smothering a sneering laugh, answered, «He believed Master Tressilian had no such
matter in his head.»

« How!» said Leicester; « what mean'st thou?
There is ever knavery in that laugh of thine,
Varney.»

«I only meant, my lord,» said Varney, «that

Tressilian has taken the sure way to avoid heart-breaking. He hath had a companion — a female companion—a mistress—a sort of player's wife or sister, as I believe,—with him in Mervyn's Bower, where I quartered him for certain reasons of my own. »

« A mistress! — mean'st thou a paramour. »

« Ay, my lord; who else waits for hours in a gentleman's chamber? »

« By my faith, time and space fitting, this were a good tale to tell, » said Leicester. « I ever distrusted those bookish, hypocritical, seeming-virtuous scholars. Well— Master Tressilian makes somewhat familiar with my house — if I look it over, he is indebted to it for certain recollections. I would not harm him more than I can help. Keep eye on him, however, Varney. »

« I lodged him for that reason, » said Varney, « in Mervyn's Tower, where he is under the eye of my very vigilant, if he were not also my very drunken servant, Michael Lambourne, whom I have told your Grace of. »

« Grace! » said Leicester : « what mean'st thou by that epithet? »

« It came unawares, my lord; and yet it sounds so very natural, that I cannot recal it. »

« It is thine own preferment that hath turned thy brain, » said Leicester, laughing; « new honours are as heady as new wine. »

« May your lordship soon have cause to say so from experience, » said Varney ; and, wishing his patron good night, he withdrew.

CHAPTER XXXIII.

Here stands the victim—there the proud betrayer,
E'en as the hind pulled down by strangling dogs
Lies, as the hunter's feet—who courteous proffers
To some high dame, the Dian of the chace,
To whom he looks for guerdon, his sharp blade,
To gash the sobbing throat.
                              The Woodsman.

- WE are now to return to Mervyn's Bower,
the apartment, or rather the prison, of the unfortunate Countess of Leicester, who for some
time kept within bounds her uncertainty and
her impatience. She was aware that, in the tumult of the day, there might be some delay ere
her letter could be safely conveyed to the hands
of Leicester, and that some time more might
elapse ere he could extricate himself from the
necessary attendance on Elizabeth, to come
and visit her in her secret bower. — « I will not
expect him, » she said, « till night — he cannot
be absent from his royal guest, even to see me.
He will, I know, come earlier if it be possible,
but I will not expect him before night. » —
And yet all the while she did expect him; and,
while she tried to argue herself into a contrary
belief, each hasty noise, of the hundred which

she heard, sounded like the hurried step of Leicester on the staircase, hasting to fold her in his arms.

The fatigue of body which Amy had lately undergone, with the agitation of mind natural to so cruel a state of uncertainty, began by degrees strongly to affect her nerves, and she almost feared her total inability to maintain the necessary self-command through the scenes which might lie before her. But, although spoiled by an overindulgent system of education, Amy had naturally a mind of great power, united with a frame which her share in her father's woodland exercises had rendered uncommonly healthy. She summoned to her aid such mental and bodily resources; and not unconscious how much the issue of her fate might depend on her own self-possession, she prayed internally for strength of body and for mental fortitude, and resolved, at the same time, to yield to no nervous impulse which might weaken either.

Yet when the great bell of the Castle, which was placed in Cæsar's Tower, at no great distance from that called Mervyn's, began to send its pealing clamour abroad, in signal of the arrival of the royal procession, the din was so painfully acute to ears rendered nervously sensitive by anxiety, that she could hardly forbear shrieking with anguish, in answer to every stunning clash of the relentless peal.

Shortly afterwards, when the small apartment was at once enlightened by the shower of artifi-

cial fires with which the air was suddenly filled,
and which crossed each other like fiery spirits,
each bent on his own separate mission, or like
salamanders executing a frolic dance in the region
of the Sylphs, the Countess felt at first as if each
rocket shot close by her eyes, and discharged its
sparks and flashes so nigh that she could feel a
sense of the heat. But she struggled against these
fantastic terrors, and compelled herself to arise,
stand by the window, look out, and gaze upon
a sight, which at another time would have appeared to her at once captivating and fearful.
The magnificent towers of the Castle were enve-
loped in garlands of artificial fire, or shrouded
with tiaras of pale smoke. The surface of the lake
glowed like molten iron, while many fire-works,
(then thought extremely wonderful, though now
common,) whose flame continued to exist in the
opposing element, dived and rose, hissed and
roared, and spouted fire, like so many dragons
of enchantment sporting upon a burning lake.

Even Amy was for a moment interested by
what was to her so new a scene. « I had thought
it magical art, » she said, « but poor Tressilian
taught me to judge of such things as they are.
Great God! and may not these idle splendours
resemble my own hoped for happiness,—a single
spark, which is instantly swallowed up by surrounding darkness,—a precarious glow, which
rises but for a brief space into the air, that its
fall may be the lower? O, Leicester! after all—
all that thou hast said—hast sworn—that Amy

was thy love, thy life, can it be that thou art
the magician at whose nod these enchantments
arise, and that she sees them, as an outcast, if
not a captive? »

The sustained, prolonged, and repeated bursts
of music, from so many different quarters, and
at so many varying points of distance, which
sounded as if not the Castle of Kenilworth only,
but the whole country around, had been at once
the scene of solemnizing some high national festival, carried the same oppressive thought still
closer to her heart, while some notes would melt
in distant and falling tones, as if in compassion
for her sorrows, and some burst close and near
upon her, as if mocking her misery, with all the
insolence of unlimited mirth. « These sounds, »
she said « are mine—mine, because they are HIS;
but I cannot say, — Be still, these loud strains
suit me not; and the voice of the meanest peasant that mingles in the dance, would have more
power to modulate the music, than the command of her who is mistress of all. »

By degrees the sounds of revelry died away,
and the Countess withdrew from the window at
which she had sate listening to it. It was night,
but the moon afforded considerable light in the
room, so that Amy was able to make the arran-
gement which she judged necessary. There was
hope that Leicester might come to her apartment
as soon as the revel in the Castle had subsided;
but there was also risk she might be disturbed by
some unauthorized intruder. She had lost con-

fidence in the key, since Tressilian had entered so easily, though the door was locked on the inside; yet all the additional security she could think of, was to place the table across the door, that she might be warned by the noise, should any one attempt to enter. Having taken these necessary precautions, the unfortunate lady withdrew to her couch, stretched herself down on it, mused in anxious expectation, and counted more than one hour after midnight, till exhausted nature proved too strong for love, for grief, for fear, nay even for uncertainty, and she slept.

Yes, she slept. The Indian sleeps at the stake, in the intervals between his tortures; and mental torments, in like manner, exhaust by long continuance the sensibility of the sufferer, so that an interval of lethargic repose must necessarily ensue, ere the pangs which they inflict can again be renewed.

The Countess slept then for several hours, and dreamed that she was in the ancient house at Cumnor Place, listening for the low whistle with which Leicester often used to announce his presence in the court-yard, when arriving suddenly on one of his stolen visits. But on this occasion, instead of a whistle, she heard the peculiar blast of a bugle-horn, such as her father used to wind on the fall of the stag, and which huntsmen then called a *mort*. She ran, as she thought, to a window that looked into the court-yard, which she saw filled with men in mourn-

ing garments. The old Curate seemed about
to read the funeral service. Mumblazen, tricked
out in an antique dress, like an ancient herald,
held aloft a scutcheon, with its usual decorations
of skulls, cross-bones, and hour-glasses, surrounding a coat-of-arms, of which she could
only distinguish that it was surmounted with an
Earl's coronet. The old man looked at her with
a ghastly smile, and said, « Amy, are they not
rightly quartered ? » Just as he spoke, the horns
again poured on her ear the melancholy yet
wild strain of the mort, or death-note, and she
awoke.

The Countess awoke to hear a real bugle-note,
or rather the combined breath of many bugles,
sounding not the *mort*, but the jolly *réveillée*, to
remind the inmates of the Castle of Kenilworth,
that the pleasures of the day were to commence
with a magnificent stag-hunting in the neighbouring Chase. Amy started up from her couch,
listened to the sound, saw the first beams of the
summer morning already twinkle through the
lattice of her window, and recollected, with feelings of giddy agony, where she was, and how
circumstanced,

« He thinks not of *me*, » she said — « he will
not come nigh me ! A Queen is his guest, and
what cares he in what corner of his huge Castle
a wretch like me pines in doubt, which is fast
fading into despair? » At once a sound at the
door, as of some one attempting to open it
softly, filled her with an ineffable mixture of

joy and fear ; and, hastening to remove the
obstacle she had placed against the door, and
to unlock it, she had the precaution to ask, « Is
it thou, my love ? »

« Yes, my Countess, » murmured a whisper
in reply.

She threw open the door, and exclaiming,
« Leicester! » flung her arms around the neck
of the man who stood without, muffled in his
cloak.

« No — not quite Leicester, » answered Michael Lambourne, for he it was, returning the
caress with vehemence, — « not quite Leicester,
my lovely and most loving duchess, but as good
a man. »

With an exertion of force of which she
would at another time have thought herself incapable, the Countess freed herself from the
profane and profaning grasp of the drunken
debauchee, and retreated into the midst of her
apartment, where despair gave her courage to
make a stand.

As Lambourne, on entering, dropped the
lap of his cloak from his face, she knew Varney's
profligate servant; the very last person, excepting his detested master, by whom she would
have wished to be discovered. But she was still
closely muffled in her travelling dress, and as
Lambourne had scarce ever been admitted to
her presence at Cumnor-Place, her person, she
hoped, might not be so well known to him as
his was to her, owing to Janet's pointing him

frequently out as he crossed the court, and telling stories of his wickedness. She might have had still greater confidence in her disguise, had her experience enabled her to discover that he was much intoxicated; but this could scarce have consoled her for the risk which she might incur from such a character, in such a time, place, and circumstances.

Lambourne flung the door behind him as he entered, and folding his arms, as if in mockery of the attitude of distraction into which Amy had thrown herself, he proceeded thus : « Hark ye, most fair Callipolis — or most lovely Countess of clouts, and divine Duchess of dark corners—if thou takest all that trouble of skewering thyself together, like a trussed fowl, that there may be more pleasure in the carving, even save thyself the labour. I like thy first frank manner the best — like thy present as little — (he made a step towards her, and staggered) — as little as — such a damned uneven floor as this, where a gentleman may break his neck, if he does not walk as upright as a posture-master on the tight-rope. »

« Stand back ! » said the Countess; « do not approach nearer to me, on thy peril. »

« My peril! — and stand off — Why, how now, madam? Must you have a better mate than honest Mike Lambourne? I have been in America, girl, where the gold grows, and have brought off such a load on't » —

« Good friend, » said the Countess, in great

terror at the ruffian's determined and audacious
manner, « I prithee begone, and leave me. »

« And so I will, pretty one, when we are
tired of each other's company — not a jot sooner. »
— He seized her by the arm, while, incapable
of further defence, she uttered shriek upon
shriek. « Nay, scream away if you like it, » said
he, still holding her fast; « I have heard the sea
at the loudest, and I mind a squalling woman
no more than a miauling kitten — Damn me!
— I have heard fifty or a hundred screaming at
once, when there was a town stormed. »

The cries of the Countess, however, brought
unexpected aid, in the person of Lawrence Staples, who had heard her exclamations from his
apartment below, and entered in good time to
save her from being discovered, if not from
more atrocious violence. Lawrence was drunk
also, from the debauch of the preceding night;
but fortunately his intoxication had taken a
different turn from that of Lambourne.

« What the devil's noise is this in the ward ? »
he said — « What! man and woman together in
the same cell? that is against rule. I will have
decency under my rule, by Saint Peter of the
Fetters. »

« Get thee down stairs, thou drunken beast, »
said Lambourne ; « Seest thou not the lady and I
would be private. »

« Good sir, worthy sir! » said the Countess,
addressing the jailor, « do but save me from him,
for the sake of mercy! »

« She speaks fairly, » said the jailor, «and I will take her part. I love my prisoners ; and I have had as good prisoners under my key, as they have had in Newgate or the Compter. And so, being one of my lambkins, as I say, no one shall disturb her in her pen-fold. So, let go the woman, or I'll knock your brains out with my keys. »

«I'll make a blood-pudding of thy midriff first, » answered Lambourne, laying his left hand on his dagger, but still detaining the Countess by the arm with his right— «So have at thee, thou old ostrich, whose only living is upon a bunch of iron keys. »

Lawrence raised the arm of Michael, and prevented him from drawing his dagger ; and as Lambourne struggled and strove to shake him off, the Countess made a sudden exertion on her side, and slipping her hand out of the glove on which the ruffian still kept hold, she gained her liberty, and escaping from the apartment, ran down stairs ; while, at the same moment, she heard the two combatants fall on the floor with a noise which increased her terror. The outer wicket offered no impediment to her flight, having been opened for Lambourne's admittance ; so that she succeeded in escaping down the stair, and fled into the Pleasance, which seemed to her hasty glance the direction in which she was most likely to avoid pursuit.

Meanwhile, Lawrence and Lambourne rolled on the floor of the apartment, closely grappled together. Neither had, happily, opportunity to draw their daggers; but Lawrence found space enough to dash his heavy keys across Michael's face, and Michael, in return, grasped the turnkey so felly by the throat, that the blood gushed from nose and mouth; so that they were both gory and obscene spectacles, when one of the other officers of the household, attracted by the noise of the fray, entered the room, and with some difficulty effected the separation of the combatants.

« A murrain on you both, » said the charitable mediator, « and especially on you, Master Lambourne! What the fiend lie you here for, fighting on the floor like two butchers' curs in the kennel of the shambles ? »

Lambourne arose, and, somewhat sobered by the interposition of a third party, looked with something less than his usual brazen impudence of visage; « We fought for a wench, an thou must know, » was his reply.

« A wench! Where is she ? » said the officer.

« Why, vanished, I think, » said Lambourne, looking around him ; « unless Lawrence hath swallowed her. That filthy paunch of his swallows as many distressed damsels and oppressed orphans, as e'er a giant in King Arthur's history : they are his prime food; he devours them body, soul, and substance. »

« Ay, ay ! It's no matter, » said Lawrence, gathering up his huge ungainly form from the floor; « but I have had your betters, Master Michael Lambourne, under the little turn of my forefinger and thumb ; and I shall have thee, before all's done, under my hatches. The impudence of thy brow will not always save thy shinbones from iron, and thy foul thirsty gullet from a hempen cord. » — The words were no sooner out of his mouth, when Lambourne again made at him.

« Nay, go not to it again, » said the sewer, « or I will call for him shall tame you both, and that is Master Varney — Sir Richard, I mean — he is stirring, I promise you — I saw him cross the court just now. »

« Didst thou, by G—? » said Lambourne, seizing on the basin and ewer which stood in the apartment ; « Nay, then, element do thy work — I thought I had enough of thee last night, when I floated about for Orion, like a cork on a cask of ale. »

So saying, he fell to work to cleanse from his face and hands the signs of the fray, and get his apparel into some order.

« What hast thou done to him? » said the sewer, speaking aside to the jailor ; « his face is fearfully swelled. »

« It is but the imprint of the key of my cabinet — too good a mark for his gallows-face. No man shall abuse or insult my prisoners ; they are my jewels, and I lock them in safe casket accordingly. — And so, mistress, leave off your wailing — Hey ! why surely there was a woman here ! »

« I think you are all mad this morning, » said the sewer ; « I saw no woman here, nor no man neither in a proper sense, but only two beasts rolling on the floor. »

« Nay, then I am undone, » said the jailor ; « the prison's broken, that is all. Kenilworth prison is broken, which was the strongest jail betwixt this and the Welch marches — ay, and a house that has had knights, and earls, and kings sleeping in it, as secure as if they had been in the Tower of London. It is broken, the prisoners fled, and the jailor in much danger of being hanged. »

So saying, he retreated down to his own den to conclude his lamentations, or to sleep himself sober. Lambourne and the sewer followed him close, and it was well for them, since the jailor, out of mere habit, was about to lock the wicket after him ; and had they not been within the reach of interfering, they would have had the pleasure of being shut up in the turret-chamber, from which the Countess had been just delivered.

That unhappy lady, as soon as she found herself at liberty, fled, as we have already mentioned, into the Pleasance. She had seen this richly ornamented space of ground from the window of Mervyn's Tower ; and it occurred to her, at the moment of her escape, that, among its numerous arbours, bowers, fountains, statues, and grottoes, she might find some recess, in which she could lie concealed until she had an opportunity of addressing herself to a protector, to whom she might communicate as much as she dared of her forlorn situation, and through whose means she might supplicate an interview with her husband.

« If I could see my guide, » she thought, « I would learn if he had delivered my letter. Even if I could see Tressilian, it were better to risk Dudley's anger, by confiding my whole situation to one who is the very soul of honour, than to run the hazard of farther insult among the insolent menials of this ill-ruled place. I will not again venture into an inclosed apartment. I will wait, I will watch — amidst so many human beings, there must be some kind heart which can judge and compassionate what mine endures. »

In truth, more than one party entered and traversed the Pleasance. But they were in joyous groupes of four or five persons together, laughing and jesting in their own fullness of mirth and lightness of heart.

The retreat which she had chosen, gave her the easy alternative of avoiding observation. It was but stepping back to the farthest recess of a grotto, ornamented with rustic work and moss-seats, and terminated by a fountain, and she might easily remain concealed, or at her pleasure discover herself to any solitary wanderer, whose curiosity might lead him to that romantic retirement. Anticipating such an opportunity, she looked into the clear basin, which the silent fountain held up to her like a mirror, and felt shocked at her own appearance, and doubtful at the same time, muffled and disfigured as her disguise made her seem to herself, whether any female, (and it was from the compassion of

her own sex that she chiefly expected sympathy,)
would engage in conference with so suspicious
an object. Reasoning thus like a woman, to
whom external appearance is scarcely in any circumstances a matter of unimportance, and like a
Beauty who had some confidence in the power of
her own charms, she laid aside her own travelling
cloak and capotaine hat, and placed them beside
her, so that she could assume them in an instant,
ere one could penetrate from the entrance of the
grotto to its extremity, in case the intrusion of
Varney or of Lambourne should render such disguise necessary. The dress which she wore under these vestments was somewhat of a theatrical
cast, so as to suit the assumed personage of one
of the females who was to act in the pageant.
Wayland had found the means of arranging it
thus upon the second day of their journey, having experienced the service arising from the
assumption of such a character on the preceding
day. The fountain, acting both as a mirror and
ewer, afforded Amy the means of a brief toilette,
of which she availed herself as hastily as possible; then took in her hand her small casket of
jewels in case she might find them useful inter-
cessors, and retiring to the darkest and most
sequestered nook, sat down on a seat of moss, and
awaited till fate should give her some chance of
rescue, or of propitiating an intercessor.

CHAPTER XXXIV.

Have you not seen the partridge quake,
Viewing the hawk approaching nigh?
She cuddles close beneath the brake,
Afraid to sit, afraid to fly.

Prior.

IT chanced upon that memorable morning, that one of the earliest of the huntress train, who appeared from her chamber in full array for the Chase, was the Princess, for whom all these pleasures were instituted, England's Maiden Queen. I know not if it were by chance, or out of the befitting courtesy due to a mistress by whom he was so much honoured, that she had scarcely made one step beyond the threshold of her chamber, ere Leicester was by her side, and proposed to her, until the preparations for the Chase had been completed, to view the Pleasance, and the gardens which it connected with the Castle-yard.

. To this new scene of pleasures they walked, the Earl's arm affording his Sovereign the occasional support which she required, where flights of steps, then a favourite ornament in a garden, conducted them from terrace, to terrace, and from parterre to parterre. The ladies in attendance, gifted with prudence, or endowed perhaps with the amiable desire of acting as they would be done by, did not conceive their duty to the Queen's person required them, though they lost not sight of her, to approach so near as to share, or perhaps disturb, the conversation betwixt the Queen and the Earl, who was not only her host, but also her most trusted, esteemed, and favoured servant. They contented themselves with admiring the grace of this illustrious couple, whose robes of state were now exchanged for hunting suits, almost equally magnificent.

Elizabeth's sylvan dress, which was of a pale blue silk, with silver lace and *aiguillettes*, approached in form to that of the ancient Amazons; and was, therefore, well suited at once to her height, and to the dignity of her mien, which her conscious rank and long habits of authority had rendered in some degree too masculine to be seen to the best advantage in ordinary female weeds. Leicester's hunting suit of Lincoln-green, richly embroidered with gold, and crossed by the gay baldric, which sustained a bugle-horn, and a woodk-n'fe instead of a sword, became its master, as did his other vestments of court or of war. For such were the perfections of his form and mien, that Leicester was always supposed to be seen to the greatest advantage in the character and dress which for the time he represented or wore.

The conversation of Elizabeth and the favourite Earl has not reached us in detail. But those who watched at some distance, (and the eyes of courtiers and court ladies are right sharp,) were of opinion, that on no occasion did the dignity of Elizabeth, in gesture and motion, seem so decidedly to soften away into a mien expressive of indecision and tenderness. Her step was not only slow, but even unequal, a thing most unwonted in her carriage; her looks seemed bent on the ground, and there was a timid disposition to withdraw from her companion, which external gesture in females often indicates exactly the opposite tendency in the secret mind. The Duchess of Rutland, who ventured nearest, was even heard to aver, that she discerned a tear in Elizabeth's eye, and a blush on her cheek; and still farther, « She bent her looks on the ground to avoid mine, » said the Duchess; « she who, in her ordinary mood, could look down a lion. To what conclusion these symptoms led is sufficiently evident; nor were they probably entirely groundless. The progress of a private conversation betwixt two persons of different sexes, is often decisive of their fate, and gives it a turn very distinct perhaps from what they themselves anticipated. Gallantry becomes mingled with conversation, and affection and passion come gradually to mix with gallantry. Nobles, as well as shepherd swains, will, in such a trying moment, say more than they intended; and Queens, like village maidens, will listen longer than they should.

Horses in the meanwhile neighed, and champed the bitts with impatience in the base-court;
hounds yelled in their couples, and yeomen,
rangers, and prickers, lamented the exhaling
of the dew, which would prevent the scent
from lying. But Leicester had another chace in
view, or, to speak more justly towards him, had
become engaged in it without premeditation,
as the high-spirited hunter which follows the
cry of the hounds that have crossed his path
by accident. The Queen — an accomplished
and handsome woman — the pride of *England*,
the hope of France and Holland, and the dread
of Spain, had probably listened with more
than usual favour to that mixture of romantic
gallantry with which she always loved to be
addressed; and the Earl had, in vanity, in ambition, or in both, thrown in more and more
of that delicious ingredient, until his importu-
nity became the language of love itself.

« No, Dudley, » said Elizabeth, yet it was
with broken accents — « No, I must be the
mother of my people. Other ties, that make
the lowly maiden happy, are denied to her
Sovereign — No, Leicester, urge it no more
— Were I as others, free to seek my own happiness — then, indeed — but it cannot — cannot
be. — Delay the chace — delay it for half an
hour — and leave me, my lord. »

« How, leave you, Madam ! » said Leicester, —
« Has my madness offended you? »

« No, Leicester, not so ! » answered the Queen

hastily ; « but it is madness, and must not be repeated. Go — but go not far from hence — and meantime let no one intrude on my privacy. »

While she spoke thus, Dudley bowed deeply, and retired with a slow and melancholy air. The Queen stood gazing after him, and murmured to herself — « Were it possible — were it *but* possible ! — but no — no — Elizabeth must be the wife and mother of England alone. »

As she spoke thus, and in order to avoid some one whose step she heard approaching, the Queen turned into the grotto in which her hapless, and yet but too successful rival lay concealed.

The mind of England's Elizabeth, if somewhat shaken by the agitating interview to which she had just put a period, was of that firm and decided character which soon recovers its natural tone. It was like one of those ancient druidical monuments, called Rocking-stones. The finger of Cupid, boy as he is painted, could put her feelings in motion, but the power of Hercules could not have destroyed their equilibrium. As she advanced with a slow pace towards the inmost extremity of the grotto, her countenance, ere she had proceeded half the length, had recovered its dignity of look, and her mien its air of command.

It was then the Queen became aware, that a female figure was placed beside, or rather partly behind, an alabaster column, at the foot of which arose the pellucid fountain, which occupied the inmost recess of the twilight grotto. The class-

ical mind of Elizabeth suggested the story of
Numa and Egeria, and she doubted not that some
Italian sculptor had here represented the Naiad,
whose inspirations gave laws to Rome. As she
advanced, she became doubtful whether she beheld a statue, or a form of flesh and blood. The
unfortunate Amy, indeed, remained motionless, betwixt the desire which she had to make
her condition known to one of her own sex,
and her awe for the stately form which approached
her, and which, though her eyes had never before beheld, her fears instantly suspected to be
the personage she really was. Amy had arisen
from her seat with the purpose of addressing
the lady, who entered the grotto alone, and, as
she at first thought, so opportunely. But when
she recollected the alarm which Leicester had
expressed at the Queen knowing aught of their
union, and became more and more satisfied that
the person whom she now beheld was Elizabeth
herself, she stood with one foot advanced and
one withdrawn, her arms, head, and hands,
perfectly motionless, and her cheek as pallid as
the alabaster pedestal against which she leaned.
Her dress was of pale sea-green silk, little distinguished in that imperfect light, and somewhat resembled the drapery of a Grecian
Nymph, such an antique disguise having been
thought the most secure, where so many masquers and revellers were assembled ; so that
the Queen's doubt of her being a living form
was well justified by all contingent circumstan-

ces, as well as by the bloodless cheek and the fixed eye.

Elizabeth remained in doubt, even after she had approached within a few paces, whether she did not gaze on a statue so cunningly fashioned, that by that doubtful light it could not be distinguished from reality. She stopped, therefore, and fixed upon this interesting object her princely look with so much keenness, that the astonishment which had kept Amy immoveable, gave way to awe, and she gradually cast down her eyes, and drooped her head under the commanding gaze of the Sovereign. Still, however, she remained in all respects, saving this slow and profound inclination of the head, motionless and silent.

From her dress, and the casket which she instinctively held in her hand, Elizabeth naturally conjectured that the beautiful but mute figure which she beheld was a performer in one of the various theatrical pageants which had been placed in different situations to surprise her with their homage, and that the poor player, overcome with awe at her presence, had either forgot the part assigned her, or lacked courage to go through it. It was natural and courteous to give her some encouragement; and Elizabeth accordingly said in a tone of condescending kindness, — « How now, fair Nymph of this lovely grotto — art thou spell-bound and struck with dumbness by the charms of the wicked enchanter whom men term Fear? — We are his sworn enemy, maiden, and can reverse his charm. Speak, we command thee. »

Instead of answering her by speech, the unfortunate Countess dropped on her knee before the Queen, let her casket fall from her hand, and clasping her palms together, looked up in the Queen's face with such a mixed agony of fear and supplication, that Elizabeth was considerably affected.

« What may this mean ? » she said ; « this is a stronger passion than befits the occasion. Stand up, damsel — what wouldst thou have with us ? »

« Your protection, Madam, » faultered forth the unhappy petitioner.

« Each daughter of England has it while she is worthy of it, » replied the Queen ; « but your distress seems to have a deeper root than a forgotten task. Why, and in what, do you crave our protection ? »

Amy hastily endeavoured to recal what she were best to say, which might secure herself from the imminent dangers which surrounded her, without endangering her husband ; and plunging from one thought to another, amidst the chaos which filled her mind, she could at length, in answer to the Queen's repeated enquiries, in what she sought protection, only faulter out, « Alas ! I know not. »

« This is folly, maiden, » said Elizabeth impatiently ; for there was something in the extreme confusion of the suppliant, which irritated her curiosity as well as interested her feelings. « The

sick man must tell his malady to the physician,
nor are WE accustomed to ask questions so oft,
without receiving an answer. »

« I request — I implore, » stammered forth
the unfortunate Countess, — «I beseech your
gracious protection—against—against one Varney. » She choaked well nigh as she uttered the
fatal word, which was instantly caught up by
the Queen.

« What, Varney—Sir Richard Varney—the
servant of Lord Leicester ! — What, damsel, are
you to him, or he to you? »

« I — I — was his prisoner — and he practised
on my life — and I broke forth to — to » —

« To throw thyself on my protection, doubtless, » said Elizabeth. « Thou shalt have it—that
is , if thou art worthy; for we will sift this matter to the uttermost. — Thou art, » she said,
bending on the Countess an eye which seemed
designed to pierce her very inmost soul, —
« thou art Amy, daughter of Sir Hugh Robsart
of Lidcote-Hall ? »

« Forgive me — forgive me — most gracious
Princess ! » said Amy, dropping once more on
her knee, from which she had arisen.

« For what should I forgive thee, silly wench? »
said Elizabeth ; « for being the daughter of thine
own father? Thou art brain-sick , surely. Well,
I see I must wring the story from thee by inches
—Thou did'st deceive thine old and honoured
father—thy look confesses it—cheated Master

Tressilian—thy blush avouches it—and married
this same Varney. »

Amy sprung on her feet, and interrupted the
Queen eagerly, with, « No, Madam, no — as
there is a God above us, I am not the sordid
wretch you would take me! I am not the wife
of that contemptible slave — of that most de-
liberate villain! I am not the wife of Varney! I
would rather be the bride of Destruction! »

The Queen, overwhelmed in her turn by
Amy's vehemence, stood silent for an instant,
and then replied, « Why, God ha' mercy! woman—I see thou can'st talk fast enough when
the theme likes thee. Nay, tell me, woman, » she
continued, for to the impulse of curiosity was
now added that of an undefined jealousy that
some deception had been practised on her, —
« tell me, woman — for by God's day, I WILL
know — whose wife, or whose paramour art
thou? Speak out, and be speedy — Thou wert
better dally with a lioness than with Elizabeth. »

Urged to this extremity, dragged as it were
by irresistible force to the verge of the precipice,
which she saw but could not avoid,—permitted
not a moment's respite by the eager words, and
menacing gestures of the offended Queen, Amy
at length uttered in despair, « The Earl of Leicester knows it all. »

« The Earl of Leicester! » said Elizabeth, in
utter astonishment — « The Earl of Leicester! »
she repeated, with kindling anger,—« Woman,

thou art set on to this—thou doest belie him—
he takes no keep of such things as thou art.
Thou art suborned to slander the noblest lord,
and the truest-hearted gentleman, in England!
But were he the right hand of our trust, or something yet dearer to us, thou shalt have thy
hearing, and that in his presence. Come with me
—come with me instantly! »

As Amy shrunk back with terror, which the
incensed Queen interpreted as that of conscious
guilt, Elizabeth hastily advanced, seized on her
arm, and hastened with swift and long steps out
of the grotto, and along the principal alley of the
Pleasance, dragging with her the terrified Countess, whom she still held by the arm, and whose
utmost exertions could but just keep pace with
those of the indignant Queen.

Leicester was at this moment the centre of a
splendid groupe of lords and ladies, assembled together under an arcade, or portico, which closed
the alley. The company had drawn together in
that place, to attend the commands of her Majesty when the hunting-party should go forward,
and their astonishment may be imagined, when
instead of seeing Elizabeth advance towards
them with her usual measured dignity of motion,
they beheld her walking so rapidly, that she was
in the midst of them ere they were aware; and
then observed, with fear and surprise, that her
features were flushed betwixt anger and agitation, that her hair was loosened by her haste of
motion, and that her eyes sparkled as they were

wont when the spirit of Henry VIII mounted highest in his daughter. Nor were they less astonished at the appearance of the pale, extenuated, half-dead, yet still lovely female, whom the Queen upheld by main strength with one hand, while with the other she waved aside the ladies and nobles who pressed towards her, under the idea that she was taken suddenly ill. « Where is my Lord of Leicester? » she said, in a tone that thrilled with astonishment all the courtiers who stood around—« Stand forth, my Lord of Leicester! »

If, in the midst of the most serene day of summer, when all is light and laughing around, a thunderbolt were to fall from the clear blue vault of heaven, and rend the earth at the very feet of some careless traveller, he could not gaze upon the smouldering chasm, which so unexpectedly yawned before him, with half the astonishment and fear which Leicester felt at the sight that so suddenly presented itself. He had that instant been receiving, with a political affectation of disavowing and misunderstanding their meaning, the half uttered, half intimated congratulations of the courtiers upon the favour of the Queen, carried apparently to its highest pitch during the interview of that morning; from which most of them seemed to augur, that he might soon arise from their equal in rank to become their master. And now, while the subdued yet proud smile with which he disclaimed those inferences was yet curling his cheek, the

Queen shot into the circle, her passions excited
to the uttermost; and, supporting with one hand,
and apparently without an effort, the pale and
sinking form of his almost expiring wife, and
pointing with the finger of the other to her half
dead features, demanded in a voice that sounded
to the ears of the astounded statesman like the
last dread trumpet-call, that is to summon body
and spirit to the judgment seat, « Knowest thou
this woman ? »

As at the blast of that last trumpet , the
guilty shall call upon the mountains to cover
them , Leicester's inward thoughts invoked the
stately arch which he had built in his pride,
to burst its strong conjunction, and overwhelm
them in its ruins. But the cemented stones,
architrave and battlement, stood fast; and it
was the proud master himself, who, as if some
actual pressure had bent him to the earth ,
kneeled down before Elizabeth, and prostrated
his brow to the marble flag-stones on which she
stood.

« Leicester , » said Elizabeth , in a voice
which trembled with passion , « could I think
thou hast practised on me — on me thy Sovereign — on me thy confiding, thy too partial
mistress , the base and ungrateful deception
which thy present confusion surmises — by all
that is holy, false lord, that head of thine were
in as great peril as ever was thy father's! »

Leicester had not conscious innocence, but
he had pride to support him. He raised slowly

his brow and features, which were black and swoln with contending emotions, and only re-plied, « My head cannot fall but by the sentence of my peers — to them I will plead, and not to a princess who thus requites my faithful service.

« What! my lords, » said Elizabeth, looking around, we are defied, I think — defied in the Castle we have ourselves bestowed on this proud man! — My Lord Shrewsbury, you are Marshall of England, attach him of high treason. »

« Whom does your Grace mean? » said Shrewsbury, much surprised, for he had that instant joined the astonished circle.

« Whom should I mean, but that traitor, Dudley, Earl of Leicester! — Cousin of Hunsdon, order out your band of gentlemen pensioners, and take him into instant custody. — I say, villain, make haste! »

Hunsdon, a rough old noble, who, from his relationship to the Boleyns, was accustomed to use more freedom with the Queen than almost any others, replied bluntly, « And it is like your Grace might order me to the Tower to-morrow, for making too much haste. I do beseech you to be patient. »

« Patient—God's life! » exclaimed the Queen, — « name not the word to me — thou know'st not of what he is guilty! »

Amy, who had by this time in some degree recovered herself, and who saw her husband, as she conceived, in the utmost danger from the rage of an offended Sovereign, instantly, (and, alas! how many women have done the same,) forgot her own wrongs, and her own danger, in her apprehensions for him, and throwing herself before the Queen, embraced her knees, while she exclaimed, « He is guiltless, Madam — he is guiltless — no one can lay aught to the charge of the noble Leicester. »

« Why, minion, » answered the Queen, « did'st not thou, thyself, say that the Earl of Leicester was privy to thy whole history? »

« Did I say so? » repeated the unhappy Amy, laying aside every consideration of consistency, and of self-interest; « O, if I did, I foully belied him. May God so judge me, as I believe he was never privy to a thought that would harm me! »

« Woman! » said Elizabeth, « I will know who has moved thee to this; or my wrath — and the wrath of kings is a flaming fire — shall wither and consume thee like a weed in the furnace. »

As the Queen uttered this threat, Leicester's better angel called his pride to his aid, and reproached him with the utter extremity of meanness which would overwhelm him for ever, if he stooped to take shelter under the generous interposition of his wife, and abandoned her, in return for her kindness, to the resentment of the Queen. He had already raised his head, with the dignity of a man of honour, to avow his marriage, and proclaim himself the protector of his Countess, when Varney, born, as it appeared, to be his master's evil genius, rushed into the presence, with every mark of disorder on his face and apparel.

« What means this saucy intrusion ? » said Elizabeth.

Varney, with the air of a man altogether overwhelmed with grief and confusion, prostrated himself before her feet, exclaiming, « Pardon, my Liege, pardon ! — or at least let your justice avenge itself on me, where it is due; but spare my noble, my generous, my innocent patron and master ! »

Amy, who was yet kneeling, started up as she saw the man whom she deemed most odious place himself so near her, and was about to fly towards Leicester, when, checked at once by the uncertainty and even timidity which his looks had reassumed as soon as the appearance of his confidant seemed to open a new scene, she hung back, and, uttering a faint scream, besought of her Majesty to cause her to be imprisoned in the lowest dungeon of the castle — to deal with her as the worst of criminals—« but spare, » she exclaimed, « my sight and hearing, what will destroy the little judgment I have left — the sight of that unutterable and most shameless villain ! »

« And why, sweetheart ? » said the Queen, moved by a new impulse; « what hath he, this false knight, since such thou accountest him, done to thee ? »

« Oh, worse than sorrow, madam, and worse than injury. — he has sown dissention where most there should be peace. I shall go mad if I look longer on him. »

« Beshrew me, but I think thou art distraught already,» answered the Queen.—« My Lord Hunsdon, look to this poor distressed young woman, and let her be safely bestowed, and in honest keeping, till we require her to be forthcoming. »

Two or three of the ladies in attendance, either moved by compassion for a creature so interesting, or by some other motive, offered their service to look after her ; but the Queen briefly answered, «Ladies, under favour, no. — You have all (give God thanks) sharp ears and nimble tongues— our kinsman Hunsdon has ears of the dullest, and a tongue somewhat rough, but yet of the slowest. — Hunsdon, look to it that none have speech of her. »

« By Our Lady ! » said Hunsdon, taking in his strong sinewy arms the fading and almost swooning form of Amy, «she is a lovely child ; and though a rough nurse, your Grace hath given her a kind one. She is safe with me as one of my own lady-birds of daughters.»

So saying, he carried her off, unresistingly and almost unconsciously; his war-worn locks and long grey beard mingling with her light-brown tresses, as her head reclined on his strong square shoulder. The Queen followed him with her eye —she had already, with that self-command which forms so necessary a part of a Sovereign's accomplishments, suppressed every appearance of agitation, and seemed as if she desired to banish all traces of her burst of passion from the recollection of those who had witnessed it. « My Lord of Hunsdon, » she said, « is but a rough nurse for so tender a babe. »

« My Lord of Hunsdon, » said the Dean of St Asaph, « I speak it not in defamation of his more noble qualities, hath a broad license in speech, and garnishes his discourse somewhat too freely with the cruel and superstitious oaths, which savour both of profaneness and of old papestrie. »

« It is the fault of his blood, Mr Dean, » said the Queen, turning sharply round upon the reverend dignitary as she spoke; « and you may blame mine for the same distemperature. The Boleyns were ever a hot and plain-spoken race, more hasty to speak their mind than careful to chuse their expressions. And by my word — I hope there is no sin in that affirmation — I question if it were much cooled by mixing with that of Tudor. »

As she made this last observation she smiled graciously, and stole her eyes almost insensibly round to seek those of the Earl of Leicester, to whom she now began to think she had spoken with hasty harshness upon the unfounded suspicion of a moment.

The Queen's eye found the Earl in no mood to accept the implied offer of conciliation. His own looks had followed, with late and rueful repentance, the faded form which Hunsdon had just borne from the presence; they now reposed gloomily on the ground, but more — so at least it seemed to Elizabeth — with the expression of one who has received an unjust affront, than of him who is conscious of guilt. She turned her face angrily from him, and said to Varney, « Speak, Sir Richard, and explain these riddles — thou hast sense, and the use of speech, at least, which elsewhere we look for in vain. »

As she said this, she darted another resentful glance towards Leicester, while the wily Varney hastened to tell his own story.

« Your Majesty's piercing eye, » he said, « has already detected the cruel malady of my beloved lady; which, unhappy that I am, I would not suffer to be expressed in the certificate of her physician, seeking to conceal what has now broken out with so much the more scandal. »

« She is then distraught? » said the Queen — « indeed we doubted not of it — her whole demeanour bears it out. I found her moping in a corner of yonder grotto; and every word which she spoke — which indeed I dragged from her as by the rack — she instantly recalled and forswore. But how came she hither? Why had you her not in safe-keeping? »

« My gracious Liege, » said Varney, « the worthy gentleman under whose charge I left her, Master Anthony Foster, has come hither but now, as fast as man and horse can travel, to shew me of her escape, which she managed with

11*

the art peculiar to many who are afflicted with
this malady. He is at hand for examination. »

« Let it be for another time, » said the Queen.
« But, Sir Richard, we envy you not your domestic felicity; your lady railed on you bitterly,
and seemed ready to swoon at beholding you. »

« It is the nature of persons in her disorder,
so please your Grace, » answered Varney, « to be
ever most inveterate in their spleen against those,
whom, in their better moments, they hold nearest
and dearest. »

« We have heard so, indeed, » said Elizabeth,
« and give faith to the saying. »

« May your Grace then be pleased, » said
Varney, « to command my unfortunate wife to
be delivered into the custody of her friends? »

Leicester partly started; but, making a strong
effort, he subdued his emotion, while Elizabeth
answered sharply, « You are something too
hasty, Master Varney; we will have first a report of the lady's health and state of mind from
Masters, our own physician, and then determine what shall be thought just. You shall have
licence, however, to see her, that if there be
any matrimonial quarrel betwixt you — such
things we have heard do occur, even betwixt
a loving couple — you may make it up, without
further scandal to our court, or trouble to ourselves. »

Varney bowed low, and made no other answer.

Elizabeth again looked towards Leicester, and
said, with a degree of condescension which

could only arise out of the most heartfelt interest, « Discord, as the Italian poet says, will
find her way into peaceful convents, as well as
into the privacy of families; and we fear our
own guards and ushers will hardly exclude her
from courts. My Lord of Leicester, you are
offended with us, and we have right to be offended with you. We will take the lion's part
upon us, and be the first to forgive. »

Leicester smoothed his brow, as by an effort,
but the trouble was too deep-seated that its
placidity should at once return. He said, however, that which fitted the occasion, « that he
could not have the happiness of forgiving, because she who commanded him to do so, could
commit no injury towards him. »

Elizabeth seemed content with this reply,
and intimated her pleasure that the sports of
the morning should proceed. The bugles sounded
— the hounds bayed — the horses pranced —
but the courtiers and ladies sought the amusement to which they were summoned with hearts
very different from those which had leaped to
the morning's *réveillée*. There was doubt, and
fear, and expectation on every brow, and sur-
mise and intrigue in every whisper.

Blount took an opportunity to whisper into
Raleigh's ear, « This storm came like a levanter
in the Mediterranean. »

« *Varium et mutabile* » — answered Raleigh,
in a similar tone.

« Nay, I know nought of your Latin, » said

Blount; « but I thank God Tressilian took not the sea during that hurricano. He could scarce have missed shipwreck, knowing as he does so little how to trim his sails to a court gale. »

« Thou wouldst have instructed him? » said Raleigh.

« Why, I have profited by my time as well as thou, Sir Walter, » replied honest Blount. « I am knight as well as thou, and of the earlier creation. »

« Now, God further thy wit, » said Raleigh; « but for Tressilian, I would I knew what were the matter with him. He told me this morning he would not leave his chamber for the space of twelve hours, or thereby, being bound by a promise. This lady's madness, when he shall learn it, will not, I fear, cure his infirmity. The moon is at the fullest, and men's brains are working like yeast. But hark! they sound to mount. Let us to horse, Blount; we *young* knights must deserve our spurs. »

CHAPTER XXXV.

——— Sincerity,
Thou first of virtues! let no mortal leave
The onward path, although the earth should gape,
And from the gulf of hell destruction cry,
To take dissimulation's winding way.
Douglas.

It was not till after a long and successful morning's sport, and a prolonged repast which followed the return of the Queen to the Castle, that Leicester at length found himself alone with Varney, from whom he now learned the whole particulars of the Countess's escape, as they had been brought to Kenilworth by Foster, who, in his terror for the consequences, had himself posted thither with the tidings. As Varney, in his narrative, took especial care to be silent concerning those practices on the Countess's health which had driven her to so desperate a resolution, Leicester, who could only suppose that she had adopted it out of jealous impatience, to attain the avowed state and appearance belonging to her rank, was not a little offended at the levity with which his wife had broken his strict commands, and exposed him to the resentment of Elizabeth.

« I have given, » he said, « to this daughter of
an obscure Devonshire gentleman, the proudest
name in England. I have made her sharer of my
bed and of my fortunes. I ask but of her a little
patience, ere she launches forth upon the full
current of her grandeur, and the infatuated woman will rather hazard her own shipwreck and
mine, will rather involve me in a thousand whirl-
pools, shoals, and quick-sands, and compel me to
a thousand devices which shame me in mine own
eyes, than tarry for a little space longer in the
obscurity to which she was born.—So lovely, so
delicate, so fond, so faithful—yet to lack in so
grave a matter the patience which one might
hope from the veriest fool — it puts me beyond
my patience. »

« We may post it over yet well enough, » said
Varney, « if my lady will be but ruled, and take
on her the character which the time commands. »

» It is but too true, Sir Richard, » said Leicester, « there is indeed no other remedy. I have
heard her termed thy wife in my presence, without contradiction. She must bear the title until
she is far from Kenilworth. »

« And long afterwards, I trust, said Varney;
then instantly added, « For I cannot but hope it
will be long after ere she bear the title of Lady
Leicester—I fear me it may scarce be with safety during the life of this Queen. But your
lordship is best judge, you alone knowing what
passages have taken place betwixt Elizabeth and
you. »

« You are right, Varney, » said Leicester ; « I
have this morning been both fool and villain; and
when Elizabeth hears of my unhappy marriage,
she cannot but think herself treated with that
premeditated slight which women never forgive.
We have once this day stood upon terms little
short of defiance; and to those, I fear, we must
again return. »

« Is her resentment, then, so implacable? » said
Varney.

« Far from it, » replied the Earl; « for, being
what she is in spirit and in station, she has even
this day been but too condescending, in giving
me opportunities to repair what she thinks my
faulty heat of temper. »

« Ay, answered Varney, » the Italians say
right—in lovers' quarrels, the party that loves
most, is always most willing to acknowledge the
greater fault. — So then, my lord, if this union
with the lady could be concealed, you stand with
Elizabeth as you did. »

Leicester sighed and was silent for a moment,
ere he replied,

« Varney, I think thou art true to me, and I
will tell thee all. I do *not* stand where I did. I
have spoken to Elizabeth—under what mad impulse I know not—on a theme which cannot be
abandoned without touching every female feeling to the quick, and which yet I dare not and
cannot prosecute. She can never, never forgive
me, for having caused and witnessed those yield-
ings to human passion. »

» We must do something, my lord, » said Varney, « and that speedily. »

« There is nought to be done, answered Leicester, despondingly; « I am like one that has long toiled up a dangerous precipice, and when he is within one perilous stride of the top, finds his progress arrested when retreat has become impossible. I see above me the pinnacle which I cannot reach—beneath me the abyss into which I must fall, as soon as my relaxing grasp and dizzy brain join to hurl me from my present precarious stance. »

« Think better of your situation, my lord, » said Varney — « let us try the experiment in which you have but now acquiesced. Keep we your marriage from Elizabeth's knowledge, and all may yet be well. I will instantly go to the lady myself — She hates me, because I have been earnest with your lordship, as she truly suspects, in opposition to what she *terms her* rights. I care not for her prejudices—She *shall* listen to me; and I will shew her such reasons for yielding to the pressure of the times, that I doubt not to bring back her consent to whatever measures these exigencies may require. »

« No, Varney, » said Leicester; « I have thought upon what is to be done, and I will myself speak with Amy. »

It was now Varney's turn to feel, upon his own account, the terrors which he affected to participate solely on account of his patron. « Your lordship will not yourself speak with the lady? »

« It is my fixed purpose, » said Leicester; « fetch me one of the livery-cloaks; I will pass the centinel as thy servant. Thou art to have free access to her. »

« But, my lord » ——

« I will have no *buts*, » replied Leicester; « it shall be even thus, and not otherwise. Hunsdon sleeps, I think, in Saintlowe's Tower. We can go thither from these apartments by the private passage, without risk of meeting any one. Or what if I do meet Hunsdon? he is more my friend than enemy, and thick-witted enough to adopt any belief that is thrust on him. Fetch me the cloak instantly. »

Varney had no alternative save obedience. In a few minutes Leicester was muffled in the mantle, pulled his bonnet over his brows, and followed Varney along the secret passage of the Castle which communicated with Hunsdon's apartments, in which there was scarce a chance of meeting any inquisitive person, and hardly light enough for any such to have satisfied their curiosity. They emerged at a door where Lord Hunsdon had, with military precaution, placed a centinel, one of his own northern retainers as it fortuned, who readily admitted Sir Richard Varney and his attendant, saying only, in his northern dialect, « I would, man, thou could'st make the mad lady be still yonder; for her moans do sae dirl through my head, that I would rather keep watch on a snow-drift, in the wastes of Catlowdie. »

11. 12

They hastily entered, and shut the door behind them.

« Now, good devil, if there be one, » said Varney within himself, « for once help a votary at a dead pinch, for my boat is amongst the breakers. »

The Countess Amy, with her hair and her garments dishevelled, was seated upon a sort of couch, in an attitude of the deepest affliction, out of which she was startled by the opening of the door. She turned hastily round, and fixing her eye on Varney, exclaimed, « Wretch! art thou come to frame some new plan of villainy? »

Leicester cut short her reproaches by stepping forward, and dropping his cloak, while he said, in a voice rather of authority than of affection, « It is with me, madam, you have to commune, not with sir Richard Varney. »

The change effected on the Countess's look and manner was like magic. « Dudley! » she exclaimed, « Dudley! and art thou come at last? » And with the speed of lightning she flew to her husband, clung around his neck, and, unheeding the presence of Varney, overwhelmed him with caresses, while she bathed his face in a flood of tears; muttering, at the same time, but in broken and disjointed monosyllables, the fondest expressions which love teaches his votaries.

Leicester, as it seemed to him, had reason to be angry with his lady for transgressing his commands, and thus placing him in the perilous situation in which he had that morning stood. But what displeasure could keep its ground before these testimonies of affection from a being so lovely, that even the negligence of dress, and the withering effects of fear and grief, which would have impaired the beauty of others, rendered her's but the more interesting. He received and repaid her caresses with fondness, mingled with melancholy, the last of which she seemed scarcely to observe, until the first transport of her own joy was over; when, looking anxiously in his face, she asked if he was ill.

« Not in my body, Amy, » was his answer.

« Then I will be well too. — O Dudley! I have been ill!—very ill, since we last met!—for I call not this morning's horrible vision a meeting. I have been in sickness, in grief, and in danger — But thou art come, and all is joy, and health, and safety. »

« Alas! Amy, » said Leicester, « thou hast undone me! »

« I, my lord, said Amy, her cheek at once losing its transient flush of joy — « how could I injure that which I love better than myself. »

« I would not upbraid you, Amy, » replied the Earl; « but are you not here contrary to my express commands — and does not your presence here endanger both yourself and me? »

« Does it, does it indeed! » she exclaimed eagerly; « then why am I here a moment longer? O if you knew by what fears I was urged to quit Cumnor Place! — but I will say nothing of my-self—only that if it might be otherwise, I would not willingly return *thither;* — yet if it concern your safety »———

« We will think, Amy, of some other retreat, » said Leicester; « and you shall go to one of my Northern castles, under the personage— it will be but needful, I trust, for a very few days—of Varney's wife. »

« How, my Lord of Leicester! » said the lady, disengaging herself from his embraces; « *is it to your wife you give the dishonourable counsel to acknowledge herself the bride of another* — and of all men, the bride of that Varney? »

« Madam, I speak it in earnest—Varney is my true and faithful servant, trusted in my deepest secrets. I had better lose my right hand than his service at this moment. You have no cause to scorn him as you do. »

« I could assign one, my lord, » replied the Countess; « and I see he shakes even under that assured look of his. But he that is necessary as your right hand to your safety, is free from any accusation of mine. May he be true to you; and that he may be true, trust him not too much or too far. But it is enough to say, that I will not go with him unless by violence, nor would I ac-knowledge him as my husband, were all »———

« It is a temporary deception, madam, » said Leicester, irritated by her opposition, « necessary for both our safeties, endangered by you through

female caprice, or the premature desire to seize
on a rank to which I gave you title, only under
condition that our marriage, for a time, should
continue secret. If my proposal disgust you, it is
yourself has brought it on both of us. There is
no other remedy—you must do what your own
impatient folly hath rendered necessary—I command you. »

« I cannot put your commands, my lord, « said
Amy, « in balance with those of honour and conscience. I will NOT, in this instance, obey you.
You may achieve your own dishonour, to which
these crooked policies naturally tend, but I will
do nought that can blemish mine. How could
you again, my lord, acknowledge me as a pure
and chaste matron, worthy to share your fortunes, when, holding that high character, I had
strolled the country the acknowledged wife of
such a profligate fellow as your servant Varney!»

« My lord », said Varney interposing, « my
lady is too much prejudiced against me, unhappily, to listen to what I can offer; yet it may
please her better than what she proposes. She
has good interest with Master Edmund Tressilian, and could doubtless prevail on him to consent to be her companion to Lidcote-hall, and
there she might remain in safety until time permitted the developement of this mystery.»

Leicester was silent, but stood looking eagerly
on Amy, with eyes which seemed suddenly to
glow as much with suspicion as displeasure.

The Countess only said, « Would to God I

were in my father's house!—When I left it, I little thought I was leaving peace of mind and honour behind me. »

Varney proceeded with a tone of deliberation, « Doubtless this will make it necessary to take strangers into my Lord's counsels; but surely the Countess will be warrant for the honour of Master Tressilian, and such of her father's family »———

« Peace, Varney, » said Leicester; « by Heaven I will strike my dagger into thee, if again thou namest Tressilian as a partner of my counsels! »

« And wherefore not? » said the Countess; « unless they be counsels fitter for such as Varney, than for a man of stainless honour and integrity.—My lord, my lord, bend no angry brows on me—it is the truth, and it is I who speak it. I once did Tressilian wrong for your sake—I will not do him the further injustice of *being* silent when his honour is brought in question. I can forbear, » she said, looking at Varney, « to pull the mask off hypocrisy, but I will not permit virtue to be slandered in my hearing. »

There was a dead pause. Leicester stood displeased, yet undetermined, and too conscious of the weakness of his cause; while Varney, with a deep and hypocritical affectation of sorrow, mingled with humility, bent his eyes on the ground.

It was then that the Countess Amy displayed, in the midst of distress and difficulty, the natural energy of character, which would have rendered her, had fate allowed, a distinguished ornament of the rank which she held. She walked up to Leicester with a composed step, a dignified air, and looks in which strong affection assayed in vain to shake the firmness of conscious truth and rectitude of principle. « You have spoke your mind, my lord, » she said, » in these difficulties with which, unhappily, I have found myself unable to comply. This gentleman — this person I would say — has hinted at another scheme, to which I object not but as it displeases you. Will your lordship be pleased to hear what a young and timid woman, but your most affectionate wife, can suggest in the present extremity ? »

Leicester was silent, but bent his head towards the Countess, as an intimation that she was at liberty to proceed.

« There hath been but one cause for all these evils, my lord, » she proceeded, « and it resolves itself into the mysterious duplicity with which you have been induced to surround yourself. Extricate yourself at once, my lord, from the tyranny of these disgraceful trammels. Be like a true English gentleman, knight, and earl, who holds that truth is the foundation of honour, and that honour is dear to him as the breath of his nostrils. Take your ill-fated wife by the hand, lead her to the footstool of Elizabeth's throne— Say, that in a moment of infatuation, moved by supposed beauty, of which none perhaps can

now trace even the remains, I gave my hand to
this Amy Robsart. — You will then have done
justice to me, my lord, and to your own honour; and should law or power require you to
part from me, I will oppose no objection—since
I may then with honour hide a grieved and broken heart in those shades from which your love
withdrew me. »

There was so much of dignity, so much of tenderness in the Countess's remonstrance, that it
moved all that was noble and generous in the soul
of her husband. The scales seemed to fall from
his eyes, and the duplicity and tergiversation of
which he had been guilty, stung him at once with
remorse and shame.·

« I am not worthy of you, Amy, » he said,
« that could weigh aught which ambition has to
give against such a heart as thine. I have a bitter penance to perform, in disentangling, before sneering foes and astounded friends, *all the*
meshes of my own deceitful policy — *And* the
Queen—but let her take my head, as she has
threatened. »

« Your head, my lord! » said the Countess;
« because you used the freedom and liberty of
an English subject in chusing a wife? For shame;
it is this distrust of the Queen's justice, this apprehension of danger, which cannot but be imaginary, that, like scare-crows, have induced you
to forsake the straight-forward path, which, as
it is the best, is also the safest. »

« Ah, Amy, thou little knowest! » said Dudley; but, instantly checking himself, he added, « Yet she shall not find in me a safe or easy victim of arbitrary vengeance.—I have friends—I have allies — I will not, like Norfolk, be dragged to the block, as a victim to sacrifice. Fear not, Amy; thou shalt see Dudley bear himself worthy of his name. I must instantly communicate with some of those friends on whom I can best rely; for, as things stand, I may be made prisoner in my own Castle. »

» O, my good lord, » said Amy, « make no faction in a peaceful state! There is no friend can help us so well as our own candid truth and honour. Bring but these to our assistance, and you are safe amidst a whole army of the envious and malignant. Leave these behind you, and all other defence will be fruitless — Truth, my noble lord, is well painted unarmed. »

« But Wisdom, Amy, » answered Leicester, « is arrayed in panoply of proof. Argue not with me on the means I shall use to render my confession — since it must be called so — as safe as may be; it will be fraught with enough of danger, do what we will. Varney, we must hence.— Farewell, Amy, whom I am to vindicate as mine own, at an expence and risk of which thou alone could'st be worthy. You shall soon hear farther from me. »

He embraced her fervently, muffled himself as before, and accompanied Varney from the apartment. The latter, as he left the room, bowed low, and, as he raised his body, regarded

Amy with a peculiar expression, as if he desired
to know how far his own pardon was included in
the reconciliation which had taken place betwixt
her and her lord. The Countess looked upon him
with a fixed eye, but seemed no more conscious
of his presence, than if there had been nothing
but vacant air on the spot where he stood.

« She has brought me to the crisis, » he muttered—« She or I are lost. There was something
— I wot not if it was fear or pity, that prompted
me to avoid this fatal crisis. It is now decided—
She or I must *perish*. »

While he thus spoke, he observed, with surprise, that a boy, repulsed by the centinel, made
up to Leicester, and spoke with him. Varney
was one of those politicians, whom not the slightest appearances escape without inquiry. He asked the centinel what the lad wanted with him,
and received for answer, that the boy had wished
him to transmit a parcel to the mad lady, but *that*
he cared not to take charge of it, such communication being beyond his commission. His curiosity satisfied in that particular, he approached
his patron, and heard him say — « Well, boy,
the packet shall be delivered. »

« Thanks, good Master Serving-man, » said
the boy, and was out of sight in an instant.

Leicester and Varney returned with hasty steps
to the Earl's private apartment, by the same passage which had conducted them to Saintlowe's
Tower.

CHAPTER XXXVI.

THEY were no sooner in the Earl's cabinet, than, taking his tablets from his pocket, he began to write, speaking partly to Varney, and partly to himself: — « There are many of them close bounden to me, and especially those in good estate and high office; many who, if they look back towards my benefits, or forward towards the perils which may befal themselves, will not, I think, be disposed to see me stagger unsupported. Let me see—Knollis is sure, and through his means Guernsey and Jersey—Horsey commands in the Isle of Wight—My brother-in-law, Huntingdon, and Pembroke, have authority in Wales—Through Bedford I lead the Puritans, with their interest, so powerful in all the boroughs—My brother of Warwick is equal, well nigh; to myself, in wealth, followers, and dependencies—Sir Owen Hopton is at my devotion; he commands the Tower of London, and the national treasure deposited there —My father and grandfather needed never to have stooped their heads to the block, had they thus forecast their enterprizes.—Why look you so sad, Varney? I tell thee, a tree so deep-rooted is not easily to be torn up by the tempest. »

« Alas! my lord, » said Varney, with well acted passion, and then resumed the same look of despondency which Leicester had before noted.

« Alas! » repeated Leicester, « and wherefore alas, Sir Richard? Doth your new spirit of chivalry supply no more vigorous ejaculation, when a noble struggle is impending? Or, if *alas* means thou wilt flinch from the conflict, thou mayest leave the Castle, or go join mine enemies, whichsoever thou thinkest best. »

« Not so, my lord, » answered his confidant; « Varney will be found fighting or dying by your side. Forgive me, if, in love to you, I see more fully than your noble heart permits *you* to do, the inextricable difficulties with which you are surrounded. You are strong, my lord, and powerful; yet, let me say it without offence, you are so only by the reflected light of the Queen's favour. While you are Elizabeth's favourite, you are all, save in name, like an actual sovereign. But let her call back the honours she has bestowed, and the Prophet's gourd did not wither more suddenly. Declare against the Queen, and I do not say that in the wide nation, or in this province alone, you would find yourself instantly deserted and outnumbered; but I will say, that

even in this very Castle, and in the midst of your
vassals, kinsmen, and dependants, you would be
a captive, nay a sentenced captive, should she
please to say the word. Think upon Norfolk,
my lord, —upon the powerful Northumberland,
— the splendid Westmoreland; — think on all
who have made head against this sage Princess.
They are dead, captive, or fugitive. This is not
like other thrones, which can be overturned by
a combination of powerful nobles; the broad
foundations which support it are in the extended
love and affections of the people. You might
share it with Elizabeth if you would; but neither
yours, nor any other power, foreign or domestic,
will avail to overthrow, or even to shake it. »

He paused, and Leicester threw his tablets
from him with an air of reckless despite. « It
may be as thou say'st, » he said; «and, in sooth,
I care not whether truth or cowardice dictate
thy forebodings. But it shall not be said I fell
without a struggle. — Give orders, that those of
my retainers who served under me in Ireland
be gradually drawn into the main Keep, and let
our gentlemen and friends stand on their guard,
and go armed, as if they expected an onset from
the followers of Sussex. Possess the town's-
people with some apprehension; let them take
arms, and be ready, at a signal given, to master
the Pensioners and Yeomen of the Guard. »

« Let me remind you, my lord, » said Varney,
with the same appearance of deep and melancholy interest, «that you have given me orders

to prepare for disarming the Queen's guard. It is an act of high treason, but you shall nevertheless be obeyed. »

« I care not, » said Leicester, desperately; — « I care not. Shame is behind me, Ruin before me; I must on. »

Here there was another pause, which Varney at length broke with the following words : « It is come to the point I have long dreaded. I must either witness, like an ungrateful beast, the downfal of the best and kindest of masters, or I must speak what I would have buried in the deepest oblivion, or told by any other mouth than mine. »

« What is that thou sayest, or would say ? » replied the Earl; « we have no time to waste on words, when the times call us to action. »

« My speech is soon made, my lord — would to God it were as soon answered. Your marriage is the sole cause of the threatened breach with your Sovereign, my lord, is it not ? »

« Thou knowest it is ! » replied Leicester. « What needs so fruitless a question ? »

« Pardon me, my lord, » said Varney; « the use lies here. Men will wager their lands and lives in defence of a rich diamond, my lord; but were it not first prudent to look if there is no flaw in it ? »

« What means this ? » said Leicester, with eyes sternly fixed on his dependant; « of whom doest thou dare to speak ? »

« It is —— of the Countess Amy, my lord, of

whom I am unhappily bound to speak; and of whom I *will* speak, were your lordship to kill me for my zeal. »

« Thou mayest happen to deserve it at my hand, » said the Earl; « but speak on, I will hear thee. »

« Nay, then, my lord, I will be bold. I speak for my own life as well as for your lordship's. I like not this lady's tampering and trickstering with this same Edmund Tressilian. You know him, my lord. You know he had formerly an interest in her, which it cost your lordship some pains to supersede. You know the eagerness with which he has pressed on the suit against me in behalf of this lady, the open object of which is to drive your lordship to an avowal of what I must ever call your most unhappy marriage, the point to which my lady also is willing, at any risk, to urge you. »

Leicester smiled constrainedly. « Thou meanest well, good Sir Richard, and would, I think, sacrifice thine own honour, as well as that of any other person, to save me from what thou think'st a step so terrible. But, remember, » — he spoke these words with the most stern decision, — «you speak of the Countess of Leicester. »

« I do, my lord, » said Varney; « but it is for the welfare of the Earl of Leicester. My tale is but begun. I do most strongly believe that this Tressilian has, from the beginning of his moving in her cause, been in connivance with her lady-ship the Countess. »

« Thou speak'st wild madness, Varney, with
the sober face of a preacher. Where , or how,
could they communicate together?»

« My lord , » said Varney, « unfortunately I can
shew that but too well. It was just before the supplication was presented to the Queen , in Tressilian's name, that I met him , to my utter astonishment, at the postern gate, which leads from
the demesne at Cumnor-Place. »

« Thou met'st him, villain! and why didst thou
not strike him dead?» exclaimed Leicester.

« I drew on him, my lord, and he on me; and
had not my foot slipped, he had not, perhaps,
been again a stumbling-block in your lordship's
path. »

Leicester seemed struck mute with surprise.
At length he answered, « What other evidence
hast thou of this, Varney, save thine own assertion?—for, as I will punish deeply, I will examine
coolly and warily. Sacred Heaven ! but no — I
will examine coldly and warily—coldly and warily. » He repeated these words more than once to
himself, as if in the very sound there was a seda-
tive quality ; and again compressing his lips, as if
he feared some violent expression might escape
from them, he asked again, « What farther
proof?»

« Enough , my lord, » said Varney, « and to
spare. I would it rested with me alone, for with
me it might have been silenced for ever. But
my servant, Michael Lambourne, witnessed the
whole, and was, indeed, the means of first intro-

ducing Tressilian into Cumnor-Place; and therefore I took him into my service, and retained him
in it, though something of a debauched fellow,
that I might have his tongue always under my
own command. » He then acquainted Lord Leicester how easy it was to prove the circumstance
of their interview true, by evidence of Anthony
Foster, with the corroborative testimonies of the
various persons at Cumnor, who had heard the
wager laid, and had seen Lambourne and Tressilian set off together. In the whole narrative, Varney hazarded nothing fabulous, excepting that,
not indeed by direct assertion, but by inference,
he led his patron to suppose that the interview
betwixt Amy and Tressilian at Cumnor-Place,
had been longer than the few minutes to which
it was in reality limited.

« And wherefore was I not told of all this? »
said Leicester, sternly. « Why did all of ye—and
in particular thou, Varney — keep back from
me such material information ? »

« Because, my lord , » replied Varney, « the
Countess pretended to Foster and to me, that
Tressilian had intruded himself upon her; and
I concluded their interview had been in all honour, and that she would at her own time tell it
to your lordship. Your lordship knows with what
unwilling ears we listen to evil surmises against
those whom we love; and I thank Heaven, I am
no make-bate or informer, to be the first to sow
them. »

« You are but too ready to receive them,

12*

however, Sir Richard, » replied his patron.
« How know'st thou that this interview was not
in all honour, as thou hast said ? Methinks the
wife of the Earl of Leicester might speak for a
short time with such a person as Tressilian,
without injury to me, or suspicion to herself. »

« Questionless, my lord, » answered Varney,
« had I thought otherwise, I had been no keeper
of the secret. But here lies the rub — Tressilian
leaves not the place without establishing a corre-
spondence with a poor man, the landlord of
an inn in Cumnor, for the purpose of carrying
off the lady. He sent down an *emissary of his*,
whom I trust soon to have in right sure keeping
under Mervyn's Tower. Killigrew and Lambsbey
are scouring the country in quest of him. The
host is rewarded with a ring for keeping counsel
— your lordship may have noted it on Tressilian's hand — here it is. This fellow, this agent,
makes his way to the Place as a pedlar, *holds*
conferences with the lady, and they *make their*
escape together by night — rob a *poor fellow*
of a horse by the way, such was their guilty
haste ; and at length reach this Castle, where
the Countess of Leicester finds refuge — I dare
not say in what place. »

« Speak, I command thee, » said Leicester ;
« speak, while I retain sense enough to hear
thee. »

« Since it must be so ; » answered Varney,
« the lady resorted immediately to the apartment of Tressilian, where she remained many

hours, partly in company with him, and partly alone. I told you Tressilian had a paramour in his chamber — I little dreamed that paramour was » ——

« Amy, thou would'st say, » answered Leicester; « but it is false, false as the smoke of hell ! Ambitious she may be — fickle and impatient — 'tis a woman's fault; but false to me! — never, never. — The proof — the proof of this ! » he exclaimed, hastily.

« Carrol, the Deputy Marshal, ushered her thither by her own desire, on yesterday afternoon — Lambourne and the Warder both found her there at an early hour this morning. »

« Was Tressilian there with her ? » said Leicester, in the same hurried tone.

« No, my lord. You may remember, » answered Varney, « that he was that night placed with Sir Nicholas Blount, under arrest. »

« Did Carrol, or the other fellows, know who she was? » demanded Leicester.

« No, my lord, » replied Varney; « Carrol and the Warder had never seen the Countess, and Lambourne knew her not in her disguise; but, in seeking to prevent her leaving the cell, he obtained possession of one of her gloves, which, I think, your lordship may know. »

He gave the glove, which had the Bear and Ragged Staff, the Earl's impress, embroidered upon it in seed-pearls.

« I do, I do recognize it, » said Leicester. « They were my own gift. The fellow of it was on the arm which she threw this very day around my neck! » — He spoke this with violent agitation.

« Your lordship, » said Varney, « might yet further inquire of the lady herself, respecting the truth of these passages. »

« It needs not — it needs not, » said the tortured Earl; « it is written in characters of burning light, as if they were branded on my very eyeballs! I see her infamy — I can see nought else; and, — gracious Heaven! — for this vile woman was I about to commit to danger the lives of so many noble friends — shake the foundation of a lawful throne — carry the sword and torch through the bosom of a peaceful land — wrong the kind mistress who made me what I am — and would, but for that hell-framed marriage, have made me all that man can be! All this I was ready to do for a woman, who trinkets and traffics with my worst foes! — And thou, villain, why didst thou not speak sooner? »

« My lord, » said Varney, « a tear from my lady would have blotted out all I could have said. Besides, I had not these proofs until this very morning, when Anthony Foster's sudden arrival, with the examinations and declarations, which he had extorted from the inn-keeper Gosling, and others, explained the manner of her flight from Cumnor-Place, and my own researches discovered the steps which she had taken here. »

«Now, may God be praised for the light he has given! so full, so satisfactory, that there breathes not a man in England who shall call my proceeding rash, or my revenge unjust.—And yet, Varney, so young, so fair, so fawning, and so false! Hence, then, her hatred to thee, my trusty, my well-beloved servant, because you withstood her plots, and endangered her paramour's life?»

»I never gave her any other cause of dislike, my lord,» replied Varney; «but she knew that my councils went directly to diminish her influence with your lordship; and that I was, and have been, ever ready to peril my life against your enemies.»

«It is too, too apparent,» replied Leicester; «yet, with what an air of magnanimity she exhorted me to commit my head to the Queen's mercy, rather than wear the veil of falsehood a moment longer! Methinks, the angel of truth himself can have no such tones of high-souled impulse. Can it be so, Varney?—Can falsehood use thus boldly the language of truth?—Can infamy thus assume the guise of purity?—Varney, thou hast been my servant from a child—I have raised thee high—I can raise thee higher. Think, think for me! Thy brain was ever shrewd and piercing—May she not be innocent? Prove her so, and all I have yet done for thee shall be as nothing — nothing — in comparison of thy recompence!»

The agony with which his master spoke, had

some effect even on the hardened Varney, who, in the midst of his own wicked and ambitious designs, really loved his patron as well as such a wretch was capable of loving any thing; but he comforted himself, and subdued his self-reproaches with the reflection, that if he inflicted upon the Earl some immediate and transitory pain, it was in order to pave his way to the throne, which, were this marriage dissolved by death or otherwise, he deemed Elizabeth would willingly share with his benefactor. He, therefore, persevered in his diabolical policy; and, after a moment's consideration, answered the anxious queries of the Earl with a melancholy look, as if he had in vain sought some exculpation for the Countess; then suddenly raising his head, he said, with an expression of hope, which instantly communicated itself to the countenance of his patron,— « Yet, wherefore, if guilty, should she have perilled herself by coming hither? Why not rather have fled to her father's, or elsewhere?— though that, indeed, might have interfered with her desire to be acknowledged as Countess of Leicester. »

« True, true, true! » exclaimed Leicester, his transient gleam of hope giving way to the utmost bitterness of feeling and expression; « thou art not fit to fathom a woman's depth of wit, Varney. I see it all. She would not quit the estate and title of the wittol who had wedded her. Ay, and if in my madness I had started into rebellion, or if the angry Queen had taken my head, as she

this morning threatened, the wealthy dower,
which law would have assigned to the Countess
Dowager of Leicester, had been no bad wind-fall
to the beggarly Tressilian. Well might she goad
me on to danger, which could not end otherwise
than profitable to her.—Speak not for her, Varney! I will have her blood!»

« My lord, » replied Varney, the wildness of
your distress breaks forth in the wildness of your
language. »

« I say, speak not for her, » replied Leicester;
« she has dishonoured me—she would have murthered me—all ties are burst between us. She
shall die the death of a traitress and adultress,
well merited both by the laws of God and man!
And—what is this casket, » he said, « which was
even now thrust into my hand by a boy, with the
desire I would convey it to Tressilian, as he
could not give it to the Countess? By Heaven!
the words surprised me as he spoke them, though
other matters chased them from my brain; but
now they return with double force.—It is her
casket of jewels!—Force it open, Varney; force
the hinges open with thy poniard. »

She refused the aid of my dagger once, thought
Varney, as he unsheathed the weapon, to cut the
string which bound a letter, but now it shall work
a mightier ministry in her fortunes.

With this reflection, by using the three-cor-
nered stiletto-blade as a wedge, he forced open the
slender silver hinges of the casket. The Earl no
sooner saw them give way, than he snatched

the casket from Sir Richard's hands, wrenched
off the cover, and tearing out the splendid contents, flung them on the floor in a transport of
rage, while he eagerly searched for some letter
or billet, which should make the fancied guilt
of his innocent Countess yet more apparent.
Then stamping furiously on the gems, he exclaimed, « Thus I annihilate the miserable toys
for which thou hast sold thyself, body and soul,
consigned thyself to an early and timeless death,
and me to misery and remorse for ever! — Tell
me not of forgiveness, Varney—She is doomed!»

So saying, he left the room, and rushed into
an adjacent closet, the door of which he locked
and bolted.

Varney looked after him, while something of
a more human feeling seemed to contend with
his habitual sneer. « I am sorry for his weakness,»
he said, « but love has made him a child. He
throws down and treads on these costly toys—
with the same vehemence would he dash to pieces
this frailest toy of all, of which he used to rave so
fondly. But that taste also will be forgotten, when
its object is no more. Well, he has no eye to
value things as they deserve, and that nature
has given to Varney. When Leicester shall be a
sovereign, he will think as little of the gales of
passion, through which he gained that royal
port, as ever did sailor in harbour, of the perils
of a voyage. But these tell-tale articles must
not remain here — they are rather too rich vails
for the drudges who dress the chamber.»

While Varney was employed in gathering together and putting them into a secret drawer of a cabinet that chanced to be open, he saw the door of Leicester's closet open, the tapestry pushed aside, and the Earl's face thrust out, but with eyes so dead, and lips and cheeks so bloodless and pale, that he started at the sudden change. No sooner did his eyes encounter the Earl's than the latter withdrew his head, and shut the door of the closet. This manœuvre Leicester repeated twice, without speaking a word, so that Varney began to doubt whether his brain was not actually affected by his mental agony. The third time, however, he beckoned, and Varney obeyed the signal. When he entered, he soon found his patron's perturbation was not caused by insanity, but by the fellness of purpose which he entertained, contending with various contrary passions. They passed a full hour in close consultation; after which the Earl of Leicester, with an incredible exertion, dressed himself, and went to attend his royal guest.

CHAPTER XXXVII.

You have displaced the mirth., broke the good meeting
With most admired disorder.

Macbeth.

It was afterwards remembered, that during the banquets and revels which occupied the remainder of this eventful day, the bearing of Leicester and of Varney were totally different from their usual demeanour. Sir Richard Varney had been held rather a man of council and of action, than a votary of pleasure. Business, whether civil or military, seemed always to be his proper sphere; and while in festivals and revels, although he well understood how to trick them up and present them, his own part was that of a mere spectator; or if he exercised his wit, it was in a rough, caustic, and severe manner, rather as if he scoffed at the exhibition and the guests, than shared the common pleasure.

But upon the present day his character seemed changed. He mixed among the younger courtiers and ladies, and appeared for the moment to be actuated by a spirit of light-hearted gaiety, which rendered him a match for the liveliest. Those who had looked upon him as a man given up to graver and more ambitious pursuits, a bitter sneerer and passer of sarcasms at the expense of those, who, taking life as they find it, were disposed to snatch at each pastime it presents, now perceived with astonishment that his wit could carry as smooth an edge as their own, his laugh be as lively, and his brow as unclouded. By what art of damnable hypocrisy he could draw this veil of gaiety over the black thoughts of one of the worst of human bosoms, must remain unintelligible to all but his compeers, if any such ever existed; but he was a man of extraordinary powers, and those powers were unhappily dedicated in all their energy to the very worst of purposes.

It was entirely different with Leicester. However habituated his mind usually was to play the part of a good courtier, and appear gay, assiduous, and free from all care but that of enhancing the pleasure of the moment, while his bosom internally throbbed with the pangs of unsatisfied ambition, jealousy, or resentment, his heart had now a yet more dreadful guest, whose workings could not be overshadowed or suppressed; and you might read in his vacant eye and troubled brow, that his thoughts were far absent from the scenes in which he was compelling himself to play a part. He looked, moved, and spoke, as if by a succession of continued efforts; and it seemed as if his will had in some degree lost the promptitude of command over the acute mind and goodly form of which it was

the regent. His actions and gestures, instead of
appearing the consequence of simple volition,
seemed, like those of an automaton, to wait the
revolution of some internal machinery ere they
could be performed; and his words fell from
him piece-meal, interrupted, as if he had first
to think what he was to say, then how it was
to be said, and as if, after all, it was only by
an effort of continued attention that he completed a sentence without forgetting both the
one and the other.

The singular effects which these distractions
of mind produced upon the behaviour and
conversation of the most accomplished courtier
of England, as they were visible to the lowest
and dullest menial who approached his person,
could not escape the notice of the most intelligent princess of the age. Nor is there the least
doubt, that the alternate negligence and irregularity of his manner, would have called down
Elizabeth's severe displeasure on the Earl of
Leicester, had it not occurred to her to account
for it, by supposing that the apprehension of
that displeasure which she had expressed towards
him with such vivacity that very morning, was
dwelling upon the spirits of her favourite, and,
spite of his efforts to the contrary, distracted
the usual graceful tenor of his mien, and the
charms of his conversation. When this idea,
so flattering to female vanity, had once obtained
possession of her mind, it proved a full and
satisfactory apology for the numerous errors

and mistakes of the Earl of Leicester; and the watchful circle around observed with astonishment, that instead of resenting his repeated negligence, and want of even ordinary attention, (although these were points on which she was usually extremely rigorous,) the Queen sought, on the contrary, to afford him time and means to recollect himself, and deigned to assist him in doing so, with an indulgence which seemed altogether inconsistent with her usual character. It was clear, however, that this could not last much longer, and that Elizabeth must finally put another and more severe construction on Leicester's uncourteous conduct, when the Earl was summoned by Varney to speak with him in a different apartment.

After having had the message twice delivered to him, he rose, and was about to withdraw, as it were, by instinct—then stopped, and turning round, entreated permission of the Queen to absent himself for a brief space upon matters of pressing importance.

« Go, my lord, » said the Queen ; « we are aware our presence must occasion sudden and unexpected occurrences, which require to be provided for on the instant. Yet, my lord, as you would have us believe ourself your welcome and honoured guest, we entreat you to think less of our good cheer, and favour us with more of your good countenance than we have this day enjoyed; for whether prince or peasant be the guest, the welcome of the host will always be the better part of the entertainment. Go, my lord; and we trust to see you return with an un-wrinkled brow, and those free thoughts which you are wont to have at the disposal of your friends. »

Leicester only bowed low in answer to this re-buke, and retired. At the door of the apartment he was met by Varney, who eagerly drew him apart and whispered in his ear, « All is well! »

« Has Masters seen her? « said the Earl.

« He has, my lord; and as she would neither answer his queries, nor allege any reason for her refusal, he will give full testimony that she la-bours under a mental disorder, and may be best committed to the charge of her friends. The op-portunity is therefore free, to remove her as we proposed. »

« But Tressilian? » said Leicester.

« He will not know of her departure for some time, » replied Varney; « it shall take place this very evening, and to-morrow he shall be cared for. »

« No, by my soul, » answered Leicester; « I will take vengeance on him with mine own hand! »

« You, my lord, and on so inconsiderable a man as Tressilian!—No, my lord, he hath long wish-ed to visit foreign parts. Let me care for him —I will take care he returns not hither to tell tales. »

« Not so, by Heaven, Varney! » exclaimed Lei-cester. — « Inconsiderable do you call an enemy, that hath had power to wound me so deeply, that my whole after life must be one scene of remorse and misery?—No; rather than forego the right of doing myself justice with my own hand on that accursed villain, I will unfold the whole truth at Elizabeth's footstool, and let her vengeance descend at once on them and on myself. »

Varney saw with great alarm that his lord was wrought up to such a pitch of agitation, that if he gave not way to him, he was perfectly capable of adopting the desperate resolution which he had announced, and which was instant ruin to all the schemes of ambition which Varney had formed for his patron and for himself. But the Earl's rage seemed at once uncontroulable and deeply concentrated; and while he spoke, his eyes shot fire, his voice trembled with excess of passion, and the light foam stood on his lip.

His confidant made a bold and successful effort to obtain the mastery of him even in this hour of emotion—« My lord, » he said, leading him to a mirror, « behold your reflection in that glass, and think if these agitated features belong to one who, in a condition so extreme, is capable of forming a resolution for himself. »

« What, then, would'st thou make me? » said Leicester, struck at the change in his own physiognomy, though offended at the freedom with which Varney made the appeal. « Am I to be thy ward, thy vassal,—the property and subject of my servant? »

« No, my lord, » said Varney, firmly, « but be master of yourself, and of your own passion. My lord, I, your born servant, am shamed to see how

poorly you bear yourself in the storm of fury.
Go to Elizabeth's feet, confess your marriage—
impeach your wife and her paramour of adulte-
ry—and avow yourself, amongst all your peers,
the wittol who married a country girl, and was
cozened by her and her book-learned gallant.—
Go, my lord—but first take farewell of Richard
Varney, with all the benefits you ever conferred
on him. He served the noble, the lofty, the high-
minded Leicester, and was more proud of de-
pending on him, than he would be of commanding thousands. But the abject lord who stoops
to every adverse circumstance, whose judicious
resolves are scattered like chaff before every
wind of passion, him Richard Varney serves not.
He is as much above him in constancy of mind,
as beneath him in rank and fortune. »

· Varney spoke thus without hypocrisy, for,
though the firmness of mind which he boasted
was hardness and impenetrability, yet he *really*
felt the ascendancy which he vaunted; while the
interest which he actually felt in the *fortunes* of
Leicester, gave unusual emotion to his voice and
manner.

Leicester was overpowered by his assumed superiority; it seemed to the unfortunate Earl as
if his last friend was about to abandon him. He
stretched his hand towards Varney, as he uttered
the words, « Do not leave me — What would'st
thou have me do ? »

« Be thyself, my noble master, » said Varney,
touching the Earl's hand with his lips, after ha-

ving respectfully grasped it in his own; « be yourself, superior to those storms of passion which wreck inferior minds. Are you the first who has been cozened in love? The first whom a vain and licentious woman has cheated into an affection, which she has afterwards scorned and misused? And will you suffer yourself to be driven frantic, because you have not been wiser than the wisest men whom the world has seen? Let her be as if she had not been — let her pass from your memory, as unworthy of ever having held a place there. Let your strong resolve of this morning, which I have both courage and zeal enough to execute, be like the fiat of a superior being, a passionless act of justice. She hath deserved death—let her die ! »

While he was speaking, the Earl held his hand fast, compressed his lips hard, and frowned, as if he laboured to catch from Varney a portion of the cold, ruthless, and dispassionate firmness which he recommanded. When he was silent, the Earl still continued to grasp his hand, until, with an effort at calm decision, he was able to articulate, « Be it so—she dies !—But one tear might be permitted. »

« Not one, my lord, » interrupted Varney, who saw by the quivering eye and convulsed cheek of his patron, that he was about to give way to a burst of emotion, — « Not a tear — the time permits it not— Tressilian must be thought of. »———

« That indeed is a name, » said the Earl, « to
convert tears into blood. Varney, I have thought
on this, and I have determined — neither en-
treaty nor argument shall move me—Tressilian
shall be my own victim. »

« It is madness, my lord; but you are too
mighty for me to bar your way to your revenge.
Yet resolve at least to chuse fitting time and opportunity, and to forbear him until those shall
be found. »

« Thou shalt order me in what thou *wilt*, »
said Leicester, « only thwart me not *in this*. »

« Then, my lord, » said Varney, « I first request of you to lay aside the wild, suspected,
and half-frenzied demeanour, which hath this
day drawn the eyes of all the court upon you;
and which, but for the Queen's partial indulgence, which she hath extended towards you
in a degree far beyond her nature, she had never given you the opportunity to atone for. »

« Have I indeed been so negligent ? » said Leicester, as one who awakes from a dream; « I
thought I had coloured it well; but fear nothing,
my mind is now eased — I am calm. My horoscope shall be fulfilled; and that it may be fulfilled, I will tax to the highest every faculty of
my mind. Fear me not, I say — I will to the
Queen instantly — not thine own looks and language shall be more impenetrable than mine. —
Hast thou aught else to say ? »

« I must crave your signet-ring, » said Varney,

gravely, «in token to those of your servants whom I must employ, that I possess your full authority in commanding their aid.»

Leicester drew off the signet-ring, which he commonly used, and gave it to Varney with a haggard and stern expression of countenance, adding only, in a low half-whispered tone, but with terrific emphasis, the words, «What thou doest, do quickly.»

Some anxiety and wonder took place, meanwhile, in the Presence-hall, at the prolonged absence of the noble Lord of the Castle, and great was the delight of his friends, when they saw him enter as a man, from whose bosom, to all human seeming, a weight of care had been just removed. Amply did Leicester that day redeem the pledge he had given to Varney, who soon saw himself no longer under the necessity of maintaining a character so different from his own, as that which he had assumed in the earlier part of the day, and gradually relapsed into the same grave, shrewd, caustic observer of conversation and incident, which constituted his usual part in society.

With Elizabeth, Leicester played his game as one, to whom her natural strength of talent, and her weakness in one or two particular points, were well known. He was too wary to exchange on a sudden, the sullen personage which he had played before he retired with Varney; but on approaching her, it seemed softened into a melancholy, which had a touch of tenderness in it,

and which, in the course of conversing with
Elizabeth, and as she dropped in compassion
one mark of favour after another to console him,
passed into a flow of affectionate gallantry, the
most assiduous, the most delicate, the most insinuating, yet at the same time the most respectful, with which a Queen was ever addressed
by a subject. Elizabeth listened, as in a sort of
enchantment; her jealousy of power was lulled
asleep; her resolution to forsake all social or
domestic ties, and dedicate herself *exclusively*
to the care of her people, began *to be shaken*,
and once more the star of Dudley culminated
in the court-horizon.

But Leicester did not enjoy this triumph over
nature, and over conscience, without its being
embittered to him, not only by the internal
rebellion of his feelings against the violence
which he exercised over them, but by many
accidental circumstances, which in the *course*
of the banquet, and during the subsequent amusements of the evening, jarred upon *that nerve*,
the least vibration of which was agony.

The courtiers were, for example, in the great
hall, after having left the banquetting-room,
awaiting the appearance of a splendid masque,
which was the expected entertainment of this
evening, when the Queen interrupted a wild
career of wit, which the Earl of Leicester was
running against Lord Willoughby, Raleigh, and
some other courtiers, by saying—« We will impeach you of high treason, my lord, if you pro-

ceed in this attempt to slay us with laughter. And here comes a thing may make us all grave at his pleasure, our learned physician Masters, with news belike of our poor suppliant, Lady Varney — nay, my lord, we will not have you leave us, for this being a dispute betwixt married persons, we do not hold our own experience deep enough to decide thereon, without good counsel—How now, Masters, what think'st thou of the run-away bride? »

The smile with which Leicester had been speaking, when the Queen interrupted him, remained arrested on his lips, as if it had been carved there by the chisel of Michael Angelo, or of Chauntry; and he listened to the speech of the physician, with the same immoveable cast of countenance.

« The Lady Varney, gracious Sovereign, » said Masters, « is sullen, and would hold little conference with me touching the state of her health, talking wildly of being soon to plead her own cause before your own presence, and of answering no meaner person's inquiries. »

« Now, the heavens forefend! » said the Queen; « we have already suffered from the misconstructions and broils which seem to follow this poor brain-sick lady wherever she comes.—Think you not so, my lord? » she added, appealing to Leicester, with something in her look that indicated regret, even tenderly expressed, for their disagreement of that morning. Leicester compelled himself to bow low. The utmost force he

could exert, was inadequate to the farther effort
of expressing in words his acquiescence in the
Queen's sentiment.

« You are vindictive,» she said, «my lord;
but we will find time and place to punish you.
But once more to this same trouble-mirth, this
Lady Varney—What of her health, Masters?»

« She is sullen, madam, as I already said,» replied Masters, «and refuses to answer interro-
gatories, or be amenable to the authority of the
mediciner. I conceive her to be possessed with
a delirium, which I incline to term rather *hypo-
chondria* than *phrenesis;* and I think she were
best cared for by her husband in his own house,
and removed from all this bustle of pageants,
which disturbs her weak brain with the most
fantastic phantoms. She drops hints as if she were
some great person in disguise—some Countess
or Princess perchance. Gold help them, such
are the hallucinations of these infirm persons.»

« Nay, then,» said the Queen, « away with her
with all speed. Let Varney care for her with fitting humanity; but let them rid the Castle of her
forthwith. She will think herself lady of all, I
warrant you. It is pity so fair a form, however,
should have an infirm understanding.—What
think you, my lord?»

« It is pity, indeed,» said the Earl, repeating
the words like a task which was set him.

« But perhaps, said Elizabeth, «you do not
join with us in our opinion of her beauty; and
indeed we have known men prefer a statelier and

more Juno-like form, to that drooping fragile
one, that hung its head like a broken lily. Ay,
men are tyrants, my lord, who esteem the ani-
mation of the strife above the triumph of an
unresisting conquest, and, like sturdy champions,
love best those women who can wage contest
with them. — I could think with you, Rutland,
that give my Lord of Leicester such a piece of
painted wax for a bride, he would have wished
her dead ere the end of the honey-moon. »

« As she said this, she looked on Leicester so
expressively, that, while his heart revolted against
the egregious falsehood, he did himself so much
violence as to reply in a whisper, that Leicester's
love was more lowly than her Majesty deemed,
since it was settled where he could never command, but must ever obey.

The Queen blushed, and bid him be silent;
yet looked as if she expected that he would not
obey her commands. But at that moment the
flourish of trumpets and kettle-drums from a
high balcony which overlooked the hall, announced the entrance of the masquers, and relieved Leicester from the horrible state of con-
straint and dissimulation in which the result of
his own duplicity had placed him.

The masque which entered consisted of four
separate bands, which followed each other at
brief intervals, each consisting of six principal
persons and as many torch-bearers, and each
representing one of the various nations by which
England had at different times been occupied.

The aboriginal Britons, who first entered were
ushered in by two ancient Druids, whose hoary
hair was crowned with a chaplet of oak, and who
bore in their hands branches of mistletoe. The
masquers who followed these venerable figures
were succeeded by two Bards, arrayed in white,
and bearing harps, which they occasionally touched, singing at the same time certain stanzas of an
ancient hymn to Belus, or the Sun. The aboriginal Britons had been selected from amongst the
tallest and most robust young gentlemen in attendance on the court. Their masks were accommodated with long shaggy beards and hair; their
vestments were of the hides of wolves and bears;
while their legs, arms, and the upper parts of
their bodies, being sheathed in flesh-coloured
silk, on which were traced in grotesque lines
representations of the heavenly bodies, and of
animals and other terrestrial objects, gave them
the lively appearance of our painted ancestors,
whose freedom was first trenched upon by the
Romans.

The sons of Rome, who came to civilize as
well as to conquer, were next produced before
the princely assembly; and the manager of the
revels had correctly imitated the high crest and
military habits of that celebrated people, ac-
commodating them with the light yet strong
buckler, and the short two-edged sword, the use
of which had made them victors of the world.
The Roman eagles were borne before them by
two standard-bearers, who recited a hymn to

Mars, and the classical warriors followed with
the grave and haughty step of men who aspired
at universal conquest.

The third quadrille represented the Saxons,
clad in the bear-skins which they had brought
with them from the German forests, and bearing
in their hands the redoutable battle-axes which
made such havoc among the natives of Britain.
They were preceded by two Scalds, who chaunt-
ed the praises of Odin.

Last came the knightly Normans, in their
mail shirts and hoods of steel, with all the panoply of chivalry, and marshalled with two Minstrels, who sung of war and ladies' love.

These four bands entered the spacious hall
with the utmost order, a short pause being made, .
that the spectators might satisfy their curiosity
as to each quadrille before the appearance of
the next. They then marched completely round
the hall, in order the more fully to display themselves, and at length ranging their torch-bearers
behind them, drew up in their several ranks, on
the two opposite sides of the hall, so that the
Romans confronting the Britons, and the Saxons
the Normans, seemed to look on each other with
eyes of wonder, which presently appeared to
kindle into anger, expressed by menacing gestures. At the burst of a strain of martial music
from the gallery, the masquers drew their swords
on all sides, and advanced against each other in
the measured steps of a sort of Pyrrhic or military dance, clashing their swords against their

13*

adversaries' shields, and clattering them against
their blades as they past each other in the progress of the dance. It was a very pleasant spectacle to see how the various bands, preserving
regularity amid motions which seemed to be totally irregular, mixed together, and then disengaging themselves, resumed each their own original rank as the music varied.

In this symbolical dance was represented the
conflicts which had taken place among the various nations which had anciently inhabited Bri-
·tain.

At length, after many mazy *evolutions*, which
afforded great pleasure to the spectators, the
sound of a loud-voiced trumpet was heard, as if
it blew for instant battle, or for victory won. The
masquers instantly ceased their mimic strife, and
collecting themselves under their original leader, or presenters, for such was the appropriate
phrase, seemed to share the anxious expectation
which the spectators experienced concerning
what was next to appear.

The doors of the hall were thrown wide, and
no less a person entered than the fiend-born
Merlin, dressed in a strange and mystical attire,
suited to his ambiguous birth and magical power.
About him and behind him fluttered or gambol-
led many extraordinary forms, intended to represent the spirits who waited to do his powerful
bidding; and so much did this part of the pageant interest the menials and others of the lowel
class then in the Castle, that many of them for-

got even the reverence due to the Queen's presence, so far as to thrust themselves into the lower part of the hall.

The Earl of Leicester, seeing his officers had some difficulty to repel these intruders, without more disturbance than was fitting where the Queen was in presence, arose and went himself to the bottom of the hall ; Elizabeth at the same time, with her usual feeling for the common people, requesting that they might be permitted to remain undisturbed to witness the pageant. Leicester went under this pretext; but his real motive was to gain a moment to himself, and to relieve his mind, were it but for one instant, from the dreadful task of hiding, under the guise of gaiety and gallantry, the lacerating pangs of shame, anger, remorse, and thirst for vengeance. He imposed silence by his look and sign upon the vulgar crowd, at the lower end of the apartment; but, instead of instantly returning to wait on her Majesty, he wrapped his cloak around him, and mixing with the crowd, stood in some degree an undistinguished spectator of the progress of the masque.

Merlin having entered and advanced into the midst of the hall, summoned the presenters of the contending bands around him by a wave of his magical rod, and announced to them, in a poetical speech, that the Isle of Britain was now commanded by a Royal Maiden, to whom it was the will of fate that they should all do homage, and request of her to pronounce on the various pretensions which each set forth to be esteemed the pre-eminent stock, from which the present natives, the happy subjects of that angelical Princess, derived their lineage.

In obedience to this mandate, the bands, each moving to solemn music, passed in succession before Elizabeth; doing her as they passed, each after the fashion of the people whom they represented, the lowest and most devotional homage, which she returned with the same gracious courtesy that had marked her whole conduct since she came to Kenilworth.

The presenters of the several masques, or quadrilles, then *alleged*, each in behalf of his own troop, the reasons which they had for claiming pre-eminence over the rest; and when they had been all heard in turn, she returned them this gracious answer : « That she was sorry she was not better qualified to decide upon the doubtful question which had been propounded to her by the direction of the famous Merlin, but that it seemed to her that no single one of these celebrated nations could claim pre-eminence over the others, as having most contributed to form the Englishman of her own time, who seemed to her to derive from each of them some worthy attribute of his character. Thus, she said, « the Englishman had from the ancient Briton his bold and tameless spirit of freedom, — from the Roman his disciplined courage in war, with his love of letters and civilization in time of peace, — from the Saxon his wise and equitable laws, —

and from the chivalrous Norman his love of honour and courtesy, with his generous desire for glory. »

Merlin answered with readiness, that it did indeed require that so many choice qualities should meet in the English, as might render them in some measure the muster of the perfections of other nations, since that alone could render them in some degree deserving of the blessings they enjoyed under the reign of England's Elizabeth.

The music then sounded, and the quadrilles, together with Merlin and his assistants, had begun to remove from the crowded hall, when Leicester, who was, as we have mentioned, stationed for the moment near the bottom of the hall, and consequently engaged in some degree in the crowd, felt himself pulled by the cloak, while a voice whispered in his ear, « I do desire some instant conference with you. »

CHAPTER XXXVIII.

« How is't with me, when every noise appals me?»
MACBETH.

« I DESIRE some conference with you. » The words were simple in themselves, but *Lord Leicester* was in that alarmed and *feverish* state of mind, when the most ordinary occurrences seem fraught with alarming import; and he turned hastily round to survey the person by whom they had been spoken. There was nothing remarkable in the speaker's appearance, which consisted of a black silk doublet and short mantle, with a black vizard on his face; for it appeared he had been among the crowd of masks who had thronged into the hall in the retinue *of Merlin*, though he did not wear any of the extravagant disguises by which most of them were distinguished.

« Who are you, or what do you want with me? » said Leicester, not without betraying, by his accents, the hurried state of his spirits.

« No evil, my lord, » answered the mask, « but much good and honour, if you will rightly understand my purpose. But I must speak with you more privately. »

« I can speak with no nameless stranger, » answered Leicester, dreading he knew not precisely what from the request of the stranger; « and those who are known to me, must seek another and a fitter time to ask an interview. »

He would have hurried away, but the mask still detained him.

« Those who talk to your lordship of what your own honour demands, have a right over your time, whatever occupations you may lay aside in order to indulge them. »

« How! my honour? Who dare impeach it? » said Leicester.

« Your own conduct alone can furnish grounds for accusing it, my lord, and it is that topic on which I would speak with you. »

« You are insolent, » said Leicester, « and abuse the hospitable licence of the time, which prevents me from having you punished. I demand your name? »

« Edmund Tressilian of Cornwall, » answered the mask. « My tongue has been bound by a promise for four-and-twenty hours, — the space is passed, — I now speak, and do your lordship the justice to address myself first to you. »

The thrill of astonishment which had penetrated to Leicester's very heart at hearing that name pronounced by the voice of the man he most detested, and by whom he conceived himself so deeply injured, at first rendered him immoveable, but instantly gave way to such a thirst for revenge as the pilgrim in the desart feels for the water-brooks. He had but sense and self-government enough left to prevent his stabbing to the heart the audacious villain, who, after the ruin he had brought upon him, dared, with such unmoved assurance, thus to practise upon him farther. Determined to suppress for the moment every symptom of agitation, in order to perceive the full scope of Tressilian's purpose, as well as to secure his own vengeance, he answered in a tone so altered by restrained passion as scarce to be intelligible, — « And what does Master Edmund Tressilian require at my hand ? »

« Justice, my lord, » answered Tressilian, calmly but firmly.

« Justice, » said Leicester, « all men are entitled to — You, Master Tressilian, are peculiarly so, and be assured you shall have it. »

« I expect nothing less from your nobleness, » answered Tressilian; « but time presses, and I must speak with you to-night—May I wait on you in your chamber ? »

« No, » answered Leicester, sternly, « not under a roof, and that roof mine own —We will meet under the free cope of heaven. »

« You are discomposed or displeased, my lord, » replied Tressilian; « yet there is no occasion for distemperature. The place is equal to me, so you allow me one half hour of your time uninterrupted. »

« A shorter time will, I trust, suffice, » answered Leicester —« Meet me in the Pleasance, when the Queen has retired to her chamber. »

« Enough, » said Tressilian, and withdrew; while a sort of rapture seemed for the moment to occupy the mind of Leicester.

« Heaven, » he said, « is at last favourable to me, and has put within my reach the wretch who has branded me with this deep ignominy — who has inflicted on me this cruel agony. I will blame fate no more, since I am afforded the means of tracing the wiles by which he means still farther to practise on me, and then of at once convicting and punishing his villainy. To my task — to my task! — I will not sink under it now, since midnight, at farthest, will bring me vengeance. »

While these reflections thronged through Leicester's mind, he again made his way amid the obsequious crowd, which divided to give him passage, and resumed his place, envied and admired, beside the person of his Sovereign. But, could the bosom of him whom they universally envied, have been laid open before the inhabitants of that crowded hall, with all its dark thoughts of guilty ambition, blighted affection, deep vengeance, and conscious sense of meditated cruelty, crossing each other like spectres in the circle of some foul enchantress; which of them, from the most ambitious noble in the courtly circle, down to the most wretched menial, who lived by shifting of trenchers, would have desired to change characters with the favourite of Elizabeth , and the Lord of Kenilworth!

New tortures awaited him as soon as he had rejoined Elizabeth.

« You come in time, my lord, » she said, « to decide a dispute between us ladies. Here has Sir Richard Varney asked our permission to depart from the Castle with his infirm lady, having, as he tells us, your lordship's consent to his absence, so he can obtain ours. Certes, we have no will to withhold him from the affectionate charge of this poor young person—but you are to know, that Sir Richard Varney hath this day shewn *himself* so much captivated with these ladies of ours , that here is our Duchess of Rutland says, he will carry his poor insane wife no farther than the lake, plunge her in, to tenant the crystal palaces that the enchanted nymph told us of, and return a jolly widower, to dry his tears, and to make up the loss among our train. How say you , my lord?—We have seen Varney under two or three different guises — you know what are his proper attributes — think you he is capable of playing his lady such a knave's trick ? »

Leicester was confounded, but the danger was urgent, and a reply absolutely necessary. « The ladies, » he said, « think too lightly of one of their own sex, in supposing she could deserve such a fate, or too ill of ours; to think it could be inflicted otherwise. »

« Hear him, my ladies, » said Elizabeth; « like all his sex he would excuse their cruelty by imputing fickleness to us. »

« Say not *us*, madam, » replied the Earl; « we say that meaner women, like the lesser lights of heaven, have revolutions and phases, but who shall impute mutability to the sun, or to Elizabeth? »

The discourse presently afterwards assumed a less perilous tendency, and Leicester continued to support his part in it with spirit, at whatever expense of mental agony. So pleasing did it seem to Elizabeth, that the castle-bell had sounded midnight ere she retired from the company, a circumstance unusual in her quiet and regular habits of disposing of time. Her departure was of course the signal for breaking up the company, who dispersed to their several places of repose, to dream over the pastimes of the day, or to anticipate those of the morrow.

The unfortunate Lord of the Castle, and founder of the proud festival, retired to far different thoughts. His direction to the valet who attended him, was to send Varney instantly to his apartment. The messenger returned after some delay, and informed him that an hour had elapsed since Sir Richard Varney had left the Castle, by the postern-gate, with three other persons, one of whom was transported in a horse-litter. »

« How came he to leave the Castle after the watch was set? » said Leicester; « I thought he went not till day-break. »

« He gave satisfactory reasons, as I understand, » said the domestic, « to the guard, and, as
I hear, shewed your lordship's signet »——

« True — true, » said the Earl; « yet he has
been hasty — Do any of his attendants remain
behind ? »

« Michael Lambourne, my lord, » said the valet, » was not to be found when Sir Richard Varney departed, and his master was much incensed at his absence. I saw him but now saddling
his horse to gallop after his master. »

« Bid him come hither instantly, » said Leicester; « I have a message to his master. »

The servant left the apartment, and Leicester
traversed it for some time in deep meditation —
.« Varney is over zealous, » he said, « over pressing — He loves me, I think — but he hath his
own ends to serve, and he is inexorable in pursuit of them. If I rise he rises, and he hath
shewn himself already but too eager to rid me
of this obstacle which seems to stand betwixt
me and sovereignty. Yet I will not stoop to bear
this disgrace. She shall be punished, but it
shall be more advisedly. I already feel, even in
anticipation, that over-haste would light the
flames of hell in my bosom. No — one victim
is enough at once, and that victim already waits
me. »

He seized upon writing materials, and hastily
traced these words :— « Sir Richard Varney, we
have resolved to defer the matter entrusted to
your care, and strictly command you to proceed

no farther in relation to our Countess, until our further order. We also command your instant return to Kenilworth, as soon as you have safely bestowed that with which you are entrusted. But if the safe-placing of your present charge shall detain you longer than we think for, we command you, in that case, to send back our signet-ring by a trusty and speedy messenger, we having present need of the same. And requiring your strict obedience in these things, and commending you to God's keeping, we rest your assured good friend and master,

R. Leicester.

Given at our Castle of Kenilworth, the tenth of July, in the year of Salvation one thousand five hundred and seventy-five. »

As Leicester had finished and sealed this mandate, Michael Lambourne, booted up to mid thigh, having his riding-cloak girthed around him with a broad belt, and a felt-cap on his head, like that of a courier, entered his apartment, ushered in by the valet.

« What is thy capacity of service? » said the Earl.

« Equerry to your lordship's master of the horse, » answered Lambourne, with his customary assurance.

« Tie up thy saucy tongue, sir, » said Leicester; « the jests that may suit Sir Richard Varney's presence, suit not mine. How soon wilt thou overtake thy master? »

« In one hour's riding, my lord, if man and

horse hold good, » said Lambourne, with an instant alteration of demeanour, from an approach to familiarity to the deepest respect. The Earl measured him with his eye from top to toe.

« I have heard of thee, » he said; « men say thou art a prompt fellow in thy service, but too much given to brawling and to wassail to be trusted with things of moment. »

« My lord, » said Lambourne, « I have been soldier, sailor, traveller, and adventurer; and these are all trades in which men enjoy to-day, because they have no surety of to-morrow. But though I may misuse mine own leisure, I have never neglected the duty I owe my master. »

« See that it be so in this instance, » said Leicester, « and it shall do thee good. Deliver this letter speedily and carefully into Sir Richard Varney's hands. »

« Does my commission reach no farther? » said Lambourne.

« No, » answered Leicester, « but it deeply concerns me that it be carefully as well as hastily executed. »

« I will spare neither care nor horse-flesh, » answered Lambourne, and immediately took his leave. « So, this is the end of my private audience, from which I hoped so much, » he muttered to himself, as he went through the long gallery, and down the back stair-case. « Cogsbones! I thought the Earl had wanted a cast of mine office in some secret intrigue, and it all ends in carrying a letter! Well, his pleasure shall be

done, however, and as his lordship well says,
it may do me good another time. The child must
creep ere he walk, and so must your infant courtier. I will have a look into this letter, however,
which he hath sealed so sloven-like. » — Having
accomplished this, he clapped his hands together
in ecstacy, exclaiming, « The Countess — the
Countess! — I have the secret that shall make
or mar me.—But come forth, Bayard, » he added, leading his horse into the court-yard, « for
your flanks and my spurs must be presently acquainted. »

Lambourne mounted, accordingly, and left
the Castle by the postern-gate, where his free
passage was permitted, in consequence of a
message to that effect left by Sir Richard Varney.

As soon as Lambourne and the valet had left
the apartment, Leicester proceeded to change
his dress for a very plain one, threw his mantle around him, and taking a lamp in his hand,
went by the private passage of communication
to a small secret postern-door which opened
into the court-yard, near to the entrance of the
Pleasance. His reflections were of a more calm
and determined character than they had been at
any late period, and he endeavoured to claim,
even in his own eyes, the character of a man
more sinned against than sinning.

I have suffered the deepest injury, » such
was the tenor of his meditations, « yet I have
restricted the instant revenge which was in my

power, and have limited it to that which is manly and noble. But shall the union which this
false woman has this day disgraced, remain an
abiding fetter on me, to check me in the noble
career to which my destinies invite me? No —
there are other means of disengaging such ties,
without unloosing the cords of life. In the sight
of God, I am no longer bound by the union she
has broken. Kingdoms shall divide us — oceans
roll betwixt us, and their waves, whose abysses
have swallowed whole navies, shall be the sole
depositaries of the deadly mystery. »

By such a train of argument did Leicester
labour to reconcile his conscience to the prosecution of plans of vengeance, so hastily adopted, and of schemes of ambition, which had
become so woven in with every purpose and
action of his life, that he was incapable of the
effort of relinquishing them; until his revenge
appeared to him to wear a face of justice, and
even of generous moderation.

In this mood, the vindictive and ambitious
Earl entered the superb precincts of the Pleasance, then illumined by the full moon. The
broad yellow light was reflected on all sides from
the white freestone, of which the pavement,
balustrades, and architectural ornaments of the
place were constructed; and not a single fleecy
cloud was visible in the azure sky, so that the
scene was nearly as light as if the sun had but just
left the horizon. The numerous statues of white
marble glimmered in the pale light, like so

many sheeted ghosts just arisen from their sepulchres, and the fountains threw their jets into the air, as if they sought that their waters should be silvered by the moon-beams, ere they fell down again upon their basins in showers of sparkling silver. The day had been sultry, and the gentle night-breeze, which sighed along the terrace of the Pleasance, raised not a deeper breath than the fan in the hand of youthful beauty. The bird of summer night had built many a nest in the bowers of the adjacent garden, and the tenants now indemnified themselves for silence during the day, by a full chorus of their own unrivalled warblings, now joyous, now pathetic, now united, now responsive to each other, as if to express their delight in the placid and delicious scene to which they poured their melody.

Musing on matters far different from the fall of waters, the gleam of moon-light, or the song of the nightingale, the stately Leicester walked slowly from the one end of the terrace to the other, his cloak wrapped around him, and his sword under his arm, without seeing any thing resembling the human form.

« I have been fooled by my own generosity, » he said, « if I have suffered the villain to escape me — ay, and perhaps to go to the rescue of the Adultress, who is so poorly guarded. »

These were his thoughts, which were instantly dispelled, when, turning to look back towards the entrance, he saw a human form advancing slowly from the portico, and darkening the various objects with its shadow, as passing them successively, in its approach towards him.

« Shall I strike, ere I again hear his detested voice ? » was Leicester's thought, as he grasped the hilt of his sword. « But no ! I will see which way his vile practice tends. I will watch, disgusting as it is, the coils and mazes of the loathsome snake, ere I put forth my strength and crush him. »

His hand quitted the sword-hilt, and he advanced slowly towards Tressilian, collecting, for their meeting, all the self-possession he could command, until they came front to front with each other.

Tressilian made a profound reverence, to which the Earl replied with a haughty inclination of the head, and the words, « You sought secret conference with me, sir — I am here, and attentive. »

« My lord, » said Tressilian, « I am so earnest in that which I have to say, and so desirous to find a patient, nay, a favourable hearing, that I will stoop to exculpate myself from whatever might prejudice your lordship against me. You think me your enemy ? »

« Have I not some apparent cause ? » answered Leicester, perceiving that Tressilian paused for a reply.

« You do me wrong, my lord. I am a friend, but neither a dependant nor partisan of the Earl of Sussex, whom courtiers call your rival; and it is some considerable time since I ceased to consider either courts, or court-intrigues, as suited to my temper or genius. »

«No doubt, sir, » answered Leicester; «there are other occupations more worthy a scholar, and for such the world holds Master Tressilian — Love has his intrigues as well as Ambition. »

« I perceive, my lord, » replied Tressilian, « you give much weight to my early attachment for the unfortunate young person of whom I am about to speak, and perhaps think I am prosecuting her cause out of rivalry, more than a sense of justice. »

« No matter for my thoughts, sir, » said the Earl; « proceed. You have as yet spoken of yourself only; an important and worthy subject doubtless, but which, perhaps, does not altogether so deeply concern me, that I should postpone my repose to hear it. Spare me farther prelude, sir, and speak to the purpose, if indeed you have aught to say that concerns me. When you have done, I, in my turn, have something to communicate. »

« I will speak, then, without farther prelude, my lord, » answered Tressilian; «having to say that which, as it concerns your lordship's honour, I am confident you will not think your time wasted in listening to. I have to request an account from your lordship of the unhappy Amy Robsart, whose history is too well known to you. I regret deeply that I did not at once take this course, and make yourself judge be-

tween me and the villain by whom she is injured.
My lord, she extricated herself from an unlaw-
ful and most perilous state of confinement, trusting to the effects of her own remonstrance upon
her unworthy husband, and extorted from me
a promise, that I would not interfere in her behalf until she had used her own efforts to have
her rights acknowledged by him. »

« Ha ! » said Leicester, « remember you to
whom you speak ? »

« I speak of her unworthy husband, my lord, »
repeated Tressilian, « and my respect can find no
softer language. The unhappy young woman is
withdrawn from my knowledge, and sequestered
in some secret place of this Castle ;—if she be not
transferred to some place of seclusion better fitted for bad designs. This must be reformed,
my lord, —I speak it as authorized by her father,—and this ill-fated marriage must be avouch-
ed and proved in the Queen's presence, and the
lady placed without restraint, and at her own
free disposal. And, permit me to say, it concerns
no one's honour that these most just demands
of mine should be complied with, so much as
it does that of your lordship. »

The Earl stood as if he had been petrified, at
the extreme coolness with which the man, whom
he considered as having injured him so deeply,
pleaded the cause of his criminal paramour, as
if she had been an innocent woman, and he a
disinterested advocate ; nor was his wonder les-
sened by the warmth with which Tressilian seem-

ed to demand for her the rank and situation which she had disgraced, and the advantages of which she was doubtless to share with the lover who advocated her cause with such effrontery. Tressilian had been silent for more than a minute ere the Earl recovered from the excess of his astonishment; and, considering the prepossessions with which his mind was occupied, there is little wonder that his passion gained the mastery of every other consideration. « I have heard you, Master Tressilian, » said he, « without interruption, and I bless God that my ears were never before made to tingle by the words of so frontless a villain. The task of chastising you is fitter for the hangman's scourge than the sword of a nobleman, but yet—— Villain, draw and defend thyself! »

As he spoke the last words, he dropped his mantle on the ground, struck Tressilian smartly with his sheathed sword, and instantly drawing his rapier, put himself into a posture of assault. The vehement fury of his language at first filled Tressilian, in his turn, with surprise equal to what Leicester had felt when he addressed him. But astonishment gave rise to resentment, when the unmerited insults of his language were followed by a blow, which immediately put to flight every thought save that of instant combat. Tressilian's sword was instantly drawn, and though perhaps somewhat inferior to Leicester in the use of the weapon, he understood it well enough to maintain the contest with great spirit, the rather that of the two he was for the time the more cool, since he could not help imputing Leicester's conduct either to actual frenzy, or to the influence of some strong delusion.

The rencontre had continued for several minutes, without either party receiving a wound, when of a sudden, voices were heard beneath the portico, which formed the entrance of the terrace, mingled with the steps of men advancing hastily. « We are interrupted , » said Leicester to his antagonist ; « follow me. »

At the same time a voice from the portico said, » The jackanape is right — they are tilting here. »

Leicester, meanwhile, drew off Tressilian into a sort of recess behind one of the fountains, which served to conceal them , while six of the yeomen of the Queen's guard passed along the middle walk of the Pleasance, and they could hear one say to the rest, » We will never find them to-night amongst all these squirting funnels, squirrel-cages, and rabbit-holes; but if we light not on them before we reach the farther end , we will return , and mount a guard at the entrance, and so secure them till morning. »

« A proper matter, » said another, « the drawing of swords so near the Queen's presence, ay, and in her very Palace as 'twere ! — Hang it, they must be some poor drunken game - cocks fallen to sparring—'twere pity almost we should find them — the penalty is chopping off a hand,

is it not? — 'twere hard to lose hand for hand-
ling a bit of steel, that comes so natural to one's
gripe. »

« Thou art a brawler thyself, George, » said
another; « but take heed, for the law stands as
thou say'st. »

« Ay, » said the first, « an the act be not mildly construed; for thou know'st 'tis not the Queen's
Palace, but my Lord of Leicester's.»

« Why, for that matter, the penalty may be
as severe, » said another; « for an our gracious
Mistress be Queen, as she is, God save her, my
Lord of Leicester is as good as King. »

« Hush! thou knave! » said a third; » how
know'st thou who may be within hearing? »

They passed on, making a kind of careless
search, but seemingly more intent on their
own conversation than bent on discovering the
persons who had created the nocturnal disturbance.

They had no sooner passed forward along the
terrace, than Leicester, making a sign to Tressilian to follow him, glided away in an opposite
direction, and escaped through the portico un-
discovered. He conducted Tressilian to Mervyn's Tower, in which he was now again lodged; and then, ere parting with him, said these
words, « If thou hast courage to continue and
bring to an end what is thus broken off, be near
me when the court goes forth to-morrow — we
shall find a time, and I will give you a signal when
it is fitting. »

« My lord, » said Tressilian, « at another time I might have inquired the meaning of this strange and furious inveteracy against me. But you have laid that on my shoulder, which only blood can wash away; and were you as high as your proudest wishes ever carried you, I would have from you satisfaction for my wounded honour. »

On these terms they parted, but the adventures of the night were not yet ended with Leicester. He was compelled to pass by Saintlowe's Tower, in order to gain the private passage which led to his own chamber, and in the entrance thereof he met Lord Hunsdon half-clothed, and with a naked sword under his arm.

« Are you awakened too, with this 'larum, my Lord of Leicester? » said the old soldier. « 'Tis well — By gog's-nails, the nights are as noisy as the days in this Castle of yours. Some two hours since, I was waked by the screams of that poor brain-sick Lady Varney, whom her husband was forcing away. I promise you, it required both your warrant and the Queen's, to keep me from entering into the game, and cutting that Varney of your's over the head; and now there is a brawl down in the Pleasance, or what call you the stone terrace walk, where all yonder gimcracks stand? »

The first part of the old man's speech went through the Earl's heart like a knife; to the last he answered that he himself had heard the clash of swords, and had come down to take order with those who had been so insolent so near the Queen's presence.

« Nay then, » said Hunsdon, « I will be glad of your lordship's company. »

Leicester was thus compelled to turn back with the rough old Lord to the Pleasance, where Hunsdon heard from the yeomen of the guard, who were under his immediate command, the unsuccessful search they had made for the authors of the disturbance; and bestowed for their pains some round dozen of curses on them, as lazy knaves and blind whoresons. Leicester also thought it necessary to seem angry that no discovery had been effected; but at length suggested to Lord Hunsdon, that after all it could only be some foolish young men, who had been drinking healths pottle-deep, and who would be sufficiently scared by the search which had taken place after them. Hunsdon, who was himself attached to his cup, allowed that a pint-flagon might cover many of the follies which it had caused. « But, » added he, « unless your lordship will be less liberal in your house-keeping, and restrain the overflow of ale, and wine, and wassail, I foresee it will end in my having some of these good fellows into the guard-house, and treating them to a doze of the strappadoe — And with this warning, good night to you. »

Joyful at being rid of his company, Leicester took leave of him at the entrance of his lodging,

14*

where they had first met, and entering the private passage, took up the lamp which he had left there, and by its expiring light found the way to his own apartment.

●●●

CHAPTER XXXIX.

Room! room! for my horse will wince
If he come within so many yards of a prince;
For to tell you true, and in rhyme,
He was foal'd in Queen Elizabeth's time;
When the great Earl of Lester
In his castle did feast her.
Masque of Owls.—BEN JONSON.

THE amusement with which Elizabeth and
her court were next day to be regaled, was an
exhibition by the true-hearted men of Coventry,
who were to represent the strife between the
English and the Danes, agreeably to a custom
long preserved in their ancient borough, and
warranted for truth by old histories and chro-
nicles. In this pageant, one party of the town's
folks presented the Saxons and the other the
Danes, and set forth both in rude rhymes and
with hard blows, the contentions of these two
fierce nations, and the Amazonian courage of
the English women, who, according to the
story, were the principal agents in the general
massacre of the Danes, which took place at
Hock-tide, in the year of God 1012. This sport,
which had been long a favourite pastime with
the men of Coventry, had, it seems, been put

down by the influence of some zealous clergy-
men, of the more precise cast, who chanced
to have considerable influence with the magis-
trates. But the generality of the inhabitants had
petitioned the Queen that they might have their
play again, and be honoured with permission
to represent it before her Highness. And when
the matter was canvassed in the little council,
which usually attended the Queen for dispatch
of business, the proposal, although opposed by
some of the stricter sort, found favour in the
eyes of Elizabeth, who said that such toys occupied, without offence, the minds of many,
who, lacking them, might find worse subjects
of pastime; and that their pastors, however
commendable for learning and godliness, were
somewhat too sour in preaching against the
pastimes of their flocks, and so the pageant was
permitted to proceed. .

Accordingly, after a morning repast, which
Master Laneham calls an ambrosial breakfast,
the principal persons of the court, in attendance
upon her Majesty, pressed to the Gallery-tower,
to witness the approach of the two contending
parties of English and Danes; and after a signal
had been given, the gate which opened in the
circuit of the Chase was thrown wide, to admit
them. On they came foot and horse; for some
of the more ambitious burghers and yeomen had
put themselves into fantastic dresses, resembling
knights, in order to resemble the chivalry of the
two different nations. However, to prevent fa-

tal accidents, they were not permitted to appear
on real horses, but had only license to accoutre
themselves with those hobby-horses, as they are
called, which anciently formed the chief delight
of a morrice-dance, and which still are exhibited
on the stage, in the grand battle fought at the
conclusion of Mr Bayes's tragedy. The infantry
followed in similar disguises. The whole exhibition was to be considered as a sort of anti-masque,
or burlesque of the more stately pageants, in
which the nobility and gentry bore part in the
show, and, to the best of their knowledge, imitated with accuracy the personages whom they
represented. The Hocktide play was of a different
character, the actors being persons of inferior
degree, and their habits the better fitted for the
occasion, the more incongruous and ridiculous
that they were in themselves. Accordingly their
array, which the progress of our tale allows us no
time to describe, was ludicrous enough, and
their weapons, though formidable enough to
deal sound blows, were long alder-poles instead
of lances, and sound cudgels for swords; and for
fence, both cavalry and infantry were well equipped with stout head-pieces, and targets of thick
leather.

Captain Coxe, that celebrated humourist of
Coventry, whose library of ballads, almanacks,
and penny histories, fairly wrapped up in parch-
ment, and tied round for security with a piece
of whipcord, remains still the envy of antiquaries, being himself the ingenious person under

whose direction the pageant had been set forth,
rode valiantly on his hobby-horse before the
bands of English, high-trussed, saith Laneham,
and brandishing his long sword, as became an
experienced man of war, who had fought under
the Queen's father, bluff King Henry, at the
siege of Boulogne. This chieftain was, as right
and reason craved, the first to enter the lists,
and, passing the Gallery at the head of his myr-
midons, kissed the hilt of his sword to the
Queen, and executed at the same time a gam-
bade, the like whereof had never been practised
by two-legged hobby-horse. Then passing on
with all his followers of cavaliers and infantry,
he drew them up with martial skill at the opposite extremity of the bridge, or tilt-yard, until
his antagonists should be fairly prepared for the
onset.

. This was no long interval; for the Danish cavalry and infantry, no way inferior to the English in number, valour, and equipment, instantly
arrived, with the northern bag-pipe blowing
before them in token of their country, and head-
ed by a cunning master of defence, only inferior to the renowned Captain Coxe, if to him,
in the discipline of war. The Danes, as invaders,
took their station under the Gallery-tower, and
opposite to that of Mortimer; and, when their
arrangements were completely made, a signal
was given for the encounter.

Their first charge upon each other was rather
moderate, for either party had some dread of

being forced into the lake. But as reinforcements came up on either side, the encounter grew from a skirmish into a blazing-battle. They rushed upon one another, as Master Laneham testifies, like rams inflamed by jealousy, with such furious encounter, that both parties were often overthrown, and the clubs and targets made a most horrible clatter. In many instances, that happened which had been dreaded by the more experienced warriors, who began the day of strife. The rails which defended the ledges of the bridge, had been, perhaps of purpose, left but slightly fastened, and gave way under the pressure of those who thronged to the combat, so that the hot courage of many of the combatants received a sufficient cooling. These incidents might have occasioned more serious damage than became such an affray, for many of the champions who met with this mischance could not swim, and those who could, were encumbered with their suits of leathern and of paper armour; but the case had been provided for, and there were several boats in readiness to pick up the unfortunate warriors, and convey them to the dry land, where, dripping and dejected, they comforted themselves with the hot ale and strong waters which were liberally allowed to them, without shewing any desire to re-enter so desperate a conflict.

Captain Coxe alone, that paragon of Black-Letter Antiquaries, after twice experiencing, horse and man, the perilous leap from the

bridge into the lake, equal to any extremity to
which the favourite heroes of chivalry, whose
exploits he studied in an abridged form, whether
Amadis, Belianis, Bevis, or his own Guy of
Warwick, had ever been subjected to — Captain Coxe, we repeat, did alone, after two such
mischances, rush again into the heat of conflict,
his bases, and the foot-cloth of his hobby-horse
dropping water, and twice reanimated by voice
and example the drooping spirits of the English;
so that at length their victory over the Danish
invaders became, as was just and reasonable,
complete and decisive. Worthy he was to be
rendered immortal by the pen of Ben Jonson,
who, fifty years afterwards, deemed that a
masque, exhibited at Kenilworth, could be
ushered in by none with so much propriety, as
by the ghost of Captain Coxe, mounted upon
his redoubted hobby-horse.

These rough rural gambols may not altogether
agree with the reader's preconceived idea of an
entertainment presented before Elizabeth, *in*
whose reign letters revived with such brilliancy,
and whose court, governed by a female, whose
sense of proprie y was equal to her strength of
mind, was no less distinguished for delicacy
and refinement, than her counsels for wisdom
and fortitude. But whether from the political
wish to seem interested in popular sports, or
whether from a spark of old Henry's rough
masculine spirit, which Elizabeth sometimes
displayed, it is certain the Queen laughed hear-

tily at the imitation, or rather burlesque of chivalry, which was presented in the Coventry play. She called near her person the Earl of Sussex and lord Hunsdon, partly perhaps to make amends to the former, for the long and private audiences with which she had indulged the Earl of Leicester, by engaging him in conversation upon a pastime, which better suited his taste than those pageants that were furnished forth from the stores of antiquity. The disposition which the Queen shewed to laugh and jest with her military leaders, gave the Earl of Leicester the opportunity he had been watching for withdrawing from the royal presence, which to the court around, so well had he chosen his time, had the graceful appearance of leaving his rival free access to the Queen's person, instead of availing himself of his right as her landlord, to stand perpetually betwixt others, and the light of her countenance.

Leicester's thoughts, however, had a far different object from mere courtesy; for no sooner did he see the Queen fairly engaged in conversation with Sussex and Hunsdon, behind whose back stood Sir Nicholas Blount, grinning from ear to ear at each word which was spoken, than, making a sign to Tressilian, who, according to appointment, watched his motions at a little distance, he extricated himself from the press, and walking towards the Chase, made his way through the crowds of ordinary spectators, who,

with open mouth, stood gazing on the battle of
the English and the Danes. When he had accomplished this, which was a work of some
difficulty, he shot another glance behind him
to see that Tressilian had been equally successful, and as soon as he saw him also free from
the crowd, he led the way to a small thicket,
behind which stood a lackey, with two horses
ready saddled. He flung himself on the one,
and made signs to Tressilian to mount the other,
who obeyed without speaking a single word.

Leicester then spurred his horse, and galloped without stopping until he reached a sequestered spot, environed by lofty oaks, about
a mile's distance from the Castle, and in an opposite direction from the scene to which curiosity was drawing every spectator. He there
dismounted, bound his horse to a tree, and
only pronouncing the words, « Here there is
no risk of interruption,' laid his cloak across
his saddle, and drew his sword.

Tressilian imitated his example punctually,
yet could not forbear saying, as he drew his
weapon, « My lord, as I have been known to
many as one who does not fear death, when
placed in balance with honour, methinks I may,
without derogation, ask, wherefore, in the name
of all that is honourable, your lordship has
dared to offer me such a mark of disgrace, as
places us on these terms with respect to each
other? »

« If you like not such marks of my scorn, »
replied the Earl, « betake yourself instantly to
your weapon, lest I repeat the usage you complain of. »

« It shall not need, my lord, » said Tressilian.
« God judge betwixt us! and your blood, if you
fall, be on your own head. »

He had scarce completed the sentence when
they instantly closed in combat.

But Leicester, who was a perfect master of
defence among all other exterior accomplishments of the time, had seen, on the preceding
night, enough of Tressilian's strength and skill,
to make him fight with more caution than here-
tofore, and prefer a secure revenge to a hasty
one. For some minutes they fought with equal
skill and fortune, till, in a desperate lounge
which Leicester successfully put aside, Tressilian exposed himself at disadvantage; and, in
a subsequent attempt to close, the Earl forced
his sword from his hand, and stretched him on
the ground. With a grim smile he held the point
of his rapier within two inches of the throat of
his fallen adversary, and placing his foot at the
same time upon his breast, bid him confess his
villainous wrongs towards him, and prepare for
death.

« I have no villainy nor wrong towards thee
to confess, » answered Tressilian, « and am better
prepared for death than thou. Use thine advantage as thou wilt, and may God forgive you. I
have given you no cause for this. »

« No cause ! » exclaimed the Earl, « no cause !
— but why parley with such a slave ? — Die a
liar, as thou hast lived ! »

He had withdrawn his arm for the purpose of
striking the fatal blow, when it was suddenly
seized from behind.

The Earl turned in wrath to shake off the unexpected obstacle, but was surprised to find that
a strange-looking boy had hold of his sword-
arm, and clung to it with such tenacity of grasp,
that he could not shake him off without a considerable struggle, in the course of which Tressilian had opportunity to rise and possess himself once more of his weapon. Leicester again
turned towards him with looks of unabated
ferocity, and the combat would have recom-
menced with still more desperation on both
parts, had not the boy clung to Lord Leicester's knees, and in a shrill tone implored him
to listen one moment ere he prosecuted this
quarrel.

« Stand up, and let me go, » said Leicester, « or,
by heaven, I will pierce thee with my rapier ! —
What hast thou to do to bar my way to revenge ? »

« Much — much ! » exclaimed the undaunted
boy; « since my folly has been the cause of these
bloody quarrels between you, and perchance of
worse evils. O, if you would ever again enjoy
the peace of an innocent mind, if you hope again
to sleep in peace and unhaunted by remorse,
take so much leisure as to peruse this letter,
and then do as you list. »

While he spoke in this eager and earnest manner, to which his singular features and voice
gave a goblin-like effect, he held up to Leicester a packet, secured with a long tress of woman's hair, of a beautiful light-brown colour.
Enraged as he was, nay, almost blinded with
fury to see his destined revenge so strangely
frustrated, the Earl of Leicester could not resist
this extraordinary supplicant. He snatched the
letter from his hand — changed colour as he
looked on the superscription—undid, with faultering hand, the knot which secured it — glanced over the contents, and staggering back,
would have fallen, had he not rested against
the trunk of a tree, where he stood for an instant, his eyes bent on the letter, and his sword-
point turned to the ground, without seeming to
be conscious of the presence of an antagonist,
towards whom he had shewn little mercy, and
who might in turn have taken him at advantage.
But for such revenge Tressilian was too noble-
minded — he also stood still in surprise, waiting
the issue of this strange fit of passion, but holding his weapon ready to defend himself in case
of need, against some new and sudden attack
on the part of Leicester, whom he again suspected to be under the influence of actual frenzy. The boy, indeed, he easily recognized as
his old acquaintance Dickon, whose face, once
seen, was scarcely to be forgotten; but how he
came hither at so critical a moment, why his

interference was so energetic, and above all how
it came to produce so powerful an effect upon
Leicester, were questions which he could not
solve.

But the letter was of itself powerful enough
to work effects yet more wonderful. It was that
which the unfortunate Amy had written to her
husband, in which she alleged the reasons and
manner of her flight from Cumnor-Place, informed him of her having taken refuge at Kenilworth to enjoy his protection, and mentioned the
circumstances which had compelled her to take
refuge in Tressilian's apartment, earnestly requesting he would, without delay, assign her a
more suitable asylum. The letter concluded with
the most earnest expressions of devoted attachment, and submission to his will in all things,
and particularly respecting her situation and
place of residence, conjuring him only that she
might not be placed under the guardianship or
restraint of Varney.

The letter dropped from Leicester's hand when
he had perused it. « Take my sword, » he said,
« Tressilian, and pierce my heart, as I would but
now have pierced your's! »

« My lord, » said Tressilian, you have done
me great wrong; but something within my breast
ever whispered that it was by egregious error. »

« Error, indeed! » said Leicester, and handed
him the letter; « I have been made to believe a
man of honour a villain, and the best and purest

of creatures a false profligate. — Wretched boy, why comes this letter now, and where has the bearer lingered ? »

« I dare not tell you, my lord, » said the boy, withdrawing, as if to keep beyond his reach; — « but here comes one who was the messenger. »

Wayland at the same moment came up; and, interrogated by Leicester, hastily detailed all the circumstances of his escape with Amy,—the fatal practices which had driven her to flight, — and her anxious desire to throw herself under the instant protection of her husband, — pointing out the evidence of the domestics of Kenilworth, « who could not, » he observed, « but remember her eager inquiries after the Earl of Leicester on her first arrival. »

« The villains! » exclaimed Leicester; « but O, that worst of villains, Varney!—and she is even now in his power! »

« But not, I trust in God, » said Tressilian, « with any commands of fatal import ? »

« No, no, no ! » exclaimed the Earl hastily.— « I said something in madness—but it was recalled, fully recalled, by a hasty messenger; and she is now—she must now be safe. »

« Yes, » said Tressilian, « she *must* be safe, and I *must* be assured of her safety. My own quarrel with you is ended, my lord; but there is another to begin with the seducer of Amy Robsart, who has screened his guilt under the cloak of the infamous Varney. »

« The *seducer* of Amy! » replied Leicester, with a voice like thunder; « say her husband! —her misguided, blinded, most unworthy husband!—She is as surely Countess of Leicester, as I am belted Earl. Nor can you, sir, point out that manner of justice which I will not render her at my own free will. I need scarce say, I fear not your compulsion. »

The generous nature of Tressilian was instantly turned from consideration of any thing personal to himself, and centered at once upon Amy's welfare. He had by no means undoubting confidence in the fluctuating resolutions of Leicester, whose mind seemed to him agitated beyond the government of calm reason; neither did he, notwithstanding the assurances he had received, think Amy safe in the hands of his dependants. « My lord, » he said, calmly, « I mean you no offence, and am far from seeking a quarrel. But my duty to Sir Hugh Robsart compels me to carry this matter instantly to the Queen, that the Countess's rank may be acknowledged in her person.

« You shall not need, sir, « replied the Earl, haughtily; » do not dare to interfere. No voice but Dudley's shall proclaim Dudley's infamy — To Elizabeth herself will I tell it, and then for Cumnor-Place with the speed of life and death! »

So saying, he unbound his horse from the tree, threw himself into the saddle, and rode at full gallop towards the Castle.

« Take me before you, Master Tressilian, »

said the boy, seeing Tressilian mount in the same haste — « my tale is not all told out, and I need your protection. »

Tressilian complied, and followed the Earl, though at a less furious rate. By the way the boy confessed, with much contrition, that in resentment at Wayland's evading all his inquiries concerning the lady, after Dickon conceived he had in various ways merited his confidence, he had purloined from him, in revenge, the letter with which Amy had entrusted him for the Earl of Leicester. His purpose was to have restored it to him that evening, as he reckoned himself sure of meeting with him, in consequence of Wayland's having to perform the part of Arion, in the pageant. He was indeed something alarmed when he saw to whom the letter was addressed; but he argued that, as Leicester did not return to Kenilworth until that evening, it would be again in the possession of the proper messenger as soon as, in the nature of things, it could possibly be delivered. But Wayland came not to the pageant, having been in the interim expelled by Lambourne from the Castle, and the boy, not being able to find him, or to get speech of Tressilian, and finding himself in possession of a letter addressed to no less a person than the Earl of Leicester, became much afraid of the consequences of his frolic. The caution, and indeed the alarm, which Wayland had expressed respecting Varney and Lambourne, led him to judge, that the letter must be designed for the Earl's own hand, and that he might prejudice the lady, by giving it to any of the domestics. He made an attempt or two to obtain an audience of Leicester, but the singularity of his features, and the meanness of his appearance, occasioned his being always repulsed by the insolent menials whom he applied to for that purpose. Once, indeed, he had nearly succeeded, when, in prowling about, he found in the grotto the casket, which he knew to belong to the unlucky Countess, having seen it on her journey; for nothing escaped his prying eye. Having strove in vain to restore it either to Tressilian or the Countess, he put it into the hands, as we have seen, of Leicester himself, but unfortunately did not recognize him in his disguise.

At length, the boy thought he was on the point of succeeding, when the Earl came down to the lower part of the hall; but just as he was about to accost him, he was prevented by Tressilian. As sharp in ear as in wit, the boy heard the appointment settled betwixt them, to take place in the Pleasance, and resolved to add a third to the party, in hopes that, either in coming or in returning, he might find an opportunity of delivering the letter to Leicester; for strange stories began to flit among the domestics, which alarmed him for the lady's safety. Accident, however, detained Dickon a little behind the Earl, and, as he reached the arcade, he saw them engaged in combat; in consequence of which he hastened to alarm the guard, having little doubt, that what bloodshed took place betwixt them, might arise out of his own frolic. Continuing to lurk in the portico, he heard the second appointment, which Leicester, at parting, assigned to Tressilian, and was keeping them in view during the encounter of the Coventry-men, when, to his surprise, he recognized Wayland in the crowd, much disguised, indeed, but not sufficiently so to escape the prying glance of his old comrade. They drew aside out of the crowd to explain their situation to each other. The boy confessed to Wayland what we have above told, and the artist, in return, informed him, that his deep anxiety for the fate of the unfortunate lady had brought him back to the neighbourhood of the Castle, upon his learning that morning at a village about ten miles distant, that Varney and Lambourne, whose violence he dreaded, had both left Kenilworth over-night.

While they spoke, they saw Leicester and Tressilian separate themselves from the crowd, dogged them until they mounted their horses, when the boy, whose speed of foot has been before mentioned, though he could not possibly keep up with them, yet arrived, as we have seen, soon enough to save Tressilian's life. The boy had just finished his tale when they arrived at the Gallery-Tower.

CHAPTER XL.

High o'er the eastern steep the sun is beaming,
And darkness flies with her deceitful shadows;—
So truth prevails o'er falsehood.

Old Play.

As Tressilian rode over the bridge lately the scene of so much riotous sport, he could not but observe that men's countenances had singularly changed during the space of his brief absence. The mock fight was over, but the men, still habited in their masquing suits, stood together in groupes, like the inhabitants of a city who have been just startled by some strange and alarming news.

When he reached the base-court, appearances were the same—domestics, retainers, and under officers, stood together and whispered, bending their eyes towards the windows of the great hall, with looks which seemed at once alarmed and mysterious.

Sir Nicholas Blount was the first person of his own particular acquaintance Tressilian saw, who left him no time to make inquiries, but greeted him with, « God help thy heart, Tressilian, thou art fitter for a clown than a courtier—thou can'st not attend, as becomes one who follows her Ma-

jesty.—Here you are called for, wished for, waited for—no man but you will serve the turn; and
hither you come with a misbegotten brat on thy
horse's neck, as if thou wert dry nurse to some
sucking devil, and wert just returned from air-
ing. »

« Why, what is the matter?» said Tressilian,
letting go the boy, who sprung to ground like a
feather, and himself dismounting at the same
time.

« Why, no one knows the matter, » replied
Blount; « I cannot smell it out myself, though I
have a nose like other courtiers. Only, my Lord
of Leicester has galloped along the bridge, as if
he would have rode over all in his passage, demanded an audience of the Queen, and is closet-
ed even now with her, and Burleigh and Walsingham—and you are called for—but whether
the matter be treason or worse, no one knows. »

« He speaks true, by heaven, » said Raleigh,
who that instant appeared; « you must immediately to the Queen's presence. »

« Be not rash, Raleigh, » said Blount, « remember his boots—For heaven's sake, go to my
chamber, dear Tressilian, and don my new bloom-
coloured silken hose — I have worn them but
twice. »

« Pshaw!» answered Tressilian; « do thou take
care of this boy, Blount; be kind to him, and look
he escapes you not—much depends on him. »

So saying, he followed Raleigh hastily, leaving honest Blount with the bridle of his horse in

one hand, and the boy in the other. Blount gave
a long look after him.

« Nobody, » he said, « calls me to these mysteries, — and he leaves me here to play horse-
keeper and child-keeper at once. I could excuse
the one, for I love a good horse naturally ; but
to be plagued with a bratchet whelp. —Whence
come ye, my fair-favoured little gossip ? »

« From the fens, answered the boy.

« And what didst thou learn there, forward
imp ? »

« To catch gulls, with their webbed feet and
yellow stockings, » said the boy.

« Umph ! » said blount, looking down on his
own immense roses, —« Nay, then the devil take
him asks thee more questions. »

Meantime Tressilian traversed the full length
of the great hall, in which the astonished courtiers formed various groupes, and were whispering mysteriously together, while all kept their
eyes fixed on the door, which led from the upper end of the hall into the Queen's withdrawing
apartment. Raleigh pointed to the door—Tressilian knocked, and was instantly admitted. Many
a neck was stretched to gain a view into the interior of the apartment ; but the tapestry which
covered the door on the inside, was dropped too
suddenly to admit the slightest gratification of
curiosity.

Upon entrance, Tressilian found himself, not
without a strong palpitation of heart, in the presence of Elizabeth, who was walking to and fro

in a violent agitation, which she seemed to scorn to conceal, while two or three of her most sage and confidential counsellors exchanged anxious looks with each other, but seemed to delay speaking till her wrath had abated. Before the empty chair of state in which she had been seated, and which was half pushed aside by the violence with which she had started from it, knelt Leicester, his arms crossed, and his brows bent on the ground, still and motionless as the effigies upon a sepulchre. Beside him stood the Lord Shrewsbury, then Earl Marshal of England, holding his baton of office—the Earl's sword was unbuckled, and lay before him on the floor.

« Ho, sir ! » said the Queen, coming close up to Tressilian, and stamping on the floor with the action and manner of Henry himself; « *you* knew of this fair work —*you* are an accomplice in this deception which has been practised on us —*you* have been a main cause of our doing injustice ? » Tressilian dropped on his knee before the Queen, his good sense shewing him the risk of attempting any defence at that moment of irritation. « Art dumb, sirrah ! » she continued; « thou know'st of this affair —doest thou not ? »

« Not, gracious Madam, that this poor lady was Countess of Leicester. »

« Nor shall any one know her for such, » said Elizabeth, « Death of my life! Countess of Leicester ! —I say Dame Amy Dudley—and well if she have not cause to write herself widow of the traitor Robert Dudley. »

« Madam, » said Leicester, « do with me what it may be your will to do — but work no injury on this gentleman — he hath in no way deserved it. »

« And will he be the better for thy intercession, » said the Queen, leaving Tressilian, who slowly arose, and rushing to Leicester, who continued kneeling, — « the better for thy intercession, thou doubly false — thou doubly forsworn ? — of thy intercession, whose villainy hath made me ridiculous to my subjects, and odious to myself ? — I could tear out mine own eyes for their blindness! »

Burleigh here ventured to interpose.

« Madam, » he said, « remember that you are a Queen — Queen of England — mother of your people. Give not way to this wild storm of passion. »

Elizabeth turned round to him, while a tear actually twinkled in her proud and angry eye. « Burleigh, » she said, « thou art a statesman — thou doest not, thou canst not, comprehend half the scorn — half the misery, that man has poured on me. »

With the utmost caution — with the deepest reverence, Burleigh took her hand at the moment he saw her heart was at the fullest, and led her aside to an oriel window, apart from the others.

« Madam, » he said, « I am a statesman, but I am also a man — a man already grown old in your councils, who have not and cannot have a

wish on earth but your glory and happiness
— I pray you to be composed. »

« Ah, Burleigh, » said Elizabeth, « thou little
knowest » — here her tears fell over her cheeks
in despite of her.

« I do — I do know, my honoured Sovereign.
O beware that you lead not others to guess that
which they know not ! »

« Ha ! » said Elizabeth, pausing as if a new
train of thoughts had suddenly shot across her
brain. « Burleigh, thou art right — thou art right
— any thing but disgrace — any thing but a confession of weakness — any thing rather than
seem the cheated — slighted — 'Sdeath ! to think
on it is distraction ! »

« Be but yourself, my Queen , » said Burleigh ;
« and soar far above a weakness which no Englishman will ever believe his Elizabeth could
have entertained , unless the violence of her disappointment carries a sad conviction to his bosom. »

« What weakness, my lord ? » said Elizabeth,
haughtily; « would you too insinuate that the favour in which I held yonder proud traitor, derived its source from aught » — But here she
could no longer sustain the proud tone which
she had assumed, and again softened as she said,
« But why should I strive to deceive even thee,
my good and wise servant ! »

Burleigh stooped to kiss her hand with affection, and — rare in the annals of courts — a tear

15*

of true sympathy dropped from the eye of the minister on the hand of his Sovereign.

. It is probable that the consciousness of possessing this sympathy, aided Elizabeth in supporting her mortification, and suppressing her extreme resentment; but she was still more moved by fear that her passion would betray to the public the affront and the disappointment, which, alike as a woman and a Queen, she was so anxious to conceal. She turned from Burleigh, and sternly paced the hall till her features had recovered their usual dignity, and her mien its wonted stateliness of regular motion.

« Our Sovereign is her noble self once more, » whispered Burleigh to Walsingham ; « mark what she does, and take heed you thwart her not. »

She then approached Leicester, and said, with calmness, « My Lord Shrewsbury, we discharge you of your prisoner. — My Lord of Leicester, rise and take up your sword. — A quarter of an hour's restraint, under the custody of our Marshal, my lord, is, we think, no high penance for months of falsehood practised upon us. We will now hear the progress of this affair. » — She then seated herself in her chair, and said, « You, Tressilian, step forward, and say what you know. »

Tressilian told his story generously, suppressing as much as he could what affected Leicester, and saying nothing of their having twice actually fought together. It is very probable that in doing so, he did the Earl good service; for had the Queen at that instant found any thing on account of which she could vent her wrath upon him, without laying open sentiments of which she was ashamed, it might have fared hard with him. She paused when Tressilian had finished his tale.

« We will take that Wayland, » she said « into our own service, and place the boy in our Secretary-office for instruction, that he may in future use discretion towards letters. For you, Tressilian, you did wrong in not communicating the whole truth to us, and your promise not to do so was both imprudent and undutiful. Yet, having given your word to this unhappy lady, it was the part of a man and a gentleman to keep it; and on the whole, we esteem you for the character you have sustained in this matter. — My Lord of Leicester, it is now your turn to tell us the truth, an exercise to which you seem of late to have been too much a stranger. »

Accordingly, she extorted by successive questions, the whole history of his first acquaintance with Amy Robsart — their marriage — his jealousy — the causes on which it was founded, and many particulars besides. Leicester's confession, for such it might be called, was extorted from him piece-meal, yet was upon the whole accurate, excepting that he totally omitted to mention that he had, by implication, or otherwise, assented to Varney's designs upon the life

of his Countess. Yet the consciousness of this
was what at that moment lay nearest to his
heart; and although he trusted in great measure
to the very positive counter-orders which he
had sent by Lambourne, it was his purpose to
set out for Cumnor-Place in person, as soon as
he should be dismissed from the presence of the
Queen, who, he concluded, would presently
leave Kenilworth.

But the Earl reckoned without his host. It is
true, his presence and his communications were
gall and wormwood to his once partial mistress.
But, barred from every other and more direct
mode of revenge, the Queen perceived that she
gave her false suitor torture by these inquiries,
and dwelt on them for that reason, no more
regarding the pain which she herself experienced, than the savage cares for the searing of
his own hands with the hot pincers with which
he tears the flesh of his captive enemy.

At length, however, the haughty lord, like
a deer that turns to bay, gave intimation that
his patience was failing. « Madam, » he said, « I
have been much to blame — more than even
your just resentment has expressed. Yet, Madam,
let me say, that my guilt, if it be unpardonable,
was not unprovoked; and that if beauty and
condescending dignity could seduce the frail
heart of a human being, I might plead both, as
the causes of my concealing this secret from
your Majesty. »

The Queen was so much struck by this reply,

whieh Leicester took care should be heard by
no one but herself, that she was for the moment
silenced, and the Earl had the temerity to pursue his advantage. « Your Grace, who has par-
doned so much, will excuse my throwing
myself on your royal mercy for those expressions, which were yester-morning accounted
but a light offence. »

The Queen fixed her eyes on him while she
replied, « Now, by heaven, my lord, thy effrontery passes the bounds of belief, as well as patience! But it shall avail thee nothing. — What,
ho! my lords, come all and hear the news — My
Lord of Leicester's stolen marriage has cost me
a husband, and England a King. His lordship
is patriarchal in his tastes — one wife at a time
was insufficient, and he designed us the honour
of his left hand. Now, is not this too insolent,
— that I could not grace him with a few marks
of court-favour, but he must presume to think
my hand and crown at his disposal? — You,
however, think better of me; and I can pity
this ambitious man, as I could a child, whose
bubble of soap has burst between his hands.
We go to the presence-chamber — My Lord of
Leicester, we command your close attendance
on us. »

All was eager expectation in the hall, and
what was the universal astonishment, when the
Queen said to those next her, « The revels of
Kenilworth are not yet exhausted, my lords and

ladies — we are to solemnize the noble owner's marriage. »

There was an universal expression of surprise.

« It is true, on our royal word, » said the Queen; « he hath kept this a secret even from us ; that he might surprise us with it at this very place and time. I see you are dying of curiosity to know the happy bride — It is Amy Robsart, the same who, to make up the May-game yesterday, figured in the pageant as the wife of his servant Varney. »

« For God's sake, Madam, » said the Earl, approaching her with a mixture of humility, vexation, and shame in his countenance, and speaking so low as to be heard by no one else, « take my head, as you threatened in your anger, and spare me these taunts! Urge not a falling man — tread not on a crushed worm. »

« A worm, my lord? » said the Queen, in the same tone; « nay, a snake is the nobler reptile, and the more exact similitude—the frozen snake you wot of, which was warmed in a certain bosom »———

« For your own sake—for mine, madam, » said the Earl —« while there is yet some reason left in me »———

« Speak aloud, my lord, » said Elizabeth, « and at farther distance, so please you—your breath thaws our ruff. What have you to ask of us ? »

« Permission, » said the unfortunate Earl, humbly, « to travel to Cumnor-Place. »

« To fetch home your bride belike ? — Why, ay, — that is but right—for, as we have heard, she is indifferently cared for there. But, my lord, you go not in person — we have counted upon passing certain days in this Castle of Kenilworth, and it were slight courtesy to leave us without a landlord during our residence here. Under your favour, we cannot think to incur such disgrace in the eyes of our subjects. Tressilian shall go to Cumnor-Place instead of you, and with him some gentleman who hath been sworn of our chamber, lest my Lord of Leicester should be again jealous of his old rival.—Whom wouldst thou have to be in commission with thee, Tressilian ? »

Tressilian, with humble deference, suggested the name of Raleigh.

« Why, ay, » said the Queen; « so God ha' me, thou hast made a good choice. He is a young knight besides, and to deliver a lady from prison is an appropriate first adventure.—Cumnor-Place is little better than a prison, you are to know, my lords and ladies. Besides, there are certain faitours there whom we would willingly have in fast keeping. You will furnish them, Master Secretary, with the warrant necessary to secure the bodies of Richard Varney and the foreign Alasco, dead or alive. Take a sufficient force with you, gentlemen—bring the lady here in all honour—lose no time, and God be with you. »

They bowed, and left the presence.

Who shall describe how the rest of that day way spent at Kenilworth? The Queen, who seemed to have remained there, for the sole purpose of mortifying and taunting the Earl of Leicester, shewed herself as skilful in that female art of vengeance, as she was in the science of wisely governing her people. The train of state soon caught the signal, and, as he walked among his own splendid preparations, the Lord of Kenilworth, in his own Castle, already experienced the lot of a disgraced courtier, in the slight regard and cold manners of alienated friends, and the ill-concealed triumph of avowed and open enemies. Sussex, from his natural military frankness of disposition, Burleigh and Walsingham, from their penetrating and prospective sagacity, and some of the ladies, from the compassion of their sex, were the only persons in the crowded court who retained towards him the countenance they had borne in the morning.

So much had Leicester been accustomed to consider court-favour as the principal object of his life, that all other sensations were, for the time, lost in the agony which his haughty spirit felt at the succession of petty insults and studied neglects to which he had been subjected; but when he was retired to his own chamber for the night, that long fair tress of hair which had once secured Amy's letter, fell under his observation, and, with the influence of a counter-charm, awakened his heart to nobler and more natural feelings. He kissed it a thousand times; and while he recollected that he had it always in his power to shun the mortifications which he had that day undergone, by retiring into a dignified and even princelike seclusion, with the beautiful and beloved partner of his future life, he felt that he could rise above the revenge which Elizabeth had condescended to take.

Accordingly, on the next day, the whole conduct of the Earl displayed so much dignified equanimity; he seemed so solicitous about the accommodations and amusements of his guests, yet so indifferent to their personal demeanour towards him; so respectfully distant to the Queen, yet so patient of her harassing displeasure, that Elizabeth changed her manner to him, and though cold and distant, ceased to offer him any direct affront. She intimated also with some sharpness to others around her, who thought they were consulting her pleasure in shewing a neglectful conduct to the Earl, that, while they remained at Kenilworth, they ought to shew the civility due from guests to the Lord of the Castle. In short, matters were so far changed in twenty-four hours, that some of the more experienced and sagacious courtiers foresaw a strong possibility of Leicester's restoration to favour, and regulated their demeanour towards him, as those who might one day claim merit for not having deserted him in adversity. It is time, however, to leave these intrigues and to follow Tressilian and Raleigh on their journey.

The troop consisted of six persons; for, besides Wayland, they had in company a royal pursuivant and two stout serving-men. All were well armed, and travelled as fast as it was possible with justice to their horses, which had a long journey before them. They endeavoured to procure some tidings as they rode along of Varney and his party, but could hear none, as they had travelled in the dark. At a small village about twelve miles from Kenilworth, where they gave some refreshment to their horses, a poor clergyman, the curate of the place, came out of a small cottage, and entreated any of the company who might know aught of surgery, to look in for an instant on a dying man.

The empiric Wayland undertook to do his best, and as the curate conducted him to the spot, he learned that the man had been found on the high-road about a mile from the village, by labourers, as they were going to their work on the preceding morning, and the curate had given him shelter in his house. He had received a gun-shot wound which seemed to be obviously mortal, but whether in a brawl or from robbers they could not learn, as he was in a fever, and spoke nothing connectedly. Wayland entered the dark and lowly apartment, and no sooner had the curate drawn aside the curtain, than he knew in the distorted features of the dying man the countenance of Michael Lambourne. Under pretence of seeking something which he wanted, Wayland hastily apprized his fellow-travellers of this extraordi nary circumstance; and both Tressilian and Raleigh, full of boding apprehensions, hastened to the curate's house to see the dying man.

The wretch was by this time in the agonies of death, from which a much better surgeon than Wayland could not have rescued him, for the bullet had passed clear through his body. He was sensible, however, at least in part, for he knew Tressilian, and made signs that he wished him to stoop over his bed. Tressilian did so, and after some inarticulate murmurs, in which the names of Varney and Lady Leicester were alone distinguishable, Lambourne bade him « make haste, or he would come too late. » It was in vain Tressilian urged the patient for farther information; he seemed to become in some degree delirious, and when he again made a signal to attract Tressilian's attention, it was only for the purpose of desiring him to inform his uncle, Giles Gosling of the Black Bear, that « he had died without his shoes after all. » A convulsion verified his words a few minutes after, and the travellers derived nothing from having met with him, saving the obscure fears concerning the fate of the Countess, which his dying words were calculated to convey, and which induced them to urge their journey with the utmost speed, pressing horses in the Queen's name, when those which they rode became unfit for service.

CHAPTER XLI.

The death-bell thrice was heard to ring,
An aerial voice was heard to call;
And thrice the raven flapped its wing,
Around the towers of Cumnor-hall.
Mickle.

WE are now to return to that part of our story
where we intimated that Varney, possessed of the
authority of the Earl of Leicester, and of the
Queen's permission to the same effect, hastened
to secure himself against discovery of his perfidy,
by removing the Countess from Kenilworth
Castle. He had proposed to set forth early in the
morning, but reflecting that the Earl might re-
lent in the interim, and seek another interview
with the Countess, he resolved to prevent, by
immediate departure, all chance of what would
probably have ended in his detection and ruin.
For this purpose he called for Lambourne, and
was exceedingly incensed to find that his trusty
attendant was abroad on some ramble in the
neighbouring village, or elsewhere. As his return was expected, Sir Richard commanded that
he should prepare himself for attending him on
an immediate journey, and follow him in case
he returned after his departure.

In the meanwhile, Varney used the ministry of a servant called Robin Tider, one to whom the mysteries of Cumnor-Place were already in some degree known, as he had been there more than once in attendance on the Earl. To this man, whose character resembled that of Lambourne, though he was neither quite so prompt nor altogether so profligate, Varney gave command to have three horses saddled, and to prepare a horse-litter, and have them in readiness at the postern-gate. The natural enough excuse of his lady's insanity, which was now universally believed, accounted for the secrecy with which she was to be removed from the Castle, and he reckoned on the same apology in case the unfortunate Amy's resistance or screams should render such necessary. The agency of Anthony Foster was indispensible, and that Varney now went to secure.

This person, naturally of a sour unsocial disposition, and somewhat tired, besides, with his journey from Cumnor to Warwickshire, in order to bring the news of the Countess's escape, had early extricated himself from the crowd of wassailers, and betaken himself to his chamber, where he lay asleep, when Varney, completely equipped for travelling, and with a dark lantern in his hand, entered his apartment. He paused an instant to listen to what his associate was murmuring in his sleep, and could plainly distinguish the words, « *Ave Maria — ora pro nobis* — No — it runs not so — deliver us from evil — Ay, so it goes. »

« Praying in his sleep, » said Varney; « and confounding his old and new devotions — He must have more need of prayer ere I have done with him.—What ho! holy man — most blessed penitent!'— Awake — awake! — The devil has not discharged you from service yet! »

As Varney at the same time shook the sleeper by the arm, it changed the current of his ideas, and he roared out, « Thieves! — thieves! I will die in defence of my gold — my hard won gold, that has cost me so dear. — Where is Janet? — Is Janet safe? »

« Safe enough, thou bellowing fool, » said Varney; « art thou not ashamed of thy clamour? »

Foster by this time was broad awake, and, sitting up in his bed, asked Varney the meaning of so untimely a visit. « It augurs nothing good, » he added.

« A false prophecy, most sainted Anthony, » returned Varney, « it augurs that the hour is come for converting thy leasehold into copyhold — What say'st thou to that? »

Had'st thou told me in broad day, » said Foster, « I had rejoiced' — but at this dead hour, and by this dim light, and looking on thy pale face, which is a ghastly contradiction to thy light words, I cannot but rather think of the work that is to be done, than the guerdon to be gained by it. »

Why, thou fool, it is but to escort thy charge back to Cumnor-Place. »

« Is that indeed all ? » said Foster; « thou look'st deadly pale, and thou art not moved by trifles — is that indeed all? »

« Ay, that — and may be a trifle more, » said Varney.

« Ah, that trifle more! » said Foster; « still thou look'st paler and paler. »

« Heed not my countenance, said Varney, you see it by this wretched light. Up and be doing, man — Think of Cumnor-Place—thine own proper copyhold—Why, thou may'st found a weekly lecture-shop, besides endowing Janet like a baron's daughter. — Seventy pounds and odds. »

« Seventy nine pounds, five shillings and five pence half-penny, besides the value of the wood, » said Foster; « and I am to have it all as copyhold? »

« All, man — squirrels and all — no gipsey shall cut the value of a broom — no boy so much as take a bird's nest, without paying thee a quittance. — Ay, that is right — don thy matters as fast as possible — horses and every thing is ready, all save that accursed villain Lambourne, who is out on some infernal gambol. »

Ay, Sir Richard, said Foster, « you would take no advice. I ever told you that drunken profligate would fail you at need. Now I could have helped you to a sober-young man. »

« What, some slow-spoken, long-breathed

brother of the congregation? — Why, we shall have use for such also, man — Heaven be praised, we shall lack labourers of every kind. — Ay, that is right — forget not your pistols — Come now, and let us away. »

« Whither? » said Anthony.

« To my lady's chamber — and, mind — she *must* along with us. Thou art not a fellow to be startled by a shriek? »

« Not if Scripture-reason can be rendered for it; and it is written, 'wives obey your husbands.' But will my lord's commands bear us out if we use violence? »

Tush, man! here is his signet, » answered Varney; and, having thus silenced the objections of his associate, they went together to Lord Hunsdon's apartment, and, acquainting the centinel with their purpose, as a matter sanctioned by the Queen and the Earl of Leicester, they entered the apartment of the unfortunate Countess.

The horror of Amy may be conceived, when, starting from a broken slumber, she saw at her bed-side Varney, the man on earth she most feared and hated. It was even a consolation to see that he was not alone, though she had so much reason to dread his sullen companion.

« Madam, » said Varney, « there is no time for ceremony. My Lord of Leicester, having fully considered the exigencies of the time, sends you his orders immediately to accompany us on our return to Cumnor-Place. See, here is his signet, in token of his instant and pressing commands. »

« It is false! » said the Countess; « thou hast stolen the warrant, — thou, who art capable of every villainy, from the blackest to the basest! »

« It is TRUE, madam, » replied Varney; « so true, that if you do not instantly arise, and prepare to attend us, we must compel you to obey our orders. »

« Compel! — thou darest not put it to that issue, base as thou art, » exclaimed the unhappy Countess.

« That remains to be proved, madam, » said Varney, who had determined on intimidation as the only means of subduing her high spirit; « if you put me to it, you will find me a rough groom of the chambers. »

It was at this threat that Amy screamed so fearfully, that had it not been for the received opinion of her insanity, she would quickly have had Lord Hunsdon and others to her aid. Perceiving, however, that her cries were vain, she appealed to Foster in the most affecting terms, conjuring him, as his daughter Janet's honour and purity was dear to him, not to permit her to be treated with unwomanly violence.

« Why, madam, wives must obey their husbands, — there's Scripture-warrant for it, » said Foster; « and if you will dress yourself, and come with us patiently, there's no one shall lay finger on you while I can draw a pistol-trigger. »

Seeing no help arrive, and comforted even by the dogged language of Foster, the Countess promised to arise and dress herself, if they would agree to retire from the room. Varney at the same time assured her of all safety and honour while in their hands, and promised, that he himself would not approach her, since his presence was so displeasing. Her husband, he added, would be at Cumnor-Place within twenty-four hours after they had reached it.

Somewhat comforted by this assurance, upon which, however, she saw little reason to rely, the unhappy Amy made her toilette by the assistance of the lantern, which they left with her when they quitted the apartment.

Weeping, trembling, and praying, the unfortunate lady dressed herself, — with sensations how different from the days in which she was wont to decorate herself in all the pride of conscious beauty! She endeavoured to delay the completing her dress as long as she could, until, terrified by the impatience of Varney, she was obliged to declare herself ready to attend them.

When they were about to move, the Countess clung to Foster with such an appearance of terror at Varney's approach, that the latter protested to her, with a deep oath, that he had no intention whatsoever of even coming near her. « If you do but consent to execute

your husband's will in quietness « you shall, »
he said, « see but little of me. I will leave you
undisturbed to the care of the usher whom your
good taste prefers. »

« My husband's will! » she exclaimed. « But
it is the will of God, and let that be sufficient
to me. — I will go with Master Foster as unresistingly as ever did a literal sacrifice. He is
a father at least; and will have decency, if not
humanity. For thee, Varney, were it my latest
word, thou art an equal stranger to both. »

Varney replied only, she was at liberty to
chuse, and walked some paces before them to
shew the way; while, half leaning on Foster,
and half carried by him, the Countess was transported from Saintlowe's Tower to the postern-
gate, where Tider waited with the litter and
horses.

The Countess was placed in the former without resistance. She saw with some satisfaction,
that while Foster and Tider rode close by the
litter, which the latter conducted, the dreaded
Varney lingered behind, and was soon lost in
darkness. A little while she strove, as the road
winded round the verge of the lake, to keep
sight of those stately towers which called her
husband lord, and which still, in some places,
sparkled with lights, where wassailers were yet
revelling. But when the direction of the road
rendered this no longer possible, she drew back
her head, and, sinking down in the litter,
recommended herself to the care of Providence.

Besides the desire of inducing the Countess to proceed quietly on her journey, Varney had it also in view to have an interview with Lambourne, by whom he every moment expected to be joined, without the presence of any witnesses. He knew the character of this man, prompt, bloody, resolute, and greedy, and judged him the most fit agent he could employ in his farther designs. But ten miles of their journey had been measured ere he heard the hasty clatter of horse's hoofs behind him, and was overtaken by Michael Lambourne.

Fretted as he was with his absence, Varney received his profligate servant with a rebuke of unusual bitterness. « Drunken villain, » he said, « thy idleness and debauched folly will stretch a halter ere it be long; and, for me, I care not how soon. »

This style of objurgation, Lambourne, who was elated to an unusual degree, not only by an extraordinary cup of wine, but by the sort of confidential interview he had just had with the Earl, and the secret of which he had made himself master, did not receive with his wonted humility. « He would take no insolence of language, » he said, « from the best knight that ever wore spurs. Lord Leicester had detained him on some business of import, and that was enough for Varney, who was but a servant like himself. »

Varney was not a little surprised at his unusual tone of insolence; but, ascribing it to liquor, suffered it to pass as if unnoticed, and then began to tamper with Lambourne, touching his willingness to aid in removing out of the Earl of Leicester's way an obstacle to a rise, which would put it in his power to reward his trusty followers to their utmost wish. And upon Michael Lambourne's seeming ignorant what was meant, he plainly indicated «the litter-load, yonder,» as the impediment which he desired should be removed.

.« Look you, Sir Richard, and so forth,» said Michael,« some are wiser than some, that is one thing, and some are worse than some, that's another. I know my lord's mind on this matter better than thou, for he hath trusted me fully.in the matter. Here are his mandates, and his last words were, Michael Lambourne,—for his lordship speaks to me as a gentleman of the sword, and useth not the words drunken villain, or such like phrases, of those who know not how to bear new dignities. — Varney, says he, must pay the utmost respect to my Countess — I trust to you for looking to it, Lambourne, says his lordship, and you must bring back my signet from him peremptorily.»

« Ay,» replied Varney, « said he so, indeed? You know all, then?»

« All — all — and you were as wise as make a friend of me while the weather is fair betwixt us.

« And was there no one present,» said Varney, « when my lord so spoke? »

« Not a breathing creature,» replied Lambourne. «Think you my lord would trust any

one with such matters, save an approved man
of action like myself?»

«Most true,» said Varney; and, making a
pause, he looked forward on the moonlight
road. They were traversing a wide and open
heath. The litter being at least a mile before
them, was both out of sight and hearing. He
looked behind, and there was an expanse, lighted
by the moonbeams, without one human being
in sight. He resumed his speech to Lambourne:
» And will you turn upon your master, who has
introduced you to this career of court-like favour
—whose apprentice you have been, Michael—
who has taught you the depths and shallows of
court intrigue ?»

« Michael not me, » said Lambourne, «I have
a name will brook a *master* before it as well as
another; and as to the rest, if I have been an
apprentice, my indenture is out, and I am resolute to set up for myself.»

« Take thy quittance first, thou fool!» said
Varney; and with a pistol, which he had for
some time held in his hand, shot Lambourne
through the body.

The wretch fell from his horse, without a single groan; and Varney, dismounting, rifled his
pockets, turning out the lining, that it might
appear he had fallen by robbers. He secured
the Earl's packet, which was his chief object,
but he also took Lambourne's purse, containing
some gold pieces, the reliques of what his de-
bauchery had left him, and, from a singular com-

bination of feelings, carried it in his hand only
the length of a small river, which crossed the
road, into which he threw it as far as he could
fling. Such are the strange remnants of conscience which remain after she seems totally subdued, that this cruel and remorseless man would
have felt himself degraded had he pocketed the
few pieces belonging to the wretch whom he
had thus ruthlessly slain.

The murderer reloaded his pistol, after clean-
sing the lock and barrel from the appearances of
late explosion, and rode calmly after the litter,
satisfying himself that he had so adroitly removed a troublesome witness to many of his intrigues, and the bearer of mandates which he
had no intentions to obey, and which, therefore, he was desirous it should be thought had
never reached his hand.

The remainder of the journey was made with
a degree of speed, which shewed the little care
they had for the health of the unhappy Countess. They paused only at places where all was
under their command, and where the tale of
the insane Lady Varney would have obtained
ready credit, had she made any attempt to appeal to the compassion of the few persons admitted to see her. But Amy saw no chance of
obtaining a hearing from any to whom she had
an opportunity of addressing herself, and besides, was too terrified for the presence of Varney to violate the implied condition, under

which she was to travel free from his company. The authority of Varney, often so used, during the Earl's private journies to Cumnor, readily procured relays of horses where wanted, so that they approached Cumnor-Place upon the night after they left Kenilworth.

At this period of the journey, Varney came up to the rear of the litter, as he had done before repeatedly during the journey, and asked, « What does she ? »

« She sleeps , » said Foster; « I would we were home — her strength is exhausted. »

« Rest will restore her, » answered Varney. « She shall soon sleep sound and long — we must consider how to lodge her in safety. »

« In her own apartments to be sure , » said Foster. « I have sent Janet to her aunt's, with a proper rebuke, and the old women are truth itself — for they hate this lady cordially. »

« We will not trust them, however, friend Anthony, » said Varney; « we must secure her in that stronghold where you keep your gold, »

« My gold! » said Anthony, much alarmed; « why, what gold have I ? — God help me, I have no gold — I would I had. »

« Now, marry hang thee, thou stupid brute — who thinks of or cares for thy gold? — If I did, could I not find an hundred better ways to come at it? — In one word, thy bed-chamber, which thou hast fenced so curiously, must be her place of seclusion; and thou, thou hind, shalt press her pillows of down. — I dare to say the Earl will never ask after the rich furniture of these four rooms. »

This last consideration rendered Foster tractable ; he only asked permission to ride before, to make matters ready, and, spurring his horse, he posted before the litter, while Varney falling about threescore paces behind it, it remained only attended by Tider.

When they had arrived at Cumnor-Place, the Countess asked eagerly for Janet, and shewed much alarm when informed that she was no longer to have the attendance of that amiable girl.

« My daughter is dear to me, madam, » said Foster, gruffly ; « and I desire not that she should get the court-tricks of lying and scaping — somewhat too much of that has she learned already, an it please your ladyship. »

The Countess, much fatigued and greatly terrified by the circumstances of her journey, made no answer to this insolence, but mildly expressed a wish to retire to her chamber.

« Ay, ay, » muttered Foster, « 'tis but reasonable; but, under favour, you go not to your gew-gaw toy-house yonder — you will sleep tonight in better security. »

« I would it were in my grave, » said the Countess ; « but that mortal feelings shiver at the idea of soul and body parting. »

« You, I guess, have no chance to shiver at that, » replied Foster. « My lord comes hither to-

16*

morrow, and doubtless you will make your own
ways good with him. »

« But does he come hither?—does he indeed,
good Foster? »

« O ay, good Foster! » replied the other. « But
what Foster shall I be to-morrow, when you
speak of me to my lord—though all I have done
was to obey his own orders. »

« You shall be my protector—a rough one indeed — but still a protector, » answered the
Countess. « O, that Janet were but here! »

« She is better where she is, » answered Foster — « one of you is enough to perplex a plain
head — but will you taste any refreshment? »

« O no, no — my chamber — my chamber. I
trust, » she said, « I may secure it on the inside. »

« With all my heart, » answered Foster, « so
I may secure it on the outside; » and taking a
light, he led the way to a part of the building
where Amy had never been, and conducted her
up a stair of great height, preceded by one of
the old women with a lamp. At the head of
the stair, which seemed of almost immeasurable
height, they crossed a short wooden gallery,
formed of black oak, and very narrow, at the farther end of which was a strong oaken door, which
opened and admitted them into the miser's apartment, homely in its accommodations in the very
last degree, and, except in name, little different
from a prison-vault.

Foster stopped at the door, and gave the lamp

to the Countess, without either offering or permitting the attendance of the old woman who had carried it. The lady stood not on ceremony, but taking it hastily, barred the door, and secured it with the ample means provided on the inside for that purpose.

Varney, meanwhile, had lurked behind on the stairs, but hearing the door barred, he now came up on tiptoe, and Foster, winking to him, pointed with self-complacence to a piece of concealed machinery in the wall, which, playing with much ease and little noise, dropped a part of the wooden gallery, after the manner of a drawbridge, so as to cut off all communication between the door of the bed-room, which he usually inhabited, and the landing-place of the high winding-stair which ascended to it. The rope by which this machinery was wrought was generally carried within the bed-chamber, it being Foster's object to provide against invasion from without; but now that it was intended to secure the prisoner within, the cord had been brought over to the landing-place, and was there made fast, when Foster, with much complacency, had dropped the unsuspected trap-door.

Varney looked with great attention at the machinery, and peeped more than once down the deep abyss which was opened by the fall of the trap-door. It was dark as pitch, and seemed profoundly deep, going, as Foster informed his confederate in a whisper, nigh to the lowest vault of the Castle. Varney cast once more a fix-

ed and long look down into this sable gulph, and
then followed Foster to the part of the manor-
house most usually inhabited.

When they arrived in the parlour which we
have mentioned, Varney requested Foster to
get them supper, and some of the choicest wine.
« I will seek Alasco, » he added; « we have work
for him to do, and we must put him into good
heart. »

Foster groaned at this intimation, but made
no remonstrance. The old woman assured Varney that Alasco had scarce eaten or drunken
since her master's departure, living perpetually
shut up in the laboratory, and talking as if the
world's continuance depended on what he was
doing there.

« I will teach him that the world hath other
claims on him, » said Varney, seizing a light,
and going in quest of the alchemist. He returned, after a considerable absence, very pale, but
yet with his habitual sneer on his cheek and nos-
tril—« Our friend, » he said, « has exhaled.

« How! what mean you? » said Foster —
« Run away—fled with my forty pounds, that
should have been multiplied a thousand fold?
I will have Hue and Cry. »

« I will tell thee a surer way, » said Varney.

» How! which way? » exclaimed Foster; « I
will have back my forty pounds—I deemed them
as surely a thousand times multiplied—I will
have back my in-put, at the least. »

« Go hang thyself then, and sue Alasco in the

Devil's Court of Chancery, for thither he has carried the cause.»

« How!—what doest thou mean—is he dead?»

« Ay, truly is he, » said Varney; «and properly swoln already in the face and body — He had been mixing some of his devil's medicines, and the glass mask which he used constantly had fallen from his face, so that the subtle poison entered the brain, and did its work.»

« *Sancta Maria!* » said Foster; — « I mean, God in his mercy preserve us from covetousness and deadly sin! — Had he not had projection, think you? Saw you no ingots in the crucibles?«

« Nay, I looked not but at the dead carrion, » answered Varney; « an ugly spectacle — he was swoln like a corpse three days exposed on the wheel — Pah! give me a cup of wine.»

« I will go, » said Foster, «I will examine myself»——He took the lamp, and hastened to the door, but there hesitated, and paused. « Will you not go with me?» said he to Varney.

« To what purpose?» said Varney; «I have seen and smelled enough to spoil my appetite. I broke the window, however, and let in the air — it reeked of sulphur, and such like suffocating steams, as if the very devil had been there.»

And might it not be the act of the Dæmon himself?» said Foster, still hesitating; I have heard he is powerful at such times, and with such people. »

« Still, if it *were* that Satan of thine, « answer-

ed Varney, "who thus jades thy imagination,
thou art in perfect safety, unless he is a most
unconscionable devil indeed. He hath had two
good sops of late."

"How, *two* sops — what mean you?" said Foster—"what mean you?"

"You will know in time," said Varney;—"and
then this other banquet — but thou wilt esteem
Her too choice a morsel for the fiend's tooth —
she must have her psalms, and harps, and se-
raphs."

Anthony Foster heard, and came slowly back
to the table : "God! Sir Richard, and must that
then be done?"

"Ay, in very truth, Anthony, or there comes
no copyhold thy way."

"I always foresaw it would land there," said
Foster; "but how, Sir Richard, how?— for not
to win the world would I put hands on her."

"I cannot blame thee, said Varney; "I should
be reluctant to do that myself—we miss Alasco
and his manna sorely; ay, and the dog Lambourne."

"Why, where tarries Lambourne?" said Anthony.

"Ask no questions," said Varney, "thou wilt
see him one day, if thy creed is true.—But to our
graver matter.—I will teach thee a springe, Tony,
to catch a pewit — yonder trap-door — yonder
gimcrack of thine, will remain secure in appearance, will it not, though the supports are
withdrawn beneath?"

"Ay, marry, will it, " said Foster; "so long
as it is not trodden on. "

" But were the lady to attempt an escape over
it," replied Varney, "her weight would carry it
down ? "

" A mouse's weight would do it, " said Foster.

" Why, then, she dies in attempting her escape,
and what could you or I help it, honest Tony?
Let us to bed, we will adjust our project to-
morrow.

On the next day, when evening approached,
Varney summoned Foster to the execution of
their plan. Tider and Foster's old man-servant
were sent on a feigned errand down to the village, and Anthony himself, as if anxious to see
that the Countess suffered no want of accommodation, visited her place of confinement. He was
so much staggered at the mildness and patience
with which she seemed to endure her confinement, that he could not help earnestly recommending to her not to cross the threshold of her
room on any account whatsoever, until Lord
Leicester should come, "Which, " he added,
I trust in God, will be very soon, " Amy patiently promised that she would resign herself to her
fate, and Foster returned to his hardened companion with his conscience half-eased of the perilous load that weighed on it. " I have warned
her, " he said; " surely in vain is the snare set
in the sight of any bird.. "

He left, therefore, the Countess's door un-
secured on the outside, and under the eye of

Varney, withdrew the supports which sustained the falling trap, which, therefore, kept its level position merely by a slight adhesion. They withdrew to wait the issue on the ground-floor adjoining, but they waited long in vain. At length Varney, after walking long to and fro, with his face muffled in his cloak, threw it suddenly back, and said, « Surely never was a woman fool enough to neglect so fair an opportunity of escape ! »

« Perhaps she is resolved, » said Foster, « to await her husband's return. »

« True ! — most true, » said Varney, rushing out, « I had not thought of that before. »

In less than two minutes, Foster, who remained behind, heard the tread of a horse in the court-yard, and then a whistle similar to that which was the Earl's usual signal ; — the instant after the door of the Countess's chamber opened, and in the same moment the drapdoor gave way. There was a rushing sound — a heavy fall — a faint groan — and all was over.

At the same instant, Varney called in at the window, in an accent and tone which was an indescribable mixture betwixt horror and raillery, « Is the bird caught ? — Is the deed done ? »

« O God, forgive us ! » replied Anthony Foster.

« Why, thou fool, » said Varney, « thy toil is ended, and thy reward secure. Look down into the vault—what seest thou ? »

« I see only a heap of white clothes, like a

snow-drift, » said Foster. « O God, she moves her arm! »

« Hurl something down on her. — Thy gold chest, Tony—it is an heavy one. »

« Varney, thou art an incarnate fiend! » replied Foster; — « There needs nothing more — she is gone! »

« So pass our troubles, said Varney, entering the room; « I dreamed not I could have mimicked the Earl's call so well. »

« Oh, if there be judgment in heaven, thou hast deserved it, » said Foster, » and wilt meet it! — Thou hast destroyed her by means of her best affections—It is a seething of the kid in the mother's milk. »

« Thou art a fanatical ass, » replied Varney; « let us now think how the alarm should be given, —the body is to remain where it is. »

But their wickedness was to be permitted no longer; — for, even while they were at this consultation, Tressilian and Raleigh broke in upon them, having obtained admittance by means of Tider and Foster's servants, whom they had secured at the village.

Anthony Foster fled on their entrance; and, knowing each corner and pass of the intricate old house, escaped all search. But Varney was taken on the spot; and, instead of expressing compunction for what he had done, seemed to take a fiendish pleasure in pointing out to them the remains of the murdered Countess, while at the same time he defied them to shew that

he had any share in her death. The despairing
grief of Tressilian, on viewing the mangled and
yet warm remains of what had lately been so
lovely and so beloved, was such, that Raleigh
was compelled to have him removed from the
place by force, while he himself assumed the
direction of what was to be done.

Varney, upon a second examination, made
very little mystery either of the crime or of its
motives; alleging, as a reason for his frankness,
that though much of what he confessed could
only have attached to him by suspicion, yet
such suspicion would have been sufficient to
deprive him of Leicester's confidence, and to
destroy all his towering plans of ambition. « I
was not born, » he said, « to drag on the remainder of life a degraded outcast, — nor will
I so die, that my fate shall make a holiday to
the vulgar herd. »

From these words it was apprehended he had
some design upon himself, and he was carefully
deprived of all means, by which such could be
carried into execution. But like some of the
heroes of antiquity, he carried about his person
a small quantity of strong poison, prepared
probably by the celebrated Demetrius Alasco.
Having swallowed this potion over-night, he
was found next morning dead in his cell; nor
did he appear to have suffered much agony,
his countenance presenting, even in death, the
habitual expression of sneering sarcasm, which
was predominant while he lived. The wicked

man, saith Scripture, hath no bonds in his death.

The fate of his colleague in wickedness was long unknown. Cumnor-Place was deserted immediately after the murder; for, in the vicinity of what was called the Lady Dudley's Chamber, the domestics pretended to hear groans and screams, and other supernatural noises. After a certain length of time, Janet, hearing no tidings of her father, became the uncontrouled mistress of his property, and conferred it with her hand upon Wayland, now a man of settled character, and holding a place in Elizabeth's household. But it was after they had been both dead for some years, that their eldest son and heir, in making some researches about Cumnor-Hall, discovered a secret passage, closed by an iron door, which, opening from behind the bed in the Lady Dudley's Chamber, descended to a sort of cell, in which they found an iron chest containing a quantity of gold, and a human skeleton stretched above it. The fate of Anthony Foster was now manifest. He had fled to this place of concealment, forgetting the key of the spring-lock; and being barred from escape, by the means he had used for preservation of that gold, for which he had sold his salvation, he had there perished miserably. Unquestionably the groans and screams heard by the domestics were not entirely imaginary, but were those of this wretch, who, in his agony, was crying for relief and succour.

The news of the Countess's dreadful fate put a sudden period to the pleasures of Kenilworth. Leicester retired from court, and for a considerable time abandoned himself to his remorse. But as Varney in his last declaration had been studious to spare the character of his patron, the Earl was the object rather of compassion than resentment. The Queen at length recalled him to court; he was once more distinguished as a statesman and favourite, and the rest of his career is well known to history. But there was something retributive in his death, if, according to an account very generally received, it took place from his swallowing a draught of poison, which was designed for another person.

Sir Hugh Robsart died very soon after his daughter, having settled his estate on Tressilian. But neither the prospect of rural independence, nor the promises of favour which Elizabeth held out to induce him to follow the court, could remove his profound melancholy. Wherever he went, he seemed to see before him the disfigured corpse of the early and only object of his affection. At length, having made provision for the maintenance of the old friends and old servants who formed sir Hugh's family at Lidcote-Hall, he himself embarked with his friend Raleigh for the Virginia expedition, and, young in years but old in griefs, died before his day in that foreign land.

Of inferior persons it is only necessary to say, that Blount's wit grew brighter as his yellow roses faded; and that, doing his part as a brave commander in the wars, he was much more in his element, than during the short period of his following the court; and that Flibbertigibbet's acute genius raised him to favour and distinction, in the employment both of Burleigh and Cecil.

The outlines of this melancholy tale may be found, at length, in Ashmole's Antiquities of Berkshire, and it is alluded to in many other works which treat of Leicester's history. The ingenious translator of « Camoens, » William Julius Mickle, has made the Countess's tragedy the subject of a beautiful elegy, called Cumnor-Hall, which concludes with these lines:

> The village maids, with fearful glance,
>   Avoid the ancient moss-grown wall,
> Nor ever lead the merry dance
>   Among the groves of Cumnor-Hall.
>
> And many a traveller has sigh'd,
>   And pensive mourn'd that lady's fall,
> As wandering onward he has spied
>   The haunted towers of Cumnor-Hall.

THE END.

TABLE

OF THE CHAPTERS OF THE SECOND VOLUME.

CPSIA information can be obtained at www.ICGtesting.com

228317LV00004B/23/P